5th CORPS, 3rd DIV.

6th CORPS, 2nd DIV.

7th CORPS, 1st DIV.

8th CORPS, 3rd DIV.

## CORPS BADGES ARMY OF THE UNITED STATES

HANCOCK'S 1st CORPS VETERANS

ENGINEER & PONTONIER CORPS

LIEUTENANT GENERAL

LIEUT. COLONEL—ARTILLERY

MAJOR GENERAL

MAJOR—INFANTRY

BRIGADIER GENERAL

CAPTAIN—CAVALRY

COLONEL—INFANTRY

FIRST LIEUTENANT—INFANTRY

SECOND LIEUT.—ARTILLERY

## SHOULDER STRAPS U.S. ARMY

9th CORPS, 4th DIV.

10th CORPS, 1st DIV.

11th CORPS, 2nd DIV.

U.S. SIGNAL CORPS

16th CORPS, 2nd DIV.

15th CORPS, 3rd DIV.

14th CORPS, 1st DIV.
(13th CORPS, NO BADGE ADOPTED)

12th CORPS, 3rd DIV.

# ARMS AND EQUIPMENT
# OF THE CIVIL WAR

JACK COGGINS

# ARMS AND EQUIPMENT
# OF THE CIVIL WAR

ILLUSTRATED BY THE AUTHOR

DOUBLEDAY & COMPANY, INC.
GARDEN CITY, NEW YORK

TO MY WIFE

*Chief-of-Staff, Quartermaster General, and Vivandière*

ISBN: 0-385-00288-2 TRADE
0-385-02735-4 PREBOUND

*Library of Congress Catalog Card Number 61-11810*
*Copyright © 1962 by Jack Coggins*
*All Rights Reserved*
*Printed in the United States of America*
9  8  7  6

# CONTENTS

# AUTHOR'S PREFACE

THERE are no battles in this book—no grand strategy—no descriptions of glorious charges or fighting retreats. The *why* and *where* and *when* of the war has been ably and amply discussed in shelf after shelf of books. This is a book of *how* and *what with*.

To fully understand the tactics and strategy; the reasons for victory or defeats; the "ifs" and "almosts" that make up the Civil War, it is necessary also to understand a little about the actual weapons and equipment with which that war was fought.

The fact that the Rattlesnake Rifles are still armed with the old .69 Minié, while the opposing Zaynsville Zouaves have just been issued the Spencer repeater, may have more to do with the outcome of the battle than General Dundreary's craftily planned, double-simultaneous enveloping movement on both flanks.

A regiment of cavalry forms for a charge. McGillicudahy's battery of Napoleons sweeps up. Action front—range fifteen hundred yards—load with spherical case—Fire!

Will the cavalry be blown to bits? Will McGillicudahy be carved up with a Chicopee saber? You will be able to evaluate the battery commander's chances a little better if you know that a well-served Napoleon can fire two carefully aimed rounds a minute. That, Hollywood to the contrary, the cavalry will probably cover the first six-hundred yards at a trot, time: just under three minutes, and the next quarter mile at a gallop—say a minute and a half more. The guns are firing solid shot by now, but about this time, if McGillicudahy knows his business, he'll switch to canister. A round of canister holds twenty-seven balls, something like a lethal can of cherries. With the whites of the troopers' eyes showing now, his sweating gunners get off a round every fifteen seconds (no need for careful aim—each piece is a huge shotgun). But the last few hundred yards are at the full gallop and charge and a troop horse going all out can cover two-hundred yards in fifteen seconds. Are the horsemen yelling and brandishing their swords? Well, they are probably yelling, all right—but the *arme blanche* is not held in the same esteem in the United States as it is in Europe and there may be a ragged but rapid fire from assorted revolvers and carbines as they close.

Note, the battery commander changed from spherical case to solid shot as the horsemen's pace quickened. Fuze setting in those days was a tricky business—almost impossible to adjust against a fast-moving target. Burst on impact? No good—a Napoleon is a smoothbore—fires a spherical shell. You can only fire a percussion fuzed shell from a rifled gun.

The Civil War was a new sort of war, waged over vast areas of the damndest country men ever fought in. It saw the first battles between ironclads, and ushered in the metallic cartridge and the repeating rifle. Men laid telegraph wire under fire from sniper's rifles fitted with telescopic sights.

Armored gunboats forced through snag-studded bayous, and hastily converted ferries patrolled on blockade duty. Heavy guns were mounted on rails; artillery officers spotted from balloons; and a submarine sank a warship. And it was the first war in history in which the railroad played a major part in strategy and logistics.

It was fought by citizen soldiers—over mountains, through swamps, on sandspits, and broad rivers, with the weirdest and most heterogeneous collection of arms and equipment ever used in a war before.

This book does not attempt to classify or describe all this equipment. Nor does it delve into the minor differences between types of six-shooters or muzzle-loading .58-caliber rifles. The collector and the connoisseur must look elsewhere for such minutiae.

What it does try to do is to give the Civil War reader a better idea of the men in blue and gray; how they were clothed, equipped, and organized; and of the tools of war with which they so gallantly fought.

A word about the research. The author has included many quotes from personal recollections of participants, both Union and Confederate, believing that an eyewitness account is of more interest and has greater authenticity than a history written long after the event. However, there are few so ill-informed about the over-all picture of a battle as those taking part in it, and differences of opinion and discrepancies as to actual facts, even weapons used, often appear. Military manuals of the period contain errors, especially in the drawings, and should be approached with suspicion. When contemporary accounts vary so much, positive statements are dangerous, if not misleading. If, therefore, the text includes more than a fair share of "abouts" and "usuallys," it is due to the author's turtle-like reluctance to stick out his neck.

A vast amount of the more perishable of the equipment used in the war has vanished, rotted, or rusted away, or been destroyed (what collector can fail to shudder at accounts of armloads of surrendered muskets thrown down to corduroy muddy roads). However, some equipment remains in various museums and it is to the interest and co-operation of Col. Frederick P. Todd and Mr. Gerald C. Stowe, director and curator respectively of the West Point Museum, that I am indebted for much of the military material. The Reading (Pa.) public library has been most helpful, especially in making available the invaluable Official Records.

The layout and mechanics of this book posed some peculiar problems. For their solution, along with his kind and tactful handling of an author-artist, much credit is due to Editor Harold Kuebler. Last, but not least, without the enthusiastic help of the author's talented wife, who added to her many other duties, those of drafting, layout, research, typing, and critic, the book would not even have been attempted.

[7]

# THE ARMIES

THE evaluation of the fighting abilities of the Civil War soldier is beyond the scope of this book. The war was fought mainly between men of Anglo-Saxon stock, often between men of the same family. Their basic weapons were in a majority of cases the same. Both sides faced the same problems of discipline inherent in armies of volunteers hastily raised in a country of rugged individualists whose nationals placed freedom of speech and action above all else. Desertions and "absenteeism" plagued each side. Both sides had their moments of triumph and of defeat, of heroism and of panic.

If, as is sometimes claimed, the morale of the Southern soldier was higher, it might have been that he was, in nearly every instance, defending his home territory against an invader. Accustomed to victory, and fortunate in possession of a beloved and war-wise leader, the Confederate soldier, ill-fed and poorly equipped as he often was, performed feats seldom if ever equaled in the history of warfare. Yet few could match the stubborn valor of the men of the Army of the Potomac—often defeated, almost always outgeneraled, and sometimes outfought, but always coming back, under some new commander, to try conclusions again with the "invincible Southerners."

Often studiedly casual in attire, informal in dealings with his superiors, and lax in matters of discipline, the men whom Moltke referred to as an armed rabble could yet, on occasion, dress ranks under fire and advance again and again over ground swept by the deadliest musketry yet seen in warfare. If somewhat lacking in spit and polish;

in ingenuity and inventiveness, they were the superior of any troops on earth. Certainly they were a breed of soldier the like of which the world had never seen, and will never see again.

In organization the opposing armies were much the same. This is natural enough, as the senior officers of both sides were West Pointers, often from the same regiments in the regular army. The regiment was the basic unit of infantry and cavalry, and the battery, of the artillery. Regiments were grouped into brigades, brigades into divisions, divisions into corps, and corps into armies.

The regiment, infantry or cavalry, theoretically numbered about one thousand men. It seldom mustered one half of that, and was constantly increasing or decreasing, usually the latter, as losses through battle or disease were seldom equaled by drafts of new recruits.

Confederate regiments tended to be a little stronger than Union regiments. Until late in the war the average strength of Union Army corps or divisions was about half that of the Confederates. This should be borne in mind, as it can lead to considerable confusion. For instance, the four Confederate divisions which bore the brunt of the first days fighting at Gettysburg, those of Early, Heth, Pender, and Rodes, totaled some 25,000 men. The six divisions of the I and XI corps of the Union army which opposed them totaled a little under 20,000 (the figures are General Longstreet's).

A strong Confederate infantry brigade might contain almost as many men as a weak Federal division, but the fighting effectiveness would not be the same, as the Federal formation, being a division, might include all arms, while the Confederates would be all infantry.

In 1864 the Army of the Potomac was reorganized, and the five corps consolidated into three, at which time each corps averaged some 26,000 men.

Union commanders seldom held as high rank as their opponents. Thus Union Army corps were commonly commanded by major generals, while a Confederate corps would be under a lieutenant general. Lee was a full general, while McClellan, Hooker, Meade, and other commanders of the Army of the Potomac were only major generals, and Grant was only made a lieutenant general in March 1864. Confederate divisional commanders were major generals, while Federal divisions were usually headed by brigadiers. A

brigade, while theoretically commanded by a brigadier general, was more often commanded in the Union Army by a colonel.

At Gettysburg, the Army of the Potomac was made up of seven army corps, with fifty-one infantry brigades, grouped in nineteen divisions, sixteen of which were commanded by brigadiers. Twenty-two of the brigades were commanded by brigadier generals and twenty-nine by colonels. The Army of Northern Virginia consisted of three army corps, divided into nine divisions, with thirty-seven brigades. Of these brigades, only three were commanded by colonels.

While much mention is often made of the sizes of various commands, it is actually almost impossible to assess numerical strengths of units in either army at any one time. Numbers given were often for strengths listed on the rolls. Actual strengths of bayonets carried into battle were much smaller. Some of the loss can be attributed to sickness, but by far the greater proportion must be set down to straggling. Stragglers, skulkers, absentees, and deserters were the curse of both armies throughout the war.

Meade declared that over 8000 men, including 250 officers, had quit the ranks of Hooker's corps before or during the Battle of Antietam. Jackson's division lost 700 out of 1600 effectives at the same battle, yet less than two weeks later, as the laggards drifted in, mustered 3900. Rapid marching accounted for some of the straggling, but the tendency of both Union and Confederate troops to stray whenever they felt like it was the main reason.

Accustomed as we are to the rules, regulations, and red tape of soldiering in the twentieth century, it seems incredible that thousands of men of both armies should wander off, many to rejoin the colors later, others to keep going "over the hill."

"The states of the North are flooded with deserters and absentees" wrote McClellan, and Lee complained that "the absent are scattered broadcast over the land."

It is safe to estimate that, given twenty thousand infantry to start with, a general would be lucky if, after two or three weeks of maneuvering, he would be able to put sixteen thousand into the line of battle.

Of the Southerners, Henderson wrote:

"Many, without going through the formality of asking leave, would make for their homes, and had no idea that their conduct was in any way peculiar. They had done their duty . . . the enemy had been driven from Virginia, and they considered that they were fully entitled to some short repose."

Neither orders, appeals, or arrests and punishments seemed to have any effect; nor could cavalry patrols or provost marshal's guards check the constant drifting away. True, a lot of these absentees "drifted" back, but, as many a despairing regular must have exclaimed, "This is a helluva way to run an army."

For while in bravery, hardihood, and self-reliance the Civil War soldier was second to none, yet time and again, through lack of discipline, a battle was lost and the results of a hard-won fight thrown away. Both sides prided themselves in relying more on wits and natural intelligence than on blind obedience. Yet such discipline need not imply a mere machine-soldier, an automaton with every ounce of initiative whipped or drilled out of him. There is a happy medium, the product of careful and intelligent training in which initiative and the habits of unhesitating obedience are combined. Unfortunately such schooling takes time, and a superior and well-trained type of officer. Neither North nor South had either time or such officers; and so Johnny Reb and Billy Yank went their own sweet ways, fighting like demons and straying like school boys; in the ranks today and off to help with the plowing tomorrow.

THE cavalry regiments at Gettysburg were grouped in brigades of which the Confederates had seven and the Union forces, eight. The Army of the Potomac by this time had organized its cavalry brigades into divisions and the divisions into a cavalry corps. The Confederates under Stuart were in a division and two separate brigades.

The Southern guns were mostly in battalions —each battalion consisting of four four-gun batteries. Each corps had five battalions assigned to it—a battalion to each division plus two in the reserve. A Union corps had an artillery brigade (four or five batteries) attached, and an army reserve of some twenty-four batteries.

Each general officer had his own staff of assistants, a group of specialists in which were represented all the services, and who bore much the same relationship to their commanding officer as the heads of departments do to the president of a large company. The staff was usually divided. The military staff included the chief of artillery, chief or inspector of cavalry, the chief engineer, the provost marshal general, and the chief signal officer, while the administrative staff included the chief ordnance officer, chief quartermaster, commissary, chief paymaster, and medical director. A chief of staff headed all these, and took much of the administrative load off the commanding officer, writing orders and seeing that they were carried out, thus relieving his general of all petty details and annoyances and leaving him free to concentrate on strategic and tactical problems.

Aides-de-camp were attached to the general's personal staff, usually in a non-technical capacity. They were in a sense glorified messengers, but also acted to a certain extent as their commander's eyes as well as his mouth. For this reason, they had to be capable of giving a concise and accurate description of the situation in the parts of the field to which they were sent. They might also, as staff members (and as such presumably knowing their general's intentions) give orders in emergencies where there was no time to consult the commanding officer himself.

All staffs were (or should have been) kept as small as possible, and occasionally heads of services were omitted, or did double duty: for instance, a chief of artillery might take over the duty of ordnance officer. In smaller organizations, such as divisional staffs, aides might perform the duties of ordnance officers, engineer officers, etc.

The staff organizations were repeated on a smaller scale down through divisions and brigades. There were also military secretaries, clerks, messengers, etc.

Armies in the Civil War were usually referred to by locality, such as the Army of the Potomac, the Army of the Ohio, and the Army of the Cumberland of the Union forces, and the Army of Northern Virginia, the Army of Tennessee, the Army of the West of the Confederacy.

Corps were usually organized into three divisions. Corps were numbered and the Union Army had corps insignia in the shape of badges worn on cap or hat.

Divisions were normally of three brigades each. The Union corps insignia was worn as a divisional badge, red for the first division, white for the second, blue for the third, and, if more than three, green for the fourth and orange for the fifth division. The Confederates wore no division or corps insignia.

Cartridge box for .58 cal.
Minié. Tin compartments.
Implement pocket.

Cartridge box for twenty 56-50
Spencer cartridges. Most cap and
cartridge boxes had double flaps.

Quick-loading cartridge box held
ten tube magazine loads for
Spencer repeating carbine. Wood,
leather covered.

The Forage Cap

OPPOSITE PAGE: *Union infantrymen. Blanket roll was usually substituted for more cumbersome blanket and knapsack. Leggings, when issued, were soon discarded or gave way to socks rolled up over trouser legs.*

ABOVE: *Union officers. The lieutenant (RIGHT) is wearing the four-button blouse, often worn in the field in place of the frock coat seen on the captain at his right. The sash was seldom seen in the field toward the end of the war. The cavalryman (LEFT) is wearing the regulation sky-blue overcoat or cloak coat, double-breasted for mounted troops, single for others. While the cloak coat was one of the best-looking pieces of Civil War uniform, the hideous forage cap was certainly the worst; one of the horrors of war.*

[13]

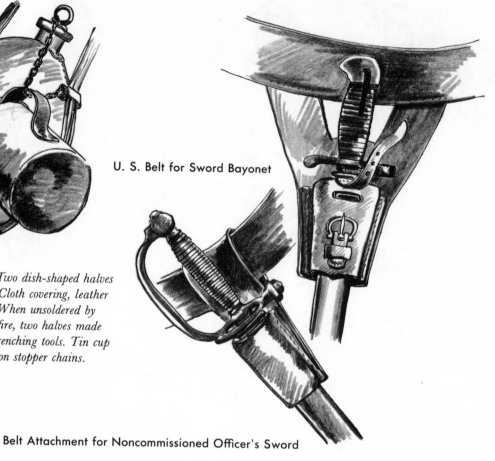

U. S. Belt for Sword Bayonet

**Union canteen.** *Two dish-shaped halves soldered together. Cloth covering, leather or canvas straps. When unsoldered by throwing in campfire, two halves made good plates or entrenching tools. Tin cup was often carried on stopper chains.*

Belt Attachment for Noncommissioned Officer's Sword

*Some of many types of hats worn by Union forces. Regulation "Jeff Davis" (*CENTER RIGHT*) looped up on the right side for officers and cavalrymen, on the left for infantry. Natty little number at lower left was worn by Phil Sheridan. Foreign legion-looking affair was a Havelock, named for the English general of Indian mutiny fame, and issued by both sides at the outset of the war. "As it is made sufficiently large to cover the neck and shoulders, the effect, when properly adjusted, was to deprive the wearer of any air he might otherwise enjoy . . . prompted their immediate transfer to the plebian uses of a dish-cloth or a coffee-strainer. . . ."*

Many Zouave regiments were formed in both North and South. The general design of the uniform was usually about the same: short jacket, baggy pantaloons, leggings, a sash, and some form of French kepi, tasseled cap or turban. Some wearers affected the French-style mustache and pointed beard. Jackets were often most ornate with many buttons, worn over colorful vests or shirts, often also bebuttoned and beribboned.

Little of this tawdry finery survived the first year of the war. Materials were often shoddy and workmanship poor.

Southern uniforms varied from the elegant to the ragged. The young captain of artillery is resplendent in kepi, sash, and high boots. The sleeve of his jacket bears the "chicken guts" appropriate to his rank. The bewhiskered private has long given up any pretense at neatness. Many of his comrades quickly discarded the haversack and some even the cartridge box, keeping a number of rounds in their pockets and a reserve in their blanket rolls, along with the rest of their worldly goods.

Confederate canteens were patterned after the U.S. canteen, but shortages of material were often met by ingenious contraptions of wood.

THE following are quotes from men of both armies concerning equipment and camp life.

"The knapsack . . . is an unwieldly burden with its . . . . contents of flannel and sole leather and sometimes twenty rounds of ammunition extra. Mixed in . . . are photographs, cards, huswife, testament, pens, ink, paper, and oftentimes stolen truck enough to load a mule. All this is crowned with a double wool blanket and half a shelter tent rolled in a rubber blanket. One shoulder and the hips support the 'commissary department.' —an odorous haversack, which often stinks with its mixture of bacon, pork, salt junk, sugar, coffee, tea, desicated vegetables, rice, bits of yesterday's dinner, and old scraps. . . ."

The early Confederate knapsack contained a similar load. "On the outside . . . were two great blankets and a rubber or oil cloth. This knapsack, etc., weighed from fifteen to twenty-five pounds, sometimes more." But "The knapsack vanished early in the struggle. It was inconvenient to change the underwear too often. . . . The better way was to dress out and out, and wear that outfit until the enemy's knapsacks, or the folks at home supplied a change."

"Reduced to the minimum, the private soldier consisted of one man, one hat, one jacket, one shirt, one pair of pants, one pair of drawers, one pair of shoes and one pair of socks. His baggage was one blanket, one rubber blanket, and one haversack."

"One blanket to each man was found to be as much as could be carried, and amply sufficient for the severest weather."

"Experience soon demonstrated that boots were not agreeable on a long march . . . good, strong brogues or brogans, with broad bottoms and big flat heels, succeeded the boots. . . ."

"Shoes are very scarce. The men get pieces of raw hide from the butchers, and, after wrapping their feet up in old rags, sew the hide around them . . . which they wear until it wears out."

"Caps . . . . finally yielded to the demands of comfort and common sense, and a good soft felt hat worn instead."

"Overcoats, an inexperienced man would think an absolute necessity for men exposed to the rigors of a northern Virginia winter. But . . . they were found to be a great inconvenience. . . . Some carried them to the last but the majority got tired of lugging them around."

"Canteens were . . . as a general thing discarded. . . . A good strong tin cup was found better than a canteen, as it was easier to fill at a well or spring, and was serviceable as a boiler for making coffee."

"In addition . . . each mess, generally composed of from five to ten men, . . . had its outfit, consisting of a large camp chest containing skillet, frying pan, coffee boiler, bucket for lard, coffee box, salt box, meal box, flour box, knives, forks, spoons, plates, cups, etc. . . . so large that eight or ten of them filled up an army wagon. . . ."

"The camp-chest soon vanished. The brigadiers and major-generals, even, found them too troublesome. . . . One skillet and a couple of frying pans, a bag of flour or meal, another bag of salt, sugar and coffee, . . . served the purpose as well."

"General Lee has just issued (July 1863) a very wise order cutting down the regimental transportation to one wagon for every 300 men. . . ."

"The cavalrymen found sabres very tiresome when swung to the belt and adopted the plan of fastening them to the saddle on the left side, with the hilt in front and in reach of the right hand." (In later years, standard practice among cavalrymen everywhere.)

"I lay down with my feet to the fire, my saddle as a pillow, the oil cloth under me and a blanket over me. . . . The fire was made some fifteen feet long. . . . In this way three or four fires could accommodate my whole company, both officers and men."

"I have no bed and water runs through my tent, as the ditch only gathers it so it can creep through my floor of dark mould, which is literally spongy with moisture, and my poor oil-cloth does not keep the dampness off me."

[17]

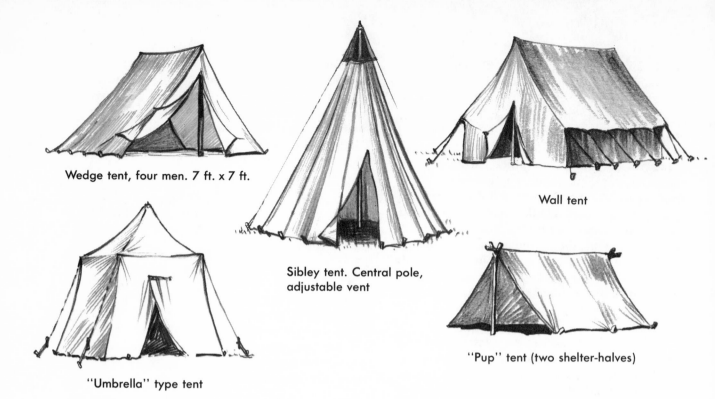

Wedge tent, four men. 7 ft. x 7 ft.

Sibley tent. Central pole, adjustable vent

Wall tent

"Umbrella" type tent

"Pup" tent (two shelter-halves)

The natural instincts of a recruit is to surround himself with all the comforts of home, including a canvas replica of home itself. The transportation problem alone proved insoluble and the larger tents with which most units encumbered themselves in 1861 speedily gave place to the little "pup" tent. These were not well received at first. They were called kennels and dog-holes and adorned with signs reading "Pups for sale," "Sons of bitches within," "Rat-terriers," and other examples of camp humor. But handiness and ease of transportation (each man carried half a tent) outweighed lack of roominess.

The Sibley—which was large enough for a stove, so large in fact, that it was not generally used in the field, but in more permanent camps, could (and usually did) sleep double its regulation number. A score or more could sleep on their sides, spoon fashion, feet to the stove in the center. At the cry "Spoon" all would roll over and settle down on the other side.

Wall tents of various sizes and patterns were used. Again, a rarity among the lower ranks in the field, although headquarters might afford the luxury of transporting a few.

But if the veteran prided himself on his ability to make do with the most meager shelter, or none at all, when campaigning, his ingenuity knew no bounds when making himself comfortable in permanent camps and winter quarters. Log or sod cabins, wood and canvas contraptions, dugouts and combinations of all these were built, drainage was carefully planned (at least by the more experienced), and much thought and labor put into chimneys and fireplaces.

[18]

*The ever-useful* **poncho** *or* **gum blanket** *served as rain cape or "pup" tent floor. It had eyelet holes and could be rigged as a small tent or joined like shelter-halves. Often the soldier merely rolled himself and his blankets up in it. On the march it was usually carried wrapped around the blanket roll.*

"We have finished our house. It is made of pickets chinked and dubbed with a tent fly for a roof. We have the best fire place and chimney in the company. The fireplace is made of brick to above the jam and from there up mud and sticks. Our house is about 12 feet square . . . our guns are in racks on the walls. Just above the fire place you will see something which we call a mantle piece and is made by making two holes one in each side of the fire place putting pegs in them and putting plank on them. . . . There are only four of us in this house."

The above excerpt from a Texan's letter is from Bell Irvin Wiley's The Life of Johnny Reb.

Chimney of burned Southern home used as improvised cookhouse

Log cabin with canvas roof. Note elaborate chimney

Confederate sapling and sod shelter. Dugout center

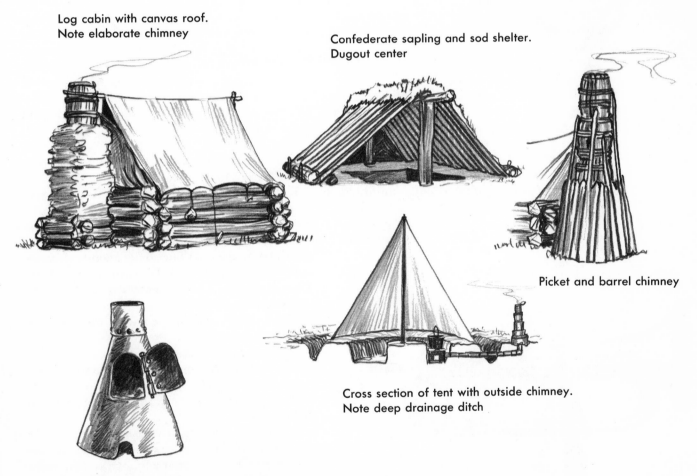

Picket and barrel chimney

Cross section of tent with outside chimney. Note deep drainage ditch

Sibley stove had sections of connecting pipe. Came in several sizes

[19]

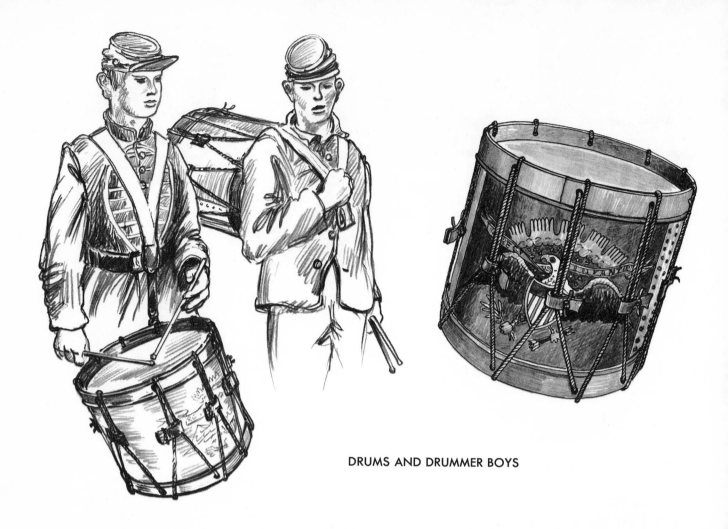

DRUMS AND DRUMMER BOYS

Bands were great morale-builders. Lee once said, "I don't believe we can have an army without music." An ex-drummer boy reminisced, "When a dozen or more of the lads, . . . led the regiment in a review with their get-out-of-the-way-old-Dan-Tuckerish style of music, it made the men in the ranks step off as though they were bound for a Donnybrook Fair."

Bands played under fire, as well as in camp and on the march. As the war progressed some regiments replaced the bands with fife and drum corps. On the other hand, General Porter reports coming across one of Sheridan's mounted bands under heavy fire at Five Forks in March of '65, "Playing 'Nelly Bly' as cheerfully as if it were furnishing music for a country picnic."

The soldier's day started with the sound of bugle and drum.

"From some commanding elevation the clear-toned bugle sounds out the reveille and another responds, . . . intermingled with this comes the beating of drums, often rattling and jarring on unwilling ears."

In the infantry there were some dozen calls, while artillery and cavalry sometimes used twenty and more. Drums were used for calls, too, and a veteran regiment could maneuver by drumbeat, no spoken commands being given.

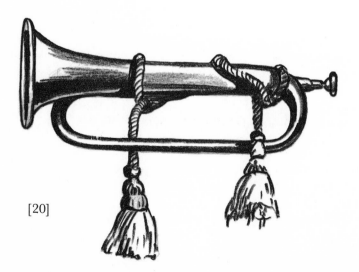

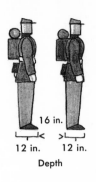

16 in.

12 in.    12 in.

Depth

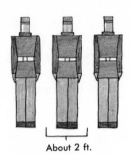

About 2 ft.

*By FRONT is meant the space in width occupied by a command, either in line or in column; by INTERVAL, an open space between elements of the same line; by DEPTH, the space from head to rear of any formation, including the leading and rear elements; by DISTANCE, an open space in the direction of depth. (From* Organization and Tactics, *by Arthur L. Wagner)*

**Unit front in battle formation equals number of men divided by number of ranks multiplied by 2 ft.**

# THE INFANTRY

WAGNER'S *Organization and Tactics* states that: "The tactical unit is the largest body of troops that can be directly commanded by a single leader, and, at the same time, be able to appear in close order on the battle-field without risk of quickly incurring ruinous losses from enemy fire." In modern times this unit has shrunk to platoon size, but at the time of the Civil War it was the regiment, nominally about one thousand men, but actually closer to the five hundred-man French battalions of the Napoleonic Wars.

The volunteer infantry regiment at full strength as prescribed in the regulations of the U. S. Army consisted of ten companies, each of ninety-seven men and three officers, as follows: one captain; one first lieutenant; one second lieutenant; one first sergeant; four sergeants; eight corporals; two musicians; one wagoner; and eighty-two privates. The regiment was commanded by a colonel assisted by a lieutenant colonel; a major; an adjutant (lieutenant); a quarter master (lieuten-

ant); a surgeon, and an assistant surgeon. There was also a sergeant major; a regimental quartermaster sergeant; one regimental commissary sergeant; one hospital steward; two principal musicians, and twenty-four bandsmen (later done away with).

The organization as listed above was seldom, if ever, up to full strength. The actual strength was likely to be half the above. The average Union regiment in the spring of '63 could muster some 425 effectives. The North usually allowed its volunteer regiments to dwindle gradually away. When they got down to some 150 to 200 men they were often broken up and new regiments formed. This vicious and demoralizing system is said to have been perpetuated by the governors of the Northern states to allow them to appoint more colonels, a form of patronage that had a very bad effect on the management of the war.

The South, in most instances, attempted to keep

[21]

its existing regiments intact by feeding in recruits. This is not to say that Southern regiments were never below strength. They were often down to mere skeletons, but the regimental *espirit de corps* was still there. Had the Union adopted such a plan, or expanded the regular regiments by using the existing personnel as cadres upon which to build, many disasters might have been averted.

In the South there was an attempt to revive the legion, a combined force of all arms under one command, but it was abandoned as too unwieldly.

The regiments brigaded together were, in the South, usually men from the same state. There was the same feeling of pride and loyalty among Southerners toward their brigades as Union troops had toward their corps or regiment. Units often took the names of their original leaders, especially in the Confederacy, and often kept them after the command had passed to another. Thus Jones might command Smith's Brigade, of Brown's division. Both Union and Confederate corps were numbered, but of the two, a Federal would be more likely to be known by its number, while a Southern corps (and there were far fewer of them) would most likely bear the name of the lieutenant general commanding it. The habit of naming commands also extended to the artillery and while some, among them the few batteries of regular artillery of the Union army, were known by their official titles, many were known by the commanding officer's name.

Regiments were almost without exception known by their number and state: The 10th New York; the 48th Mississippi, etc. Companies were designated by letters starting with A, the senior captain's company, which held the post of honor on the right flank; B, next ranking company, was on the left of the line.

The raw material being much the same, regiments were just about as good as their officers. Discipline, and training by leaders who knew their business (or were quick to learn it), who took an interest in their men's health and welfare, and who "stood fire" well, meant the difference between a regiment that "stayed put" and "took it" or one that "skedaddled." Bravery among the officers was a prime requisite, and a regiment without confidence in its leaders was not likely to have much in itself. Under the volunteer system, many newly-formed regiments were thrown into battle almost untrained. With no leavening of veterans in the ranks, none of the *espirit de corps* which a famous regimental name and tradition

can give, and often under leaders who knew no more of war than did the rank and file, it is a wonder that so many of these raw regiments "met the elephant" without panicking.

In the war's early stages there was an attempt to create morale by the use of distinctive uniforms or drill. There was a rash of Zouave regiments in both North and South, complete with baggy pants, fezzes, and vivandières, and the Zouave drill was seen on every drill ground.

The original Zouave battalions were recruited by the French during the fighting in Algeria in 1831 from a Berber tribe of that name. Later the troops became purely French, and their color and dash, their distinctive uniforms, and their exploits in the Crimean War captured the popular imagination. A famous drill team, wearing the French-type uniforms and performing evolutions based on much modified light-infantry tactics, toured the country in 1860 and put on exhibitions in many cities. Several companies were formed in emulation and at the outbreak of war were recruited and expanded into regiments.

The snappy drill, brilliant uniforms, and the fact that there was something dashing about being a light infantryman helped recruiting and Zouave regiments became all the rage.

Most of the fancy uniforms of both sides vanished during the first months of campaigning, and faded blue coats and light blue pants, or home-dyed butternut became the standard fighting and working rig.

Battle flags and regimental colors were carried into action. The color guard usually being made up of picked N.C.O.s. This was a universal custom of the time and, looking back on it from the vantage point of some hundred years, seems like a waste of manpower. The flags "drew lead like a magnet," and the brave color guards were frequently wiped out to a man. On the other hand, the colors acted as rallying points, were focal points for a regiment's strength and morale, and acted as markers (when seen from other points of the battlefield) of the regiment's progress and present position. Often, because of the smoke, they were almost all that could be seen of the battle lines.

There were also distinctive flags for armies, corps, divisions, and brigades. Some generals had distinctive flags of their own—the best known, perhaps, was Sheridan's two-starred, red and white battle flag, which streamed out behind the fiery little general in many a mad gallop.

Companies in reserve

Company guarding flank

300 yds.

500 yds.

Skirmish line—two companies

Besides the basic motions of handling his weapons, facing right, left, etc., the underlying principle of all drill and tactics was to bring the soldier expeditiously and in good order to the field of battle; and when there, to arrange him, with as little confusion and delay as possible, in a position where he might employ his weapons to the best advantage. To accomplish this with large bodies of men and where roads were narrow and few in number was no easy task.

On the march, a brigade of four regiments of six hundred men each would take up close to one thousand yards of road. In battle order (two ranks), they would extend about the same distance.

On the march, carrying some forty-five pounds of equipment, a regiment on good roads might make three miles an hour. Heat and dust might slow this to close to two. A good average, including halts, might be a distance of two and a half miles in an hour.

There was always a certain "tailing out" of a column, depending to a great extent on the discipline and morale of the troops. This "snowballed" as the size of the unit increased. Elongation of a regiment might amount to ten per cent, that of a division fifteen per cent—and an army corps, twenty per cent.

When complicated by baggage wagons, supply trains, batteries, and ambulances, the route orders called for competent staff work and good timing. A divisional train moving into the line of march at the wrong time could cause a colossal traffic jam which might cost a battle.

A REGIMENT might fight with all its companies abreast, forming a long, double line of men—or one or more companies might be held back as reserve or formed on the flanks as in the sketch above. One or more companies were usually sent forward as a skirmish line. In a divisional attack, whole regiments might be assigned as skirmishers. Later in the war skirmish lines grew heavier, in some cases consisting of half the regimental strength, the remainder being held in line of battle as a reserve. Troops in formation under fire but not actually in action were often ordered to lay down. The officers usually remained standing. Skirmishers sought to keep down enemy fire and harass his ranks with musketry. They fought in open order, taking advantage of the ground. Skirmish lines might be 400 to 500 yards in advance of the main formation. Where there was little room for deployment or when great strength was to be brought against a small part of the enemy line, attacks were sometimes made in column: a regimental attack in columns of companies, and divisional attacks in columns of regiments.

The actual distances covered in a minute, as laid down in the manuals, were: 70 yards at common time (90 steps); 86 yards at quick time (110 steps); 109 yards at double-quick time (140 steps). However, pace of an attack depended on many factors: the distance to be covered; the nature of the ground; distance already marched; temperature; whether packs, etc., had been shed before going into action; and most important of all, the morale of the attacking units.

[23]

25 yds.  250–300 yds.

ADVANTAGE OF WIDE SPACING BETWEEN "WAVES"

Bodies of men cannot be moved with the cold-blooded precision of chessmen, as generals have been finding out to their cost since time began, and many a charge which started out with a rattle of drums, glitter of fixed bayonets, and fierce shouts, lost momentum and petered out into a fire fight at a respectable distance from the enemy formations.

Attacks were often by succeeding lines or "waves" of regiments or brigades, usually at a distance of 250 to 300 yards. The second line was then more or less safe from enemy musketry, but still near enough to act as close support. Also this left room for units to swing right or left if attacked in flank. Much smaller distances between "waves" were often used, sometimes as little as 25 yards. This gave no room for maneuvering, and ensured that missiles that missed the front lines ploughed into another of the following formations.

The formations used in the first years of the war were holdovers from the days when the infantry weapon was not accurate beyond 100 yards. No attempt was made to modify existing tactics to keep pace with the development of the rifle. Consequently the slaughter was as terrible as it was unnecessary.

Finally the common sense of the veteran soldier on both sides came to his rescue. Instead of standing in ranks in the open he learned to take cover whenever possible and to entrench wherever and however he could. If time and circumstances permitted, trees were felled, breastworks were built, and trenches dug. One of Sherman's officers before Atlanta wrote:

". . . cause a hasty barricade to be constructed. The front rank take all the guns and remain on the line, while the rear rank goes off in double-quick to collect rails, logs, rocks, any thing that can assist in turning a hostile bullet. These they place on the front of the front rank, and in five minutes there is a hasty barricade, bullet-proof and breast-high, along your whole line; not a mere straight work, but one varied with its sali-

ents and re-entering angles, taking every advantage of the ground, and cross-firing on every hollow." The same officer asserted:

"This war has demonstrated that earth-works can be rendered nearly impregnable against direct assault."

As the war progressed more and more stress was laid on these temporary entrenchments. Entrenching tools were not standard issue (often shovels and axes were borrowed from a neighboring battery), but knives, bayonets, plates, and tin cups were pressed into service.

Not only did the veteran dig, but he learned to make a shrewd appraisal of his chances when attacks on fortified positions were ordered. More than once it happened that while officers raved and threatened, veteran troops refused to advance in the face of certain death, leaving the assault to "green" regiments. If he did advance, it was likely to be in short rushes, lying flat between volleys, and taking advantage of such cover as the ground afforded. Willing enough to risk his life if there was a chance of success, the veteran campaigner drew the line at throwing it away for no purpose. Shannon, writing of discipline in the Union Army, said:

"The soldier would comply with a reasonable order, but he did so because it was reasonable, not because it was an order."

The senselessness of hurling masses of men against prepared positions was also apparent to many officers. In a letter to his sister, Colonel Emory Upton wrote after Cold Harbor:

"I am disgusted with the generalship displayed. Our men have, in many instances, been foolishly and wantonly sacrificed. Assault after assault has been ordered upon the enemy's intrenchments, when they knew nothing about the strength or position of the enemy. Thousands of lives might have been spared by the exercise of a little skill."

The net result of all this was the gradual evolution by the troops in the field of realistic tactics which conformed both to the terrain and to the new and deadly weapons with which the war was being fought. That these improvised tactics later became standard practice in modern warfare reflects favorably on the intelligence and adaptability of the soldier, both Blue and Gray.

THE soldier's equipment was also modified by experience. Anything superfluous was speedily jettisoned, and the veteran campaigner soon stripped down to the essentials. This stripping down was sometimes carried to extremes, and coats and blankets discarded by hot and weary troops in the morning might be desperately missed by their shivering owners at night. Many a recruit went thirsty because his canteen had been thrown away under some hedge, and many an improvident man went hungry for lack of the rations he had neglected to draw or had consumed at one sitting, as being too much of a bother to carry.

Despite some shoddy materials palmed off on the Federal authorities by unscrupulous contractors, the equipment used by the Union was of good quality. Certainly, in the matter of uniforms, there may not have been many sizes to choose from. But the fact that most of the photographs that have come down to us represent the average soldier of the Civil War as looking like an unmade bed is due more to the sartorial customs of the times than to any malfunction of the Quartermaster Corps.

One reads that the knapsack issued to the Union troops did not "ride" well and sagged into the wearers' backs. This was probably aggravated by improper packing—and anyway many veteran campaigners threw away their knapsacks and kept their clean clothes, if any, rolled in their blankets. Although the weight of the accouterments might have been better distributed and a summer-weight uniform appreciated, all in all the Northern soldier went to war as sensibly equipped as any soldier of that era. Any shortages he felt (and Federal troops went barefoot sometimes) was only temporary and due to poor supply arrangements—or to a successful raid by Rebel cavalry.

With the Southerners it was another matter. Any form of equipment was in short supply, and although they too discarded all inessentials at an early date, the lack of the necessities was acute, and in the case of boots, painful as well. But between the spinning wheels of the womenfolk and the plunder from abundantly stocked Yankee supply depots, Johnny Reb managed to keep going, and any deficiency in his wardrobe was not reflected in his fighting ability.

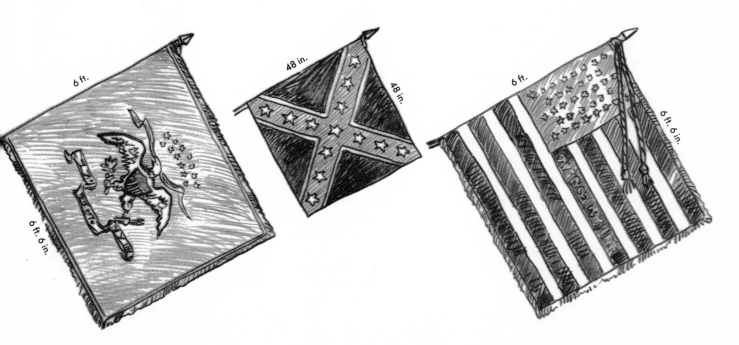

*Union Regiments had two colors. National colors, right, had name and number of regiment on center stripe. Regimental colors, left, were blue: had name of regiment on scroll beneath eagle. Confederate battle flag, center, was 48 inches square for infantry, 36 inches for artillery and 30 inches for cavalry.*

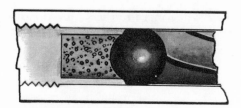

Delvigne breech chamber showing bullet expanded by ramming against shoulder

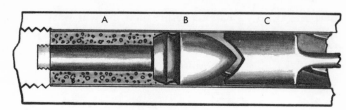

Thouvenin's carabine à tige  A. "Tige," or pillar  B. Bullet  C. Shaped rammer

## INFANTRY WEAPONS

The basic infantry weapon of the Civil War was the rifled musket. This had been developed and introduced into several armies during the preceding decade, and its effects were already making themselves felt on the battlefield. But while rifles had been used by the British and French in the Crimea, and by the French and the Austrians in Italy, the Civil War was the first great conflict in which the combination of an accurate weapon and marksmanship of a high order forced radical changes in tactical formations.

At the beginning of the war the need for firearms of any description was so great that many early types were purchased abroad and were used by both North and South until better weapons could be procured. This being the case, a brief summary of the developments leading up to the adoption of the muzzle-loading rifle as used by most infantry on both sides may be in order.

Prior to the invention of the famous Minié ball, rifles were issued only to a few special units because of the difficulty of loading. To grip the rifling properly, a ball had to be a tight fit; it often had to be hammered down, which did not help its accuracy (early rifle regiments were furnished with small mallets). Also, a greased patch had to be used, and the ball carefully centered in it. If the ball was made small enough to slip easily down a fouled barrel, it merely slid down the lands and did not bite into the groves at all. What was needed was a bullet which would expand after loading. One such system, French

Captain Delvigne's, called for a "shoulder" round the bottom of the chamber. The ball rested on this "shoulder" and was expanded by sharp blows of the ramrod. Captain Thouvenin substituted a pillar sticking up out of the bottom of the chamber, which acted as an anvil, as in the "carabine à tige," with which many units of both Northern and Southern armies were armed in the early days. This was better—but not good enough. The pillars bent, they were hard to clean, and unless the blows of the ramrod were of exactly the same force for each round the expansion differed, throwing the ballistics completely off. One thing had been accomplished, however. The round ball had given way at last to a flat-bottomed pointed bullet.

Enter Captain Minié: "Let's try a cylindrical-sided, pointed bullet with a tapered hollow in the base. In this hollow we fit a little iron cup. The force of the explosion will drive the cup up into the hollow; forcing the bullet tight into the rifling." They tried it, and it worked! The British adopted it, as did the U.S. in 1852, rifling out some of the old .69 caliber smoothbore muskets, model of 1841. Numbers of these were used during the war, and the peculiar whistle made by the Minié bullet became unpleasantly familiar to many Americans. But the Minié bullet had some drawbacks, the most serious being the tendency of the iron cup to drive right through the bullet.

The British substituted a wooden or clay plug, which worked very well, while the Americans finally did away with both the cup and plug

Minié bullet, with iron cup

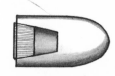

Enfield, wooden plug

Pritchett bullet for Enfield, no plug

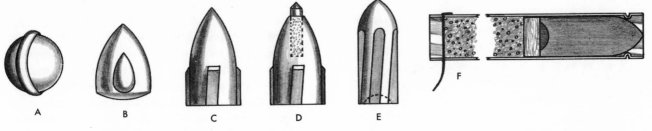

A. Belted ball for two-groove Brunswick. B. Picket bullet with two wings for two-groove rifle. C. Bullet with angled projections for four-groove Jacobs' rifle. D. Explosive bullet for Jacobs' rifle. Cylindrical copper tube with fulminate cap filled with powder and inserted in cavity cast in top of bullet. E. Whitworth bullet. F. Whitworth cartridge. Cardboard case crimped on end, powder end closed by paper slip. Cartridge was placed in muzzle, slip withdrawn, and charge rammed home by one thrust of ramrod. Lubricating wad between powder and bullet.

and relied on a hollow base bullet for expansion.

At the same time as men were experimenting with an expanding bullet, others were working on a different tack—a rifle firing a mechanically fitted ball or bullet. (I use ball here to describe a spherical projectile as opposed to an elongated one, although the term, ball, was loosely applied to any missile from a rifle or musket.)

The first of these was the Brunswick. This horror had two deep spiral grooves and used a belted ball which, naturally, was most erratic in flight. It also fouled easily and became exceedingly difficult to load. Nevertheless, it was the arm of many European rifle regiments, and numbers found their way to American units, to be relegated to the Home Guard as soon as better weapons became available.

Mr. Lancaster's rifle (he made cannon as well!) had no lands or grooves, but was slightly oval in bore. It suffered from the same defects as the Brunswick. Colonel Jacobs, of the Indian Army, developed a rifle firing a pointed projectile with four lugs which fitted corresponding grooves in

the barrel. Rifled with a quick twist (4/5 of a turn in 24 inches) the weapon showed surprising accuracy. A feature of the Jacobs bullet was that it could be cast with a hollow in the point into which a percussion tube filled with powder was fitted. With such a shell, a box of powder, 10 feet square, was exploded at the distance of 1800 yards. At such a range, the trajectory must have resembled that of a small howitzer. The writer owns one of these rifles, and the leaf sight is 5 inches long!

Explosive bullets were used during the war, although they were regarded as a bit underhanded and not gentlemanly, much as were the land mine and the booby trap. These "musket shells" were made in both .58 and .54 caliber.

Another English rifle well known to American marksmen was the Whitworth, with an hexagonal bore, spiraled with a fairly rapid twist, and firing a six-sided bullet. Like all rifles firing mechanically fitted bullets, it was hard to load after a few rounds unless swabbed out frequently. Its superior accuracy seems to have made it worth the trouble,

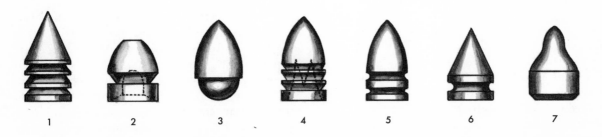

A few of the many types of bullets in use at the time of the Civil War. 1. Prussian bullet for "Tige" rifle. 2. Bullet originally used by the French Imperial Guard. 3. Bullet used with Prussian needle gun. 4. Bullet used by Belgian infantry. 5. Saxon bullet. 6. Saxon bullet for "Tige" rifle. 7. Bullet adopted by Bersaglieri.

as it was a favorite with Confederate sharp-shooters.

There was another way to load a bullet and get it to grip the rifling, and that was to load it through the breech. The years just prior to the war saw a great variety of breech-loading weapons made, though few ever received official sanction. They were mostly very ingenious affairs, using paper or linen cartridges and percussion cap ignition. They all had one major fault. They leaked gas at the breech and their mechanisms were easily fouled by the powder. Black powder, when burned, produces a residue like a hard soot, which makes even a smoothbore muzzle-loader difficult to load after a few rounds. The Sharps was the most successful of this type and was used throughout the war by both sides.

Another type, which in later years would supersede all others, used a cartridge in which the charge was enclosed in a metallic case. Some of these still relied on a separate percussion cap for ignition, but those firing a cartridge in which case, charge, and detonator were combined proved far superior. Of these the Spencer was the best known, with the Henry (direct ancestor of the Winchester) a close second. Both of these were repeaters, and while neither was used in sufficient quantities as an infantry weapon to influence the outcome of the war, they did have considerable local effect.

It should be remarked that the development of a successful breechloader was dependent on the design of a metallic cartridge containing the detonator and projectile, and capable of being mass-manufactured. Not until the difficulties of stamping, annealing, drawing, machining, and loading had been surmounted could work begin on the weapon itself. The development of such manufacturing techniques in the North was an outstanding achievement and revolutionized weapon design throughout the world.

It is hard to understand why the Federal government never made a determined effort to arm the troops with breechloaders. There was no question as to their effectiveness, and the men were so anxious to have them that in many cases companies would save their small pay and purchase the arms themselves.

While realizing the troubles of the head of the Bureau of Ordnance, Brigadier General James W. Ripley, in trying to build up and distribute stocks of ammunition for the dozens of different weapons in use, it is plain that a less conservative approach to the problem of the ideal weapon might have shortened the war and saved tens of thousands of lives. It was a great tragedy for the North that, despite the wealth of ideas, technical ability, and manufacturing facilities at its disposal, the head of the Bureau of Ordnance should have hindered the adoption of the very weapons which might have brought speedy victory to the Union. No doubt Ripley was not solely to blame, and other elderly die-hards in the ranks of the Regular Army must share some of it. In 1864 Brigadier General George D. Ramsay, who succeeded Ripley as Chief of Ordnance, wrote:

"Repeating arms are the greatest favorite in the Army, and could they be supplied in quantities to meet all requisitions I am sure no other arm would be used."

By that time it was too late to tool-up enough factories to turn out the vast numbers of weapons and the millions of cartridges required.

THERE is considerable written about accuracy in rifles, and some of it is misleading. It is all very well to speak of weapons with ranges of so many hundreds of yards. The truth is that few people are capable of hitting a man-size target offhand at more than three hundred yards, even with a modern high-powered rifle. The black-powder gun of those days was anything but high-power. A high trajectory means a small "danger space," and at any but the closest ranges, distances had to be estimated carefully. Also, many a "crack shot" woodsman had not reckoned on the fact that it is one thing to pick a squirrel out of a tree in a nice quiet wood lot and quite another to aim accurately when the woods are murky with powder smoke from bursting shells and the air full of shrieking shell fragments and whistling bullets. It takes a steady veteran to find his mark under those conditions, as the tons of wasted lead on any battlefield testified. Many company commanders preferred to hold their fire until opposing units were so close that missing was almost impossible. Accounts like the following were frequent:

"The column was in full view and about 30 yards distant . . . . just in front of me was a bush three or four feet high . . . . hitting this with my sword, I said, 'Boys, give them a volley just over this. Ready! Aim! (and jumping around my company to get from in front of their guns) fire! . . . . It seems to me that the fire of my company had cut down the head of the column that struck us as deep back as my company was long." (Oscar Jackson, 63rd Ohio Volunteers—"The Colonel's Diary")

"Now the front rank was within a few rods (a rod is 16.5 feet). . . . My rifles flamed and roared in the Federal's faces . . . . the effect was appalling. The entire front line, with few exceptions, went down in the consuming blast." (General John Gordon—"Reminiscences of the Civil War")

Volley firing also steadied the men. When loading "by the numbers" there was less chance of putting in a cartridge bullet-first, or ramming several charges one on top of the other (one musket picked up at Gettysburg had 23 loads), or any of the accidents by which a nervous and excited man might disable his musket (shooting away the ramrod was another).

After Gettysburg, of more than 37,000 muskets salvaged, 24,000 were loaded and of these 18,000 had more than one load. Many of those with a single charge were loaded with untorn cartridges or bullet-down. From this, experts judge that, figuring as many improperly loaded weapons were probably retained by their users as those that were found, 35 per cent of all troops engaged were ineffective.

There were many instances when sharpshooters made remarkable hits at seven hundred, eight hundred, or even one thousand yards, but these were by picked shots, and usually fired from steady rests. Some of these men were armed with heavy barreled target rifles with telescopic sights, but the weight of these "sniper's" rifles (some ran close to thirty pounds) precluded their use in ordinary combat.

There were several attempts to interest the armies in machine guns, and some few saw action. However, there was considerable opposition on the part of the military. Brigadier General Ripley, of course, refused to consider such weapons and few officers in authority saw any need for a rapid-fire gun.

A few were ordered by commanding officers (the only Gatlings to see service with the Union Army were purchased by General Ben Butler), but in general the Army just wasn't interested. In defense of the skeptics, it must be admitted that the early machine guns were far from perfect, and much subject to jamming and other malfunction. The Confederate Ordnance Department under General Gorgas was less conservative, but hampered by difficulties of manufacture and supply.

It is possible that given proper encouragement by those in authority, the North could have produced a reliable machine gun in sufficient quantities by 1863 to have materially influenced the course of the war.

With all the advances in metallurgy, manufacturing techniques, and explosives, it is interesting to note that one of the few multi-shot weapons that did see service was not, strictly speaking, a machine gun, but a "volley" gun that closely resembled weapons projected by Leonardo da Vinci, and which were used as early as the beginning of the sixteenth century.

The small arms used by officers and carried by some enlisted men were mostly the standard "cap and ball" revolver of the period, with five or six chambers. In addition, the infantry officer traditionally carried a sword, as did the sergeants.

While grenades were used to some extent, usually in special instances, as in the siege and trench warfare around Petersburg, they were not part of the infantryman's standard armament.

THE bayonet was carried by the infantry of both sides. It was used as an entrenching tool, can opener, roasting spit, and for a great many other purposes, but seldom as a weapon. Bayonets were fixed before a charge but, as General John Gordon, C.S.A. (who should have known, if any man did) wrote:

"The bristling points and the glitter of the bayonets were fearful to look upon as they were leveled in front of a charging line, but they were rarely reddened with blood."

In most cases the rifles of the defenders forced the attackers to halt and begin a fire fight before the bayonet could be brought into play.

Speaking of a bayonet charge and counter-charge, Oscar Jackson, in his *Colonel's Diary,* said:

". . . . Corporal Selby killed a rebel with his bayonet there, *which is a remarkable thing in a battle and was spoken of in the official report.*" (The italics are mine.)

Out of 7302 wounded during part of Grant's Wilderness campaign, only six were listed as being injured by sword or bayonet. Reporting on accounts of Union troops being caught and spitted in their tents at Shiloh, *Tribune* correspondent Richardson wrote:

"No man was bayoneted in his tent *or anywhere else to the best evidence I could obtain.*"

The day of the bayonet was over.

[29]

**Williams bullet**

**Shaler sectional bullet**

**Expanding bullet**

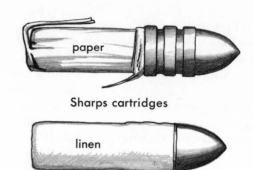

**Sharps cartridges**

paper

linen

## CARTRIDGES

Cartridges were used by the millions. The Union alone bought or made over a billion. They came in all sizes, from .31 to .79, in paper, linen, skin, brass, and copper, usually in packages of ten, in wooden cases of one thousand. The manufacture and distribution of this amazing variety was a tremendous problem to the ordnance and quartermaster departments on both sides.

The Williams bullet had a hole in its base in which fitted a lead disc and plug holding a zinc washer. When fired, the washer was jammed up against the base of the bullet and expanded, scraping the bore clean. One of these bore-cleaners was sometimes included in a package of cartridges.

The Shaler sectional bullet separated on firing and was introduced as an improvement on the buckshot or buck and ball loads. The expanding bullet shows a different method of expanding by means of a lead base plug, giving more weight than the hollow or clay-plugged projectile.

Christian Sharps brought out his self-consuming linen cartridge in 1852. It was a great improvement over the paper cartridge, holding its shape better and being able to stand rougher handling without breaking open. Colt manufactured self-consuming paper cartridges for his pistols. The paper was impregnated with a preparation containing potassium nitrate. Skin cartridges were also used for revolver ammunition. Pigs' intestines were stretched wet over forms which gave them their shape. When dry they were treated with chemicals to make them self-consuming, and then shellacked to keep out moisture.

There was a tremendous demand for percussion caps (the North bought or made nearly one and a quarter billion). They were punched by machine from thin sheets of copper. These machines could make over thirty thousand in a ten-hour day. The charge in each cap was one-half grain of fulminate, which was pressed into the base of the cap. Great care had to be taken in manufacturing, as caps occasionally exploded under the press. They were sorted and varnished by hand —a boy being able to count and varnish 7000 per hour.

Although the cartridge developed by the inventive Dr. Edward Maynard relied for ignition on a separate detonator, it achieved great popularity. For one thing, it was easily reloaded and could be used many times. It had an oversize head for ease of extraction and, of course, gave good obturation. The flame from either percussion cap or tape primer passed through a small hole in the head, blowing in a wax-paper disc and igniting the charge. The same system was used by the oddly-shaped Burnside, invented by the general, of whisker and Fredericksburg fame, for his carbine. The breechblock of this weapon tipped down, and as in the early Hall, the cartridge was pushed end-first into the chamber. One odd feature of this cartridge was its habit of tearing off the whole crimped end and sending it through the rifling still firmly attached to the bullet.

The Henry cartridge was a rim-fire. The hollow rim was filled with detonating material and exploded when struck by hammer or firing pin.

The pin-fire cartridge was the first successful

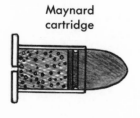

**Maynard cartridge**

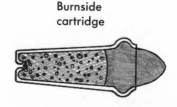

**Burnside cartridge**

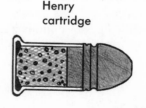

**Henry cartridge**

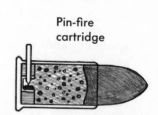

**Pin-fire cartridge**

[30]

self-exploding type, being invented in France about 1836. A cap was fixed in the base of the cartridge by a wad with a pin in contact with the detonating compound. The pin stuck out of the side of the case, and the hammer, which struck down on the cylinder instead of against the rear, drove the pin into the detonator. It was more dangerous to handle and more subject to damage in storing and transit than the rim-fire cartridge, but thousands of pin-fire revolvers were used, nevertheless.

There is not, nor can there ever be, a complete list of all the types of small arms used in the Civil War. The important weapons are well-known; but during the acute shortages of the early days, antiques of every description were rummaged out of attics or found rusting in local armories. (At Fort Henry, the 10th Tennessee—described as "the best equipped regiment in the command" was armed with Tower muskets carried by militia in 1812.)

If it comes as a shock to some of us to find (in a war in which fire control directions were telegraphed from observations balloons to batteries of rifled artillery) troops armed with flintlocks, it must be remembered that the manufacture of the flintlock had only been discontinued by the U. S. Government less than twenty years before, and many veterans had never fired anything else. In justice to the ordnance departments of both North and South, it must be said that these obsolete weapons were replaced by percussion arms as soon as possible.

In addition, there were quantities of a variety of European weapons; some, such as the two-grooved Brunswicks, were obsolete and nearly worthless; others, however, like the .577 caliber Enfield and the .45 Whitworth, were well made and accurate weapons. Most of these imports needed special ammunition in practically every caliber from .79 down. With the many different American weapons in use, this posed a tremendous problem in ordnance supply and repair. As late as 1863, the Federals listed as official over one hundred models of rifles, muskets, musketoons, and carbines.

There were some nine models of smoothbore U.S. flintlocks made at government armories or by contract after 1800, most in .69 caliber. Of these, the best known was the U. S. Flintlock, Model of 1822. A .69 caliber flintlock was also made at the Virginia Armory for that state. There was also the Hall Breech-loading Flintlock Rifle,

round ball, .53 caliber, patented 1811, made in later models in different lengths and calibers, rifled and smoothbores; some were even altered to muzzle-loaders early in the war.

The percussion system of ignition came into use in the U.S. in 1841 with the U. S. Percussion musket, Model of 1841. Many of these .69 caliber smoothbores were rifled early in the fifties and became the U. S. Minié rifle, .69 caliber. The famous "Mississippi" rifle, Model of 1841, .54 caliber, round ball (so called because Jefferson Davis' Mississippi Volunteers were armed with it in the Mexican War), also saw much service. A .69 percussion musket was made in 1852 for the State of South Carolina at Columbia. These weapons, stamped Palmetto Armory, were, with the above-mentioned Virginia Armory flintlocks, the only military muskets made in the South prior to the outbreak of the Civil War.

The advent of the Minié bullet rendered the smoothbore musket obsolete and, starting with the U. S. Model 1855, all weapons were rifled.

In appearance, the various muzzle-loading percussion smoothbores and rifles were very similar, differing only enough to confuse the amateur and delight the collector. The lock mechanisms were much alike; simple, rugged, and easily repaired. For illustrative purposes, the U. S. Model 1861 can be considered as typical of the class.

Of the many varying types of breech-loading rifles and carbines, space permits illustration of only a few. A list of breechloaders used or tested by the U. S. Ordnance Department shows fifty-two with patents dated prior to January 1865. At least thirty-six different models saw service—some of which were manufactured in very small numbers and others by the thousands.

How many of the experimental models were made and sold to individual soldiers or to small units will probably never be known. The variations were both numerous and ingenious. On some, barrels slid forward, revolved, or hinged downward like a shot gun. On others, breechblocks tipped up or down, hinged, or lowered. A few took a metallic cartridge; most used a combustible container and relied on the percussion cap for ignition. All of this latter type suffered in some degree from gas escape at the breech and subsequent fouling of the action. The Maynard and the Burnside used a combination, getting obturation with a metal case, but relying on a separate cap for ignition.

The forerunners of the U. S. Model 1861 were

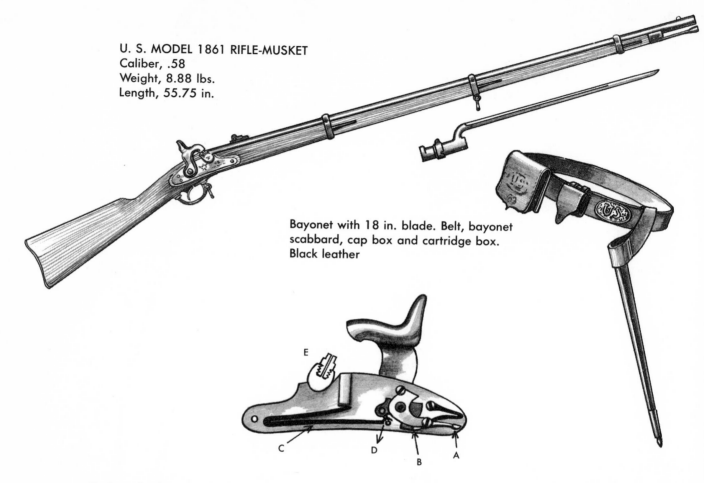

U. S. MODEL 1861 RIFLE-MUSKET
Caliber, .58
Weight, 8.88 lbs.
Length, 55.75 in.

Bayonet with 18 in. blade. Belt, bayonet scabbard, cap box and cartridge box. Black leather

*Lock mechanism was simple. When action of trigger pressed sear up,* A, *it released tumbler at* B. *Mainspring* C, *pulled tumbler down and round,* D, *bringing hammer down on nipple* E.

the U. S. Model 1855 Maynard Primer musket, and a shorter version, the U. S. Model 1855 rifle, also fitted with a Maynard primer. This primer worked like a child's roll cap pistol—a tape containing patches of fulminate feeding a cap to the nipple by action of an arm on the hammer. A good idea, but the "waterproof" tape got damp and caused misfires. Condemned in 1860, it was hastily brought out of retirement in '61.

The Model of 1861, and the subsequent, slightly changed Models of 1863 and 1864, became the standard American infantry arm. These were generally known as "Springfields," although many were made at other armories. During the war the Federal Government made over 800,000 of these guns and purchased over 670,000 more.

This weapon was rugged, simple in construc-

tion, and had an effective range of 500–600 yards. At battle ranges, 200–300 yards, it was deadly. It could also kill at 1000 yards, although at that range the chances of a hit on anything smaller than a body of troops in formation were slight. The trajectory was high. Aimed at a target 300 yards away, the bullet rose some four feet above the line of sight. Sighted at 500 yards, the rifle would send the bullet well over the head of a horseman 250 yards away. Rate of fire was slow—three shots a minute was fast shooting.

Second in numbers used was the British Enfield, .577 caliber. This fine weapon came in several models, and was considered by some to be superior in workmanship and accuracy to the American rifle. More than 800,000 were bought by North and South.

*To load: A cartridge was taken from the case, and the powder end torn open with the teeth. The powder was emptied down the barrel and the bullet pressed down with the thumb. The ramrod was then withdrawn from under the rifle barrel, the cup-shaped end pressed down on top of the bullet, and the bullet rammed firmly home till it seated on the powder. The ramrod was returned, the hammer pulled back to the half cock, and a percussion cap taken from the cap box and pressed over the nipple. When ready to fire, the hammer was pulled back to full cock.*

*Black powder fouls badly. Theoretically, the bullet expanded in the bore and scoured out the soot and clinkers left over from the preceding shot. In practice, loading became more difficult and accuracy fell off.*

A.  .69 cal. ball
B.  .69 cal. buck and ball—1 ball, 3 buckshot
C.  .69 cal. Minié ball with wooden plug
D.  .58 Minié ball
E.  .58 Buckshot, 12 shot

CUTAWAY DIAGRAMS OF MUZZLE-LOADING CARTRIDGES. ACTUAL SIZE

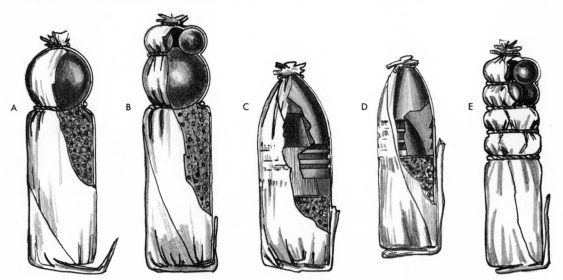

A          B          C          D          E

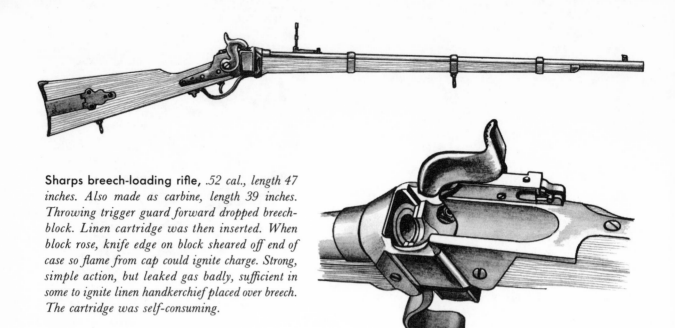

Sharps breech-loading rifle, .52 cal., length 47 inches. Also made as carbine, length 39 inches. Throwing trigger guard forward dropped breech-block. Linen cartridge was then inserted. When block rose, knife edge on block sheared off end of case so flame from cap could ignite charge. Strong, simple action, but leaked gas badly, sufficient in some to ignite linen handkerchief placed over breech. The cartridge was self-consuming.

Top view showing breechblock dropped

## THE SHARPS

Accuracy with the Sharps was probably better than with the muzzle-loaders. Some tall stories have come down about its performance in the hands of Berdan's famous Sharpshooters. However, it must be remembered that these were picked shots, and if they could drop a man at 700 yards, so could a skilled shooter with a Springfield or Enfield. The main thing was that its rate of fire was at least three times as great. Also, although a muzzle-loader could be charged while in a prone position, it was almost impossible for a marksman under cover to load such a rifle without exposing some portion of his anatomy to return fire. The advantages of a breechloader in this respect were enormous.

Even the ultra-conservative Ripley had to admit that a breechloader was a necessity for mounted troops, so it was as a cavalry carbine that this fine weapon saw most active service. Over 80,000 were purchased by the Federal Government, while government purchases of the rifles totaled less than 10,000. However, many troops were armed with Sharps rifles at their own expense, or by their state governments.

The carbine weighed less than eight pounds, and was furnished with the customary ring and slide for sling. An interesting variation was the incorporation of a small coffee mill with a detachable handle in the butt. The idea was to supply one to every company (coffee was frequently issued in the bean), but only a very few were ever so altered. Some Sharps were manufactured in the South, but reports indicate inferior workmanship and performance.

*Cutaway showing disc priming device. A magazine held a number of copper detonating pellets. As the hammer fell, it ejected a disc out of the top of the magazine into position on the nipple. A feed spring forced the next disc up into place. This did away with the necessity for capping by hand and speeded up the rate of fire. A tape primer, which fed pellets of fulminate enclosed between two strips of paper to the firing position, had been used prior to the invention of the disc primer. Not proving waterproof, the tape was replaced by the disc, although rifles fitted with tape primers were used during the war.*

**SPENCER REPEATING RIFLE**
Length, 47 in. Weight, 10 lb.

## THE SPENCER

The Spencer, made as a rifle and carbine, and in several calibers, was the most widely used and most sought after breechloader of the war. Government purchases of over 12,000 rifles and more than 94,000 carbines were supplemented by purchases by individuals, units, and states. It was a remarkable gun, and went far toward revolutionizing warfare, as it was then waged. Its eight shots (seven in the magazine and one in the chamber) could be fired as rapidly as the lever could be worked and the hammer thumbed back (lock and breech-loading mechanisms were separate). Spencer himself fired part of a Navy test at the rate of twenty-one rounds per minute. The effect of such a volume of fire was devastating. Of one Confederate attack on a regiment armed with the Spencer rifle it was written that,

"The head of the column, as it was pushed on by those behind, appeared to melt away, or sink into the earth. For although continually moving, it got no nearer."

Objections were made that reloading the magazine took too much time—but a quick-loading cartridge box, holding several tubes containing seven cartridges each, which could be loaded in the magazine in one operation, was introduced.

Tests included burying a loaded weapon and immersing it in salt water before actual firing.

"We found them simple and compact in construction and think them less liable to get out of order than any other breech-loading arm in use and are particularly pleased with the light carbine . . ." reads an excerpt from an official report.

The cartridge had a copper case, rim-fire (the detonating compound was in the rim of the cartridge like the present-day .22) with a soft lead bullet, weighing 385 grains in the .52 caliber, and with 48 grains of powder. The complete round weighed just over an ounce. The inclusion of the detonator with the charge was a great improvement—doing away with caps and discs, while the case rendered the cartridge waterproof. This also was a tremendous advantage in an age when "keeping your powder dry" was not just a saying but a matter of life or death.

The carbine, which was the deciding factor on many of the great cavalry actions of the latter part of the war, weighed just over nine pounds empty, and was a handy thirty-nine inches long.

Another point in the weapon's favor (this applied also to the Henry) was the inability of the South to manufacture cartridges for captured Spencers. When supplies of captured cartridges gave out, the guns were useless.

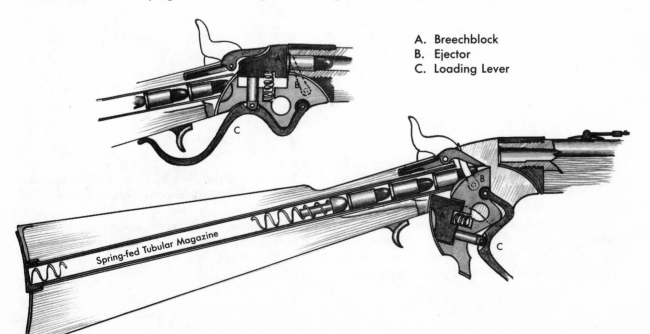

A. Breechblock
B. Ejector
C. Loading Lever

Spring-fed Tubular Magazine

[35]

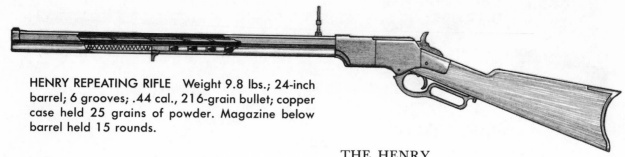

HENRY REPEATING RIFLE   Weight 9.8 lbs.; 24-inch barrel; 6 grooves; .44 cal., 216-grain bullet; copper case held 25 grains of powder. Magazine below barrel held 15 rounds.

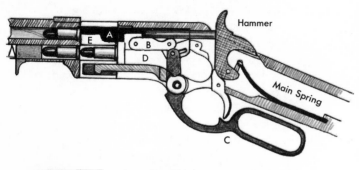

Hammer

E A
B
D

Main Spring

C

## THE HENRY

The fast-shooting Henry was in great demand. Federal orders were small, but some 10,000 were bought by state troops. The Spencer was rated less likely to get out of order, but the Henry's rate of fire was higher. The magazine could be emptied in less than 11 seconds; 120 shots were loaded and fired in 5 minutes, 45 seconds.

Simplified diagrams at left show loading system.

*Breechblock was locked by toggle. Pulling trigger-guard lever unlocked toggle, which then pulled breech-block straight back. Hammer cocked by end of block riding over it. Carrier block with round from magazine raised into line with chamber. Raising lever drove round into chamber, dropped carrier block, and locked toggle joint, securing breechblock.*

A. Breechblock and breech pin piston
B. Toggle
C. Trigger guard lever
D. Carrier lever
E. Carrier block

Hammer

E
A
D
B

Main Spring

C

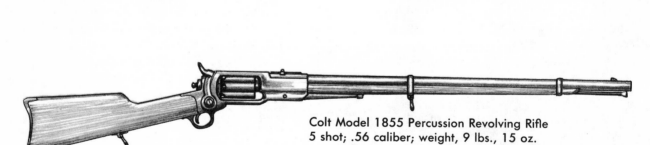

Colt Model 1855 Percussion Revolving Rifle
5 shot; .56 caliber; weight, 9 lbs., 15 oz.

## THE COLT

The Colt was the first repeating rifle adopted by the U. S. Government (an early model was used in the Seminole War in 1838). Revolving rifles were made in several lengths and calibers. Most of the smaller calibers were made with six cylinders. There was considerable sideflash and possibility of other cylinders going off at once—

taking off the shooter's left hand. There were so many accidents that some commanders ordered their men to lower the loading lever and hold the gun by it. Many were used during the war, however, and Berdan's Sharpshooters were issued the 1855 model while waiting to be rearmed with the Sharps.

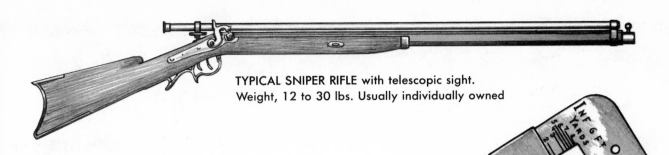

**TYPICAL SNIPER RIFLE** with telescopic sight.
Weight, 12 to 30 lbs. Usually individually owned

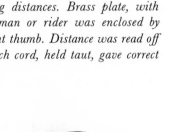

*Stadium for estimating distances. Brass plate, with sliding bar. Figure of man or rider was enclosed by pushing up bar with right thumb. Distance was read off appropriate scale. 25-inch cord, held taut, gave correct distance from eye.*

10-shot group shot in 1859 at 220 yards. Actual size

## THE SNIPER RIFLE

Marksmen were formed into sharpshooters regiments, or attached singly or in small groups to various commands. *Harper's Weekly* reported of Berdan's Sharpshooters: "The requirements are that no man is admitted to the regiment who does not shoot, at 600 feet distance, ten consecutive shots at an average of five inches from the bulls eye." With telescopic sights, and fired from a steady rest, these rifles were capable of great accuracy.

These super-accurate, heavy-barreled rifles were usually provided with false muzzles and bullet starters. The false muzzle ensured the correct seating of the bullet which was, of course, of greater diameter than the bore measured over the lands (it was not usually quite as big as the groove diameter, as most such rifles took a thin paper patch). It also protected the true muzzle from wear and damage which might destroy the fine accuracy of the weapon. Before rifling, the end of the barrel was turned down slightly, cut off, and the cut-off portion was drilled for steel pins (see below). These pins exactly fitted corresponding holes in the end of the barrel. The false muzzle was then put in place and the gun rifled. The forward end of the false muzzle was reamed out very slightly to make starting the bullet easier. The bullet starter was a piston-like arrangement, the end of which was shaped to fit the nose of the bullet, and which fitted over the false muzzle when the bullet was in place. A smart blow with the palm of the hand drove the bullet into the barrel and engaged it in the rifling. The starter was then withdrawn and the bullet pushed down onto the powder with a wooden ramrod. The metal pin on the false muzzle blocked the sight, to make sure the shooter removed the false muzzle before firing. Careful marksmen often inserted a brass or copper tube down the barrel and poured the powder down that, to ensure the full charge reaching the chamber. Bullets were carefully molded, sized, and checked for weight.

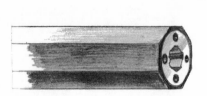

Before recording how accurate were the rifles used in the Civil War, it may be well to note how inaccurate were the smooth bores of the period. At 50 yards they were good—that is, they could be relied on to place most of their shots in an 18-inch circle. At 100 this circle was more likely to be about three to four feet—in other words, a man-target stood a fair chance at this range, although use of buck and ball increased his chances of being hit. Over 100 yards, accuracy fell off alarmingly. At 150 yards, tests made of the old British Army smoothbore showed that a target three feet wide and 11½ feet high could only be hit 75 per cent of the time. At 250 yards, although the width of the target was increased to six feet, not one out of ten shots hit. It is safe to say that a man at 200 yards stood little risk of being hit except by a stray bullet.

The rifled muskets firing a round ball did better. At 100 yards the Model 1841 "Mississippi" could hit a target the size of a man's head pretty consistently. At 200 yards the old Baker (Britain's first army rifle) could hit a man most of the time, but at 300 even the 1841 could score less than 25 per cent of hits on a target eight feet square.

The conical bullet was a vast improvement, and now a reasonable percentage of hits could be expected at 500 yards. The French carabine à

tige made 42.3 per cent of hits on a target 13 feet wide and 6½ feet high at 628 yards. A trained rifleman, with a British Enfield, could expect to hit a man-size target about half the time at 500 yards. R. T. Pritchett, the inventer of the improved bullet for the Enfield, firing one of his own rifles on a windy, rainy day, put 98 out of 100 shots within a seven-foot circle at 600 yards.

Tests in the United States gave the mean vertical deviation at 500 yards of the U. S. Model 1855 Rifle-Musket as 15 inches and horizontal, 13 inches, and that of the Enfield as 20 and 17 inches, respectively. At ranges of 1000 yards and over both Springfields and Enfields could only be depended upon to put down a volume of fire in a given area. Tests showed that at 500 yards the Enfield gave mean radial deviation of 2.24 feet; at 800, 4.2 feet; and at 1100, 8 feet. At increased distances it shot so wildly that no records could be kept.

The gun which gave the greatest accuracy at long range was the Whitworth. At 500 yards from a fixed rest, this hexagonal bore .45 caliber rifle put 20 of its mechanically-fitting bullets into a 12-inch circle. At 800 yards, mean radial deviation was only one foot; at 1100 yards, 2.62 feet; at 1400, 4.62 feet, and at 1800 yards, 11.62 feet. Fired from the prone position, in five-round

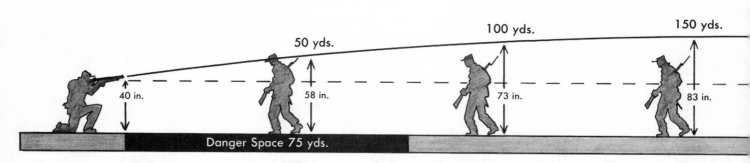

*Danger space areas for rifled musket sighted for 300 yards. Figures given are approximate heights of trajectory above line of sight, plus 40 inches. Sighted for 500 yards, at midrange bullet would pass well over head of horseman;*

strings, Whitworths tests in recent years have given three-inch groups at 200 yards, and spreads of as little as 10.75 inches at 500 yards. This is excellent accuracy and compares favorably with modern weapons. But it must be remembered that the mechanically-fitting bullet was slow to load, and, by all accounts, the rifle fouled badly.

Another group of super-accurate rifles comprised the heavy-barreled target rifles, some with telescopic sights, with which small groups of trained marksmen were armed. Many of these were too heavy (25 to 30 pounds) for field work and were only used during periods of trench warfare.

For comparison, a trained rifleman firing ten shot strings from the Springfield '06 with .30 caliber service ammunition can count, on the average, on four minute groups, that is, groups that stay within a four-inch circle at 100 yards, 12 inches at 300, 24 inches at 600 and (here is where the modern rifle and ammunition really have the advantage) 40 inches at 1000. Of course, individual scores with match ammunition better these figures, and groups of less than one inch at 300 yards have been made, but this is a highly specialized field and has little in common with battle conditions and combat shooting. Whether firing a Model 1863 muzzle-loader or a gas-oper-

ated M1, the average citizen cannot hit the proverbial bull in the behind with a bass fiddle. Training helps, but training in marksmanship was something woefully lacking in most commands during the Civil War. Little time or ammunition was allocated to actual range practice—and many recruits went into battle without having fired a single practice round. Little wonder that pounds of lead were expended for each hit made, that many a man fired his piece, unaimed, into the blue, or that front-rank men, their ears ringing or their beards singed, were known to turn about and pummel their overzealous rear-rank comrades.

What made hitting extremely difficult was the high trajectory of the hugh chunks of lead thrown by the old rifled muskets. Ranges had to be correctly estimated and sights carefully adjusted for anything but the very closest ranges. A bullet fired by a kneeling man at the belt buckle of a man running toward him at an estimated range of 300 yards would just pass over the head of a man 250 yards away. Thus, if the shooter had overestimated the range by as little as 50 yards he would have missed. The diagram below shows the so-called "danger spaces" involved. At greater ranges the heights of trajectories increased sharply and the danger spaces grew smaller.

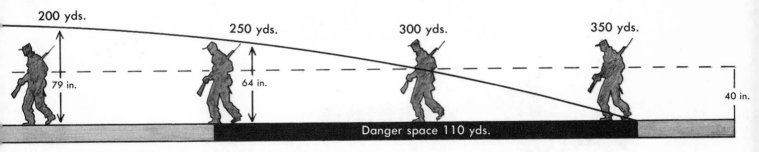

200 yds.    250 yds.    300 yds.    350 yds.

79 in.    64 in.    40 in.

Danger space 110 yds.

*danger spaces would be very small. By comparison, height of trajectory at midrange of .30 caliber M1 sighted for 300 yards is 7.2 inches above the line of sight.*

[39]

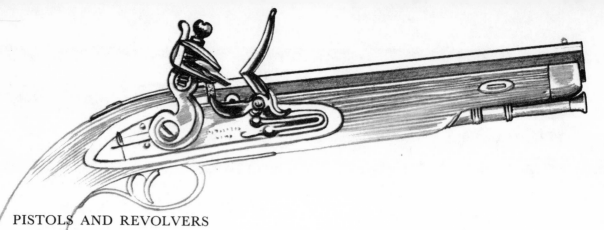

## PISTOLS AND REVOLVERS

Pistols and revolvers of all descriptions were used during the war, from ancient flintlocks to the latest double-action models. As was natural, a greater variety of antiques and oddities saw service in the weapon-poor South than in the North. Many infantry volunteers on both sides armed themselves with handguns, only to discard them later along with much of the weighty paraphernalia with which they at first burdened themselves. Nearly all cavalry carried handguns of some sort throughout the war.

Foreign arms were imported, especially into the Confederacy—where also copies of Northern weapons, mainly Colts, were made by Leech and Rigden, Tucker, Sherrod & Co., and Dance Bros., to name a few. With the exception of the metallic pin-fires, most were percussion weapons with a nipple on each chamber of the cylinder.

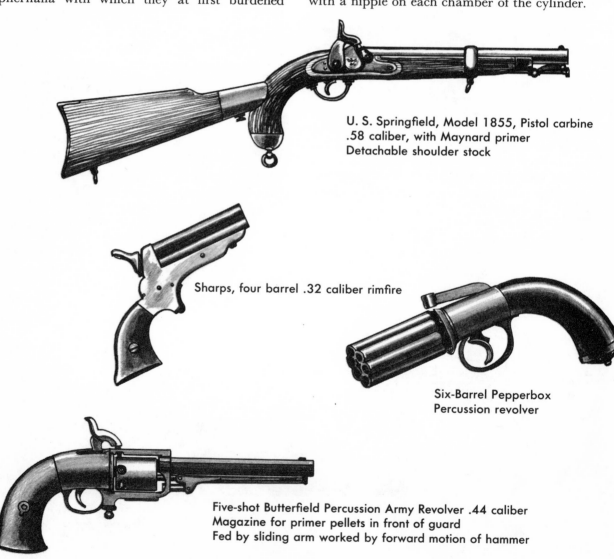

U. S. Springfield, Model 1855, Pistol carbine
.58 caliber, with Maynard primer
Detachable shoulder stock

Sharps, four barrel .32 caliber rimfire

Six-Barrel Pepperbox
Percussion revolver

Five-shot Butterfield Percussion Army Revolver .44 caliber
Magazine for primer pellets in front of guard
Fed by sliding arm worked by forward motion of hammer

COLT'S ARMY REVOLVER
Model 1860 with shoulder stock

The favorite handgun of the war was the Colt revolver. Over 146,000 were purchased by the U. S. Government during the war, and thousands of others were used by North and South. Colts were made in several models and many calibers, the most popular being the .44 caliber Army and the Navy .36. It was simple, rugged, and reliable. Cartridges were paper, foil, or skin; or the gun could be loaded with the powder and ball separate.

Shoulder stocks were provided with some models. The Navy model of 1851 had shoulder stocks containing a canteen. Bullets were round or conical. Moulds with cased sets made both kinds. Ball diameter for .44 caliber was .46, weight 216 grains, with 30 grains of powder. The .38 caliber, 145-grain ball for the Navy .36 used 17 grains of powder. Chambers were slightly less than ball diameter to ensure tight fit over powder. The loading lever was hinged under the barrel.

To load, the hammer was drawn back to half cock. This allowed the cylinder to spin freely. A cartridge, or loose powder and ball, was then loaded into a chamber and the cylinder turned under the rammer. The loading lever brought the rammer down on the bullet, which was pressed firmly down on the powder. This was repeated for all chambers. The gun was then capped and the hammer let down on the cylinder between the nipples. Cocking, which had to be done by hand (all Colts were single-action), brought the chamber in line with the barrel and locked it. Caps fit snugly, so that considerable jarring was necessary to dislodge them. A notch in the hammer at full cock formed the rear sight.

CUTAWAY OF COLT REVOLVER

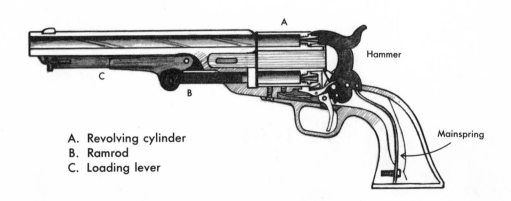

A. Revolving cylinder
B. Ramrod
C. Loading lever

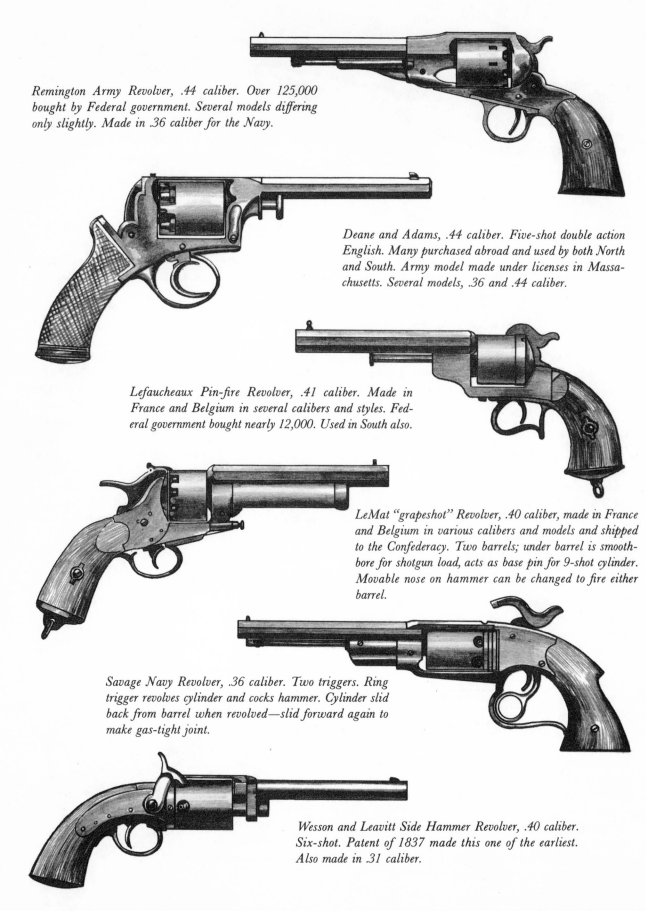

*Remington Army Revolver, .44 caliber. Over 125,000 bought by Federal government. Several models differing only slightly. Made in .36 caliber for the Navy.*

*Deane and Adams, .44 caliber. Five-shot double action English. Many purchased abroad and used by both North and South. Army model made under licenses in Massachusetts. Several models, .36 and .44 caliber.*

*Lefaucheaux Pin-fire Revolver, .41 caliber. Made in France and Belgium in several calibers and styles. Federal government bought nearly 12,000. Used in South also.*

*LeMat "grapeshot" Revolver, .40 caliber, made in France and Belgium in various calibers and models and shipped to the Confederacy. Two barrels; under barrel is smooth-bore for shotgun load, acts as base pin for 9-shot cylinder. Movable nose on hammer can be changed to fire either barrel.*

*Savage Navy Revolver, .36 caliber. Two triggers. Ring trigger revolves cylinder and cocks hammer. Cylinder slid back from barrel when revolved—slid forward again to make gas-tight joint.*

*Wesson and Leavitt Side Hammer Revolver, .40 caliber. Six-shot. Patent of 1837 made this one of the earliest. Also made in .31 caliber.*

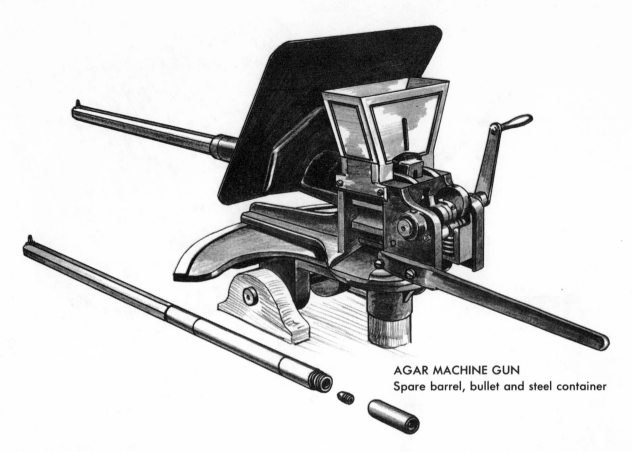

AGAR MACHINE GUN
Spare barrel, bullet and steel container

## MACHINE GUNS

Ingenious as some of them were, machine guns played little part in the war. Aside from military conservatism, there were difficulties in all such weapons of the period. One was weight. There was great weight in the carriage alone, which, in turn, cut down on maneuverability, and curtailed operation in the rough, wooded type of country in which so much of the war was fought. Coupled with this was the weight of the ammunition and the consequent difficulty of adequate supply (a paper-wrapped .58 round weighed just over 1.25 ounces). Another drawback to accurate sustained fire would have been smoke. On a still day, a few rounds would have created enough smother to have made aiming difficult.

The modern-looking weapon above, the Agar Machine Gun, was nicknamed, for obvious reasons, the "Coffee Mill," and fired a .58 Minié-type ball from a single barrel at the rate of 120 rounds a minute. The rate was kept low because of the danger of overheating the barrel, although two spares were carried. Steel containers holding either loose powder and ball, or combustible cartridges (75 grains), and with the nipple for the cap at the end, were loaded into the hopper and were gravity-fed into the recess at the back of the barrel. Containers, which also acted as firing cham-

bers, were pushed forward to form prolongation of the barrel by action of the crank, and were locked by a rising wedge. As the crank turned, the cam-operated hammer fell on the detonating cap. Further revolution of the crank released the wedge; a lever pushed the empty container out of the recess; and a fresh one dropped into place. A small shield protected the hopper and the operator from small arms fire.

An Agar machine gun and
ammunition boxes on carriage

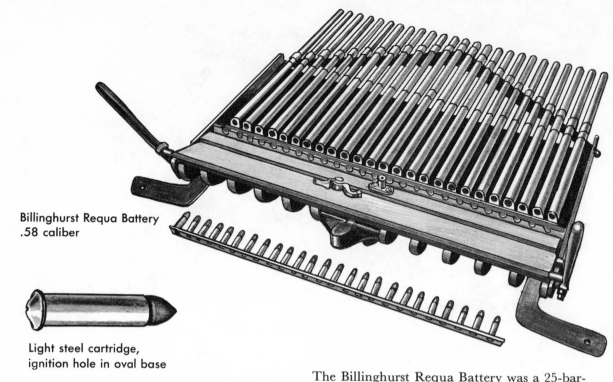

Billinghurst Requa Battery
.58 caliber

Light steel cartridge,
ignition hole in oval base

Requa Battery mounted
on carriage

The Billinghurst Requa Battery was a 25-barrel volley gun with a sliding breech worked by a lever. Cartridges were held in clips for quick loading. When the gun was loaded, the channel behind the cartridges was filled with powder. This train was ignited by a percussion cap struck by a hammer, firing all barrels simultaneously. Barrels could be moved laterally for "spread." With a crew of three, the gun could fire seven volleys per minute. A fault was that the powder train was exposed to rain, and could misfire. It was used mainly in defense of bridges, hence the nickname "covered bridge gun."

A less successful type was the Vandenberg gun, with from 85 to 451 barrels, depending on caliber. A screw-type breech slid in a key-way and forced copper sleeves into a counterbored chamber for a gas-tight seal. A center charge fired by a cap set off a whole volley; or sections of barrels could be blocked off and fired later. In tests, the 91-barrel model put 90 per cent in a six-foot square at 100 yards.

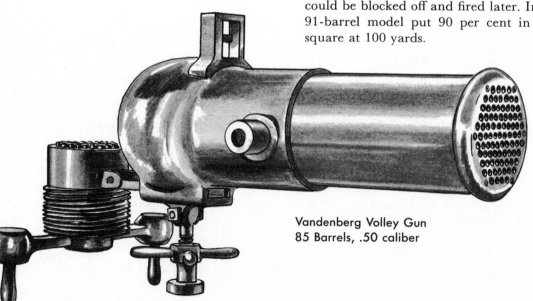

Vandenberg Volley Gun
85 Barrels, .50 caliber

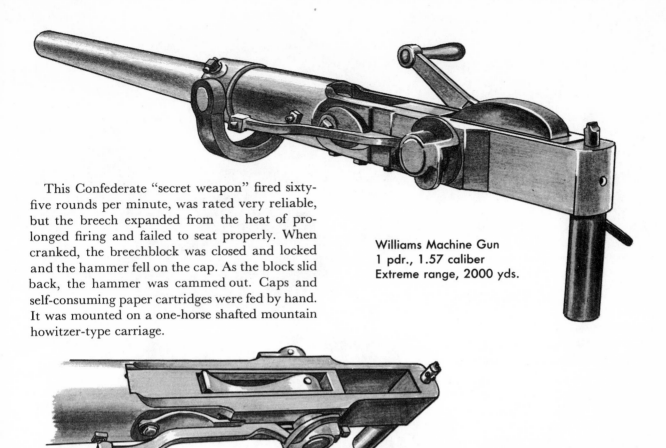

This Confederate "secret weapon" fired sixty-five rounds per minute, was rated very reliable, but the breech expanded from the heat of prolonged firing and failed to seat properly. When cranked, the breechblock was closed and locked and the hammer fell on the cap. As the block slid back, the hammer was cammed out. Caps and self-consuming paper cartridges were fed by hand. It was mounted on a one-horse shafted mountain howitzer-type carriage.

Williams Machine Gun
1 pdr., 1.57 caliber
Extreme range, 2000 yds.

Williams gun, breech closed

The Gatling model of 1862 was the forerunner of the successful 1865 model, which was adopted by the U.S. in 1866. The 1862 model fed capped steel chambers loaded with paper cartridges by gravity from a hopper. Later copper rim-fire cartridges were substituted for paper. The gun had six barrels which were revolved by a crank. Six cam-operated bolts alternately wedged, fired, and dropped chambers. One fault was that the bores were tapered (because barrels and chambers did not always exactly align), and so velocity and accuracy were impaired. U. S. Ordnance would not order any, but General Butler bought twelve after a field demonstration and used them at Petersburg. The vastly improved model of 1865 came too late for the war.

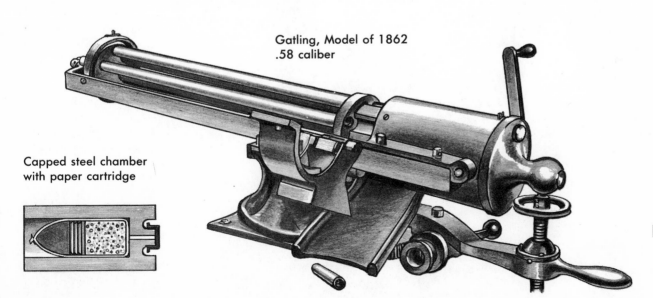

Gatling, Model of 1862
.58 caliber

Capped steel chamber
with paper cartridge

# THE CAVALRY

THE Civil War was fought under such conditions as to make the use of large bodies of cavalry inevitable. Yet at its outset none of the leaders on either side seemed to appreciate the fact. In both North and South, offers of cavalry regiments were turned down and some recruits, in disgust, enlisted in other branches. Certainly no one foresaw the masses of horsemen who would maneuver and clash in the great cavalry actions of '63 and '64.

Stuart's companies of Clarke's, Drake's, and Ashby's were a small enough beginning, and all the Federals could muster at the First Battle of Bull Run were seven troops of regulars.

If the South had any great advantage at the outset of the war, it was in the quality and leadership of its cavalry. It would be foolish to state that all Southerners were born horsemen, any more than that all Northerners were born mechanics. It was true, however, that in the mainly agrarian and communication-poor Southern states there was a greater proportion of men to whom the horse was a useful and necessary part of everyday life—as essential as an automobile is to most Americans today. There was also a considerable class of landed gentry, hard riders all, and it was from this "horsey set" that many of the excellent Rebel cavalry officers were drawn.

Coupled with this reservoir of potential cavalrymen, there was a definite "feeling" for the cavalry branch in the higher brackets of the Confederate command. Almost from the start, the Southern cavalry was handled in large bodies, and with great dash and daring.

The Northerner, even if he came from the country, was more likely to be familiar with a horse as a farm animal and beast of burden than as a mount. And, while an infantryman might be, and often was, sent into battle with a very minimum of training, it was physically impossible to do so with mounted men. A recruit's main concern was to stay in the saddle. A trooper who was probably less afraid of the enemy than he was of his mount (a mount of whose care, needless to say, he had not the remotest idea) was a liability,

[47]

not an asset. To jog-trot a conglomeration of such unhappy horsemen within reach of an aggressive enemy was to invite disaster. Yet this happened time and again, and with each reverse the moral ascendancy of the Rebel horsemen became greater. Small wonder that in the first part of the war the Southern cavalry could ride rings around almost any Northern command, capture its patrols, loot its wagon trains, burn its bridges, and escape practically unharmed.

But the Northerners learned. At the cost of many men and tens of thousands of horses there gradually evolved units of cavalry which individually could give a good account of themselves. But in the word "units" lay much of the trouble. For until Hooker organized the cavalry of the Army of the Potomac into a corps, there was almost no attempt to use it in mass, as a separate striking force. During the first two years it was frittered away in little detachments; detailed for guard duty—for provost work—for escorting anything from generals to commissary wagons. It was lacking both in self-confidence and training and there was some truth in the gibe, "Who ever saw a dead cavalryman?"

But assembled into a corps, its improvement was rapid. Always better equipped than the Southerners, the Federal cavalry soon became equal, then superior, not only to the Confederates, but to any cavalry in the world. In the opinion of McClelland, of Stuart's staff "During the last two years no branch of the Army of the Potomac contributed so much to the overthrow of Lee's army as the cavalry, both that which operated in the Valley of Virginia and that which remained at Petersburg."

Meanwhile, the strength of the Southern cavalry arm was declining. Battle and disease took their toll, and disabled horses were increasingly difficult to replace. Under the Confederate system the troopers provided their own mounts and were paid a per diem for their use, as well as for their value at mustering if killed in action. However, no compensation was given for horses lost due to the hardships of campaign or in any other way. Consequently, as horses became scarcer and more expensive, hundreds were unable to obtain mounts and so were lost to the arm. A member of General J. E. B. Stuart's staff wrote:

"We now felt the bad effect of our system of requiring men to furnish their own horses. The most dashing trooper was the one whose horse was the most apt to get shot, and when this man

was unable to remount himself he had to go to the infantry service and was lost to the cavalry. Such a penalty for gallantry was terribly demoralizing."

Coupled with this was the inability of the Confederates to supply good weapons and accouterments. Much was captured, but not enough, and the Southern cavalry lost in numbers and efficiency while the Federals gained in both.

AT THE outbreak of the war, there were five regiments of U.S. regular cavalry: the First and Second Regiments of Dragoons, the Mounted Rifles, and the First and Second Regiments of Cavalry. A regiment was composed of five squadrons of two troops each. When the Third Cavalry was organized early in 1861, another squadron of two troops was added. Shortly after, the regiments were renumbered from one to six, and the twelve-troop organization adopted for the original five. This was also adopted for volunteer regiments.

Originally a troop was supposed to consist of a hundred men, commanded by a captain, a first lieutenant, a second lieutenant, and a supernumerary lieutenant. In 1863 troops were made more flexible, with from eighty-two to one hundred men, and the supernumerary lieutenant vanished. The squadron organization was dropped, and battalions, usually of four troops, were formed when troops were to be detached for service.

Each regiment was commanded by a colonel and had a lieutenant colonel and three majors, an adjutant, a quartermaster, a commissary (usually lieutenants), and a regimental surgeon and assistant. Regimental noncoms included one sergeant major, one quartermaster sergeant, one commissary sergeant, one saddler sergeant, one chief farrier or blacksmith, and two hospital stewards.

Each troop had its first sergeant, quartermaster sergeant, and commissary sergeant, in addition, five sergeants, eight corporals, two teamsters, two farriers, one saddler, one waggoner, and two musicians.

As in all units in the war, the number and organization established by the regulations were more theoretical than actual, and the above cavalry commanders' pipe dream seldom if ever took the field in full strength.

The Southern cavalry regiment, as listed by

Major Joe Wheeler, C.S.A., was organized along somewhat similar lines. It consisted, at least on paper, of ten companies or squadrons of sixty to eighty privates, each officered by a captain, one first and two second lieutenants, and included five sergeants, four corporals, a farrier, and a blacksmith. The regimental officers were a colonel, a lieutenant colonel, a major, and an adjutant. There was also a sergeant major and a quartermaster sergeant.

Cavalry regiments of both armies were formed into brigades; brigades into divisions; and divisions into corps. A Confederate cavalry division might have as many as six brigades. The number of regiments in each brigade varied from two to six, depending partly on the strength of the units. Union divisions usually had two or three brigades each with a varying number of regiments, four to six being about normal. A corps contained two or three divisions.

Horse artillery in varying strengths was attached as occasion dictated. Where possible the cavalry was followed by its own train of ammunition and supply wagons, including rolling forges.

Cavalry was traditionally the "eyes" of the army. It was the duty of the cavalry leader to keep his commander-in-chief informed of his opponents' maneuvers, and at the same time to attempt to screen the movements of his own army from the enemy patrols. In addition to guarding the army's flanks and acting as a mobile striking force, enemy communications, supply lines, and trains were to be attacked and destroyed where possible. As the cavalry increased in numbers, this latter work was undertaken by forces involving thousands of men and horses. This occasionally had unfortunate results for, spectacular as some of the great cavalry raids were, they were frequently made at a sacrifice in men and horses disproportionate to the results obtained. Also there was the danger that, when needed most, the main body of cavalry would be away on some enterprise of its own.

Tactically, the cavalry of both North and South broke with tradition and fought with carbine or rifle, mounted or on foot, as well as with the saber. Speaking of the Battle of Beverly Ford, June 9, 1863, Wagner, in his "Organization and Tactics" says: "This was the first engagement in which the United States cavalry manifested real efficiency; and this action, more than any other, illustrates the many-sided nature of the American cavalry. In this battle a cavalry charge was re-

pulsed by cavalry mounted; an attack by cavalry dismounted against cavalry dismounted and behind cover was repulsed by sharpshooters in front, aided by mounted charges on the flanks of the assailants; a mounted charge with saber against dismounted cavalry using fire action and supported by a mounted detachment was successfully made; and two opposing brigades of cavalry met in direct charge with the saber. In brief, every possible condition of cavalry action seems to have been encountered in this remarkable engagement."

As the Union cavalry improved, it placed more reliance on the saber, while in some Confederate units the saber was used little, if at all, and the carbine, rifle, or shotgun and revolver was the principle weapon. While the Union cavalryman thought nothing of storming entrenchments or digging in to repulse an infantry attack (the development by the North of a reliable repeating carbine was of great advantage), there is no ground for the popular belief that he was little more than a mounted infantryman himself. In a report written in October 1864, General Early says ".... but the fact is, the enemy's cavalry is so much superior to ours, both in numbers and equipments, and the country is so favorable to the operations of cavalry, that it is impossible for ours to compete with his. Lomax's cavalry is armed entirely with rifles and has no sabers, and the consequence is they cannot fight on horseback, and in this open country they cannot successfully fight on foot against large bodies of cavalry."

"This," wrote General Merritt, "is a statement on which those who think our cavalry never fought mounted and with the saber should ponder."

One further quote will serve to show how highly the American cavalryman and his unique method of fighting was regarded abroad. Sir Henry Havelock, speaking of Sheridan's attacks on the Confederate rear guard at Sailor's Creek, says: "The mode in which Sheridan, from the special arming and training of his cavalry, was able to deal with this rear guard, first to overtake it in retreat, then to pass completely beyond it, to turn, face it, and take up at leisure a position strong enough to enable him to detain it in spite of its naturally fierce and determined efforts to break through, is highly characteristic of the self-reliant, all-sufficing efficiency to which at this time the Northern horsemen had been brought .... and had enabled Sheridan, and one or two more of

*Cavalry in action dismounted. The skirmish line is in advance, with the main body behind. Mounted companies are stationed on one or both flanks. The horse holders are behind the main body. In practice the number fours would hold the mounts in as sheltered a position as possible, yet near enough to be readily available.*

similar bent of mind, to shake themselves free of the unsound traditions of European cavalry theory, and to make their own horse not the jingling, brilliant, costly, but almost helpless unreality it is with us, but a force that was able, on all grounds, in all circumstances, to act freely and efficiently, without any support from infantry."

The rifled musket so weighed the balance in favor of the defense that charges against infantry in line of battle were rare, and were often met with a contempt for the sword, an occurrence new to warfare. A Southern general wrote that when charged by Northern cavalry, his men would raise the cry: "Boys, here are those fools coming again with their sabers; give it to them."

In the partisan-type warfare in the west, the hastily-equipped Southern troopers often preferred the double-barreled shotgun, with which they would charge at full gallop, firing both barrels in their opponents' faces, then drawing revolvers or laying about them with the butts of their guns.

General John H. Morgan, the great raider, developed his own tactics. The following is from General Basil W. Duke's "History of Morgan's Cavalry." If the reader will only imagine a regiment drawn up in single rank, the flank companies skirmishing, sometimes on horseback, and then thrown out as skirmishers on foot, and so deployed as to cover the whole front of the regiment, the rest of the men dismounted (one out of each set of four, and the corporals remaining to hold the horses), and deployed as circumstances required and the command indicated, to the front of, on either flank, or to the rear of the line of horses, the files two yards apart, and then imagine this line moved forward at a double-quick, or oftener a half run, he will have an idea of Morgan's style of fighting.

"Exactly the same evolutions were applicable for horseback or foot fighting, but the latter method was much oftener practised—we were in fact not cavalry, but mounted riflemen. A small body of mounted men was usually kept in reserve to act on the flanks, cover the retreat or press a victory, but otherwise our men fought very little on horseback, except on scouting expeditions."

Troops were usually maneuvered in columns of fours. When small, these columns were flexible, easy to deploy, and simplified the passage of obstacles, roads, clearings, etc.

The older army drill book called for deploying into two ranks for a charge. General St. George Cooke's drill book of '62 called for a single rank, as did that of Major General Joseph Wheeler, C.S.A.

Charges were also made in columns of fours, or double columns of fours.

The ideal position from which to launch an attack was from the flank.

(There is a military saying: "Ten men on the flank are worth more than one hundred in front.")

The ground for a mounted attack was chosen with care. When possible it was scouted first. Neglect of this precaution might cause a disaster. At Shiloh, Forrest made a charge against infantry, but when some forty paces away, was checked by a morass, which effectively stopped his attack. Fences were sometimes cleared away under fire to allow unimpeded movements. Only the best horsemen on the most carefully trained mounts could charge with unbroken ranks over fences, ditches, and broken ground. A wild gallop over such terrain was likely to do more damage to men and horses than a brush with the enemy.

On the march, cavalry could cover some thirty-five miles in an eight-hour day without undue strain on men or horses. On some of the great raids, much longer marches were made. During the Chambersburg raid in '62, Stuart's command marched eighty miles in twenty-seven hours; in 1864, Wilson's and Kautz's divisions marched three hundred miles in ten days, meanwhile destroying sixty miles of railroad; and on Morgan's great raid, the troopers were in the saddle on some days for an average of twenty-one hours a day, and once did ninety miles in thirty-five hours. Quoting General Duke again: "The men in our ranks were worn down and demoralized with the tremendous fatigue."

On such marches, troopers often slept in the saddle.

"There was no place to lie down and to stand in the snow only aggravated the discomfort. But when mounted, the men would pull the capes of their overcoats over their heads, drop their chins upon their breasts and sleep. The horses plodded along and doubtless were asleep too, doing their work as a somnambulist might, walking while they slept."

One of Stuart's columns, returning with captured horses after a raid in Pennsylvania, is described by a member of his staff:

"The column . . . was about five miles long. First there was the advance guard of one squadron, preceded by three vedettes (mounted sentries or scouts) at a distance of a hundred and fifty yards ahead; a couple of hundred yards behind the advance guard came a division of six hundred men with a section of artillery, then six hundred men leading the horses, and then six hundred bringing up the rear with a section of artillery, followed by a squadron for a rear guard, about the same distance behind that the advance guard was in front, and behind them again three men for vedettes."

Cavalry on the march took up a considerable length of road. A horse occupies approximately three yards, and there was a distance of about one yard between ranks. A troop of ninety-six men in columns of fours would be ninety-five yards long. There would, of course, be some distance between units. Colonel Kidd of the Sixth Michigan Cavalry noted that on Sheridan's great march, before Yellow Tavern, the huge column of some ten thousand troopers in three divisions and six batteries stretched for thirteen miles.

"The long column of fours thus proceeded slowly by the road while to the right and to the left, about 500 yards out, were parallel columns of flankers, marching by file, thus assuring that should the enemy attack either flank, it was only necessary to wheel by fours in this direction to be in line of battle with a strong line of skirmishers well in front."

At a walk, cavalry could cover four miles in an hour; at a slow trot, six; at a maneuvering trot, eight; at an alternate trot and walk, five; at a maneuvering gallop, twelve; and at a full extended gallop, sixteen.

Troopers fought dismounted in various circumstances: to seize and hold ground until the arrival of their infantry; to force defended places not accessible to mounted troops; to fill gaps in a line of battle or in covering the retreat of infantry, and in general where the ground was impractical for cavalry.

The number fours were horseholders in action, and the mounts were held as close to the firing line as possible, while still taking advantage of any shelter available.

[51]

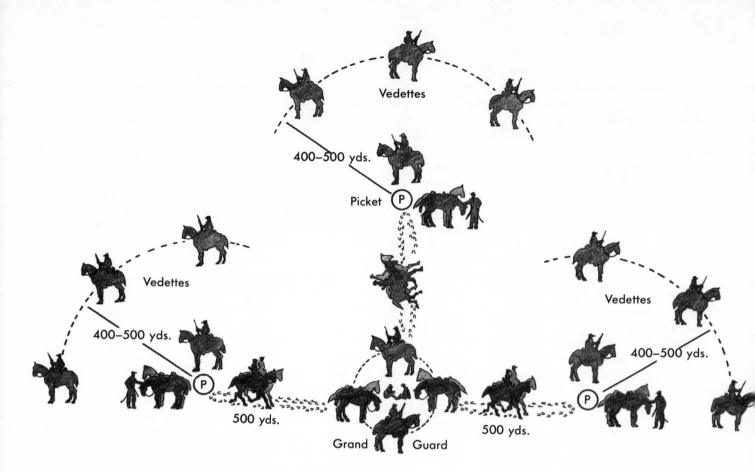

Vedettes

400–500 yds.

Picket

Vedettes

400–500 yds.

500 yds.

Grand Guard

Vedettes

400–500 yds.

500 yds.

Cavalry outposts were of varying strengths, set out to form a flexible screen against infiltrating patrols and to check and report enemy movements generally. The customary setup was an outpost, with perhaps one half the total strength forming the "grand guard." In front and on both flanks, at five hundred yards distance, were the pickets, and thrown out five hundred yards from them were the solitary vedettes. Patrols moved constantly between the grand guard and the pickets, and from 3 A.M. to sunrise were sent forward at least two miles in front of the vedettes. Units went on picket for twenty-four hours, and horses at the advanced posts remained saddled and bridled, ready for instant use.

Picket duty was hard on men and horses. At one time the Union cavalry was guarding a line nearly one hundred miles long. Cavalry leaders maintained that this picket duty could be better performed by infantry. The Confederates usually used their infantry for this duty, preferring to keep their horses in good condition and ready for concerted action.

MOUNTING the cavalry, and supplying horses for the artillery and wagon trains presented a huge problem. There are no exact figures on

the number of horses used, even in the North; but from the fact that the Federal Government spent close to $124,000,000 on horses during the war, at an average price of about $150.00, one can arrive at a figure somewhat in excess of 825,000 for the Union alone.

There were the usual shortages, especially at the beginning. But the establishment of the Cavalry Bureau in 1863 was a step in the right direction. Numbers of the horses were shipped in from the West. Many of these were only partly broken, and some not broken at all. While some of the horses were of top quality the horse traders in many cases lived up to their reputation and inspectors had a hard time detecting the frauds and tricks of the trade.

The Federal depot system of receiving those horses newly purchased, and recuperating those sick or injured in the field, as well as providing drill and training camps for the men, had a great effect on the efficiency of the cavalry service. There were six large remount depots in all, the main one at Giesboro, on the Potomac near Washington. Covering some 625, acres it was capable of handling 30,000 animals. It included stables, stockyards, forage- and storehouses, hospitals with accommodations for over 2500 horses, along with mess houses and quarters for hundreds of blacksmiths, carpenters, wagon makers, wheelwrights, farriers, and teamsters.

On one occasion, at least, even this efficient system failed to supply the needed horses. Hood was advancing on Nashville; unable to mount even half his troopers, General Wilson resorted to impressment. In his "Under the Old Flag" Wilson wrote: "Within seven days seven thousand horses were obtained in middle and Western Kentucky.... Every horse and mare that could be used was taken. All street-car and livery stable horses, and private carriage and saddle-horses, were seized. Even Andrew Johnson, the vice-president-elect, was forced to give up his pair.... a clean sweep was made of every animal that could carry a cavalry-man...."

The horse is a peculiar beast, capable of great feats of endurance on the one hand, and on the other, subject to a bewildering number of ailments. General Meade's "Baldy" was wounded twice at Bull Run, was left for dead at Antietam, recovered and was wounded again at Gettysburg, and outlived his master by ten years. Yet let a recruit allow his heated mount one swallow of water too many, and the government was minus another horse. Captain Charles D. Rhodes wrote: "The bane of the cavalry service of the Federal armies in the field was diseases of the feet. 'Hoof-rot,' 'grease-heel,' or the 'scratches' followed in the wake of days and nights spent in mud, rain, snow and exposure to cold, and caused thousands of otherwise serviceable horses to become useless for the time being.

"Sore backs became common with the hardships of campaigning, and one of the first lessons taught the inexperienced trooper was to take better care of his horse than he did of himself. The remedy against recurrence of sore backs on horses was invariably to order the trooper to walk and lead the disabled animal. With a few such lessons, cavalry soldiers of but short service became most scrupulous in smoothing out wrinkles in saddle-blankets, in dismounting to walk steep hills, in giving frequent rests to their jaded animals, and when opportunity offered, in unsaddling and cooling the backs of their mounts after hours in the saddle. Poor forage, sudden changes of forage, and overfeeding produced almost as much sickness and physical disability as no forage at all."

That the horses were not the only sufferers is evident from the following extract from Captain Vanderbilt's *History of the 10th. N. Y. Cavalry:*

"Please remember that my company had been mustered into service only about six weeks before, and had received horses less than a month prior to this march; and in the issue we drew everything on the list—bridles, lariat ropes and pins.... Many men had extra blankets, nice large quilts presented by some fond mother or maiden aunt (dear souls), sabers and belts, together with the straps that pass over the shoulders, carbines and slings, pockets full of cartridges, nose bags and extra little bags for carrying oats, haversacks, canteens, and spurs ... curry-combs, brushes, ponchos, button tents, overcoats, frying-pans, cups, coffee-pots, etc.... but my company had hardly time to get into proper shape when 'the general' was sounded, 'boots and saddles' blown.

"Such a rattling, jingling, jerking, scrabbling, cursing, I never heard before. Green horses—some of them had never been ridden—turned round and round, backed against each other, jumped up or stood up like trained circus-horses. Some of the boys had a pile in front of their saddles, and one in the rear, so high and heavy it took two men to saddle one horse and two men to help the fellow into his place.... Some of the boys had never ridden anything since they galloped on a hobby horse, and they clasped their legs close together, thus unconsciously sticking the spurs into their horses' sides. ... Blankets slipped from under saddles and hung from one corner; saddles slipped back until they were on the rumps of horses; others turned and were on the under side of the animals; horses running and kicking; tin pans, mess-kettles ... flying through the air."

VETERAN troopers traveled light and lived off the country as much as possible. Pack animals and the wagon train carried the bulk of supplies. On Wilson's great expedition through Alabama, with 12,000 horsemen, his troopers carried five days' worth of light rations in haversacks, 100 rounds of ammunition, 24 pounds of grain, and two extra horseshoes. The supply train of 250 wagons and pack animals carried the extra rations and ammunition.

On Morgan's Christmas raid, no wheeled vehicles were taken, with the exception of the artillery, which was drawn by doubled teams.

An additional blanket was standard equipment, as was an oilcloth and a canteen.

The regulation U. S. Army saddle was the McClellan, adopted through recommendations made by McClellan after his European tour of inspection just prior to the Civil War. It has been described as an adaptation of the Mexican or Texan saddle, although some claim it a copy of the Cossack saddle (McClellan was in the Crimea). It was light, strong, easy on the horse's back, and comfortable for the rider (although the rawhide with which they were originally covered often split, making them anything *but* comfortable). It was equipped with wooden stirrups with leather hoods. In a slightly modified form it remained the standard saddle for the U. S. Cavalry. Harnesses varied, and several kinds of bits can be seen in the photographs and paintings of the period. Many commanding officers were exceedingly fussy about the turnouts of their staffs, and expected them to furnish themselves with the most expensive housings and horse equipments.

The Federal Volunteer Cavalrymen were armed with sabers and revolvers, and some troops in each regiment carried carbines or rifles. Later all had carbines. The saber was usually of the long, straight, Prussian type, later replaced by a light, curved, cavalry saber. The revolver generally carried was either a Colt percussion Army or Navy model, or a Remington.

There was a great variety of carbines: muzzle-loaders, single-shot breech loaders, and repeaters. Because of the difficulty of loading a muzzle-

loader on horseback, much thought had gone in to evolving a suitable breech-loading weapon for the cavalry. The most popular single-shot breech-loading carbine was the Sharps, next in numbers purchased was the Burnside. The most famous carbine of all was the seven-shot Spencer repeater.

The Southern cavalryman was also armed with saber, revolver, and carbine. Not all of the more irregular bodies carried the saber, however, and in place of the carbine they might have carried a rifle or a muzzle-loading, double-barreled shotgun. We are told that the favorite weapon of Morgan's troopers was the medium Enfield, a muzzle-loading import. The Sharps was well liked and was copied in Richmond. It had the great advantage of firing a linen cartridge, whereas some of the other Federal weapons, like the Burnside, acquired by the Rebels, fired metallic cartridges. Manufacture of these metallic cartridges were in most cases beyond the limited resources of Southern industry. "In 1864," wrote a Southern general, "we captured some Spencer breech-loaders, but could never use them for lack of proper cartridges."

The revolvers used by the South were much the same, being in most cases captured Federal weapons, or copies made in Southern arsenals. Two were frequently carried, and some of Mosby's men (many of whom carried no sabers) favored four. The additional pair were carried in saddle holsters.

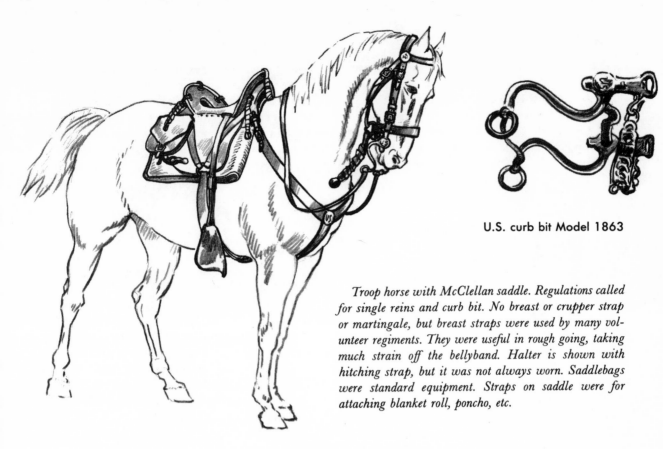

U.S. curb bit Model 1863

*Troop horse with McClellan saddle. Regulations called for single reins and curb bit. No breast or crupper strap or martingale, but breast straps were used by many volunteer regiments. They were useful in rough going, taking much strain off the bellyband. Halter is shown with hitching strap, but it was not always worn. Saddlebags were standard equipment. Straps on saddle were for attaching blanket roll, poncho, etc.*

Officer's bit
Brass plated over steel

*General officer's mount. Officers' outfits were often non-regulation. Saddles were frequently of the flat or English type, also imported and used by many Confederates of all ranks. Outfit shown has iron stirrups, breast and crupper straps, running martingale, bridoon or snaffle bit as well as curb bit. Saddle holsters were often used. Saddlecloth shows the two stars of a major general.*

Cavalry equipment varied only in unessentials, with the exception of the 6th Pennsylvania Cavalry (Rush's Lancers). They carried the nine-foot lance of Norway fir with its 11-inch steel tip from December 1861 to May 1863. It was finally discarded as being unsuitable to the wooded, broken country of Northern Virginia. At first only twelve carbines were added to each troop for scouting and picket duty. Later the regiment was rearmed with carbines and sabers. The heavy roll carried by the lancer is unusually large. Later veteran troopers shed much of their super-fluous gear. Note the brass shoulder scales, also discarded later in the war.

*The corporal watering his horse is wearing another victim of hard campaigning, the regulation "Jeff Davis" hat of stiff felt.*

*The Southern Cavalier drawing his sword is an officer of the 1st Virginia Cavalry, resplendent with plumed and tasseled hat, befrogged tunic, and yellow sash. The trooper on his right is armed with pistol and carbine, in this case the .577 Enfield muzzle-loader, a favorite with Southern cavalry because of its accuracy and availability of ammunition.*

Carbine sling
and snap hook

Cavalry saber
and scabbard

Belt holster
and cartridge box

[57]

## BREECH-LOADING CARBINES

Carbines were well suited to cavalry operations. They were shorter and handier than rifles (average length was about thirty-eight inches, as compared to fifty-six inches for the rifled musket) and weighed considerably less. Rate of fire was high, as a majority, at least in the Federal service, were breechloaders, and many were repeaters. Accuracy was fair, considering the short barrels and comparatively weak loads. Some were capable of making a good percentage of hits at 500 yards (machine rest), but 150–200 yards was considered effective range. There were more than 30 different makes and models, though not all used different ammunition.

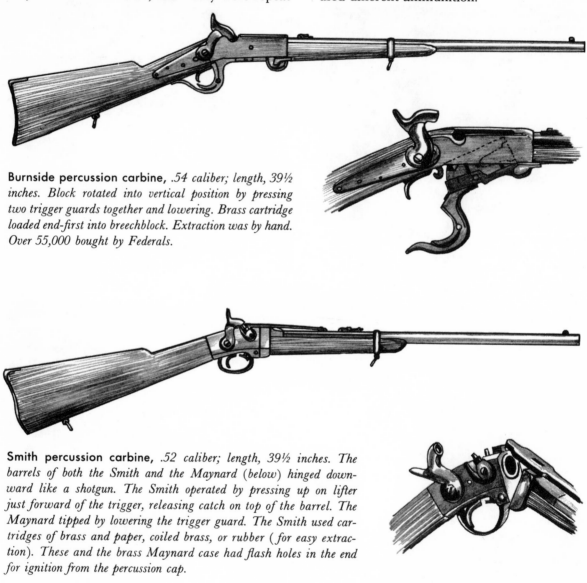

Burnside percussion carbine, .54 caliber; length, 39½ inches. Block rotated into vertical position by pressing two trigger guards together and lowering. Brass cartridge loaded end-first into breechblock. Extraction was by hand. Over 55,000 bought by Federals.

Smith percussion carbine, .52 caliber; length, 39½ inches. The barrels of both the Smith and the Maynard (below) hinged downward like a shotgun. The Smith operated by pressing up on lifter just forward of the trigger, releasing catch on top of the barrel. The Maynard tipped by lowering the trigger guard. The Smith used cartridges of brass and paper, coiled brass, or rubber (for easy extraction). These and the brass Maynard case had flash holes in the end for ignition from the percussion cap.

Maynard percussion carbine, .50 caliber, length 36⅞ inches.

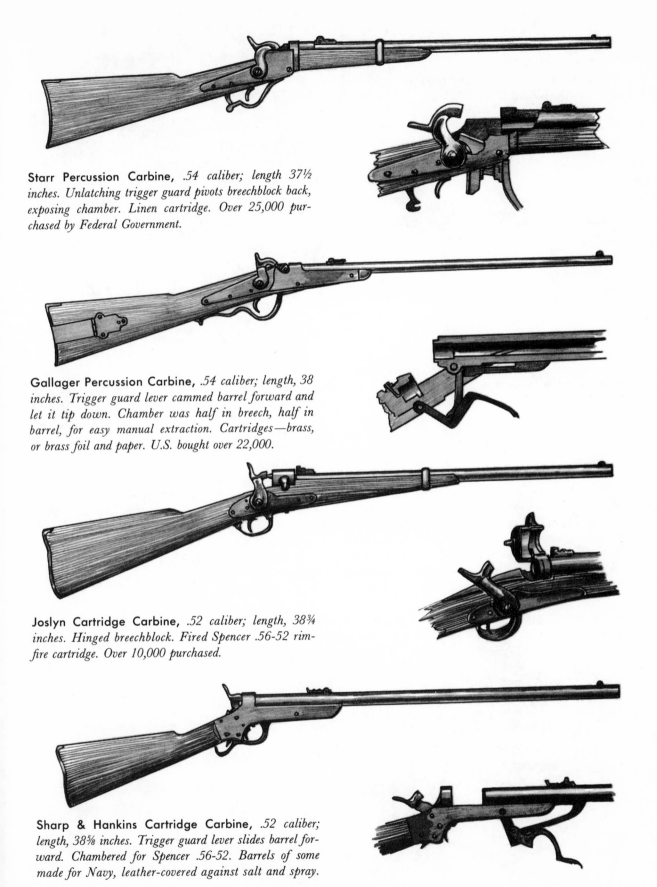

**Starr Percussion Carbine**, *.54 caliber; length 37½ inches. Unlatching trigger guard pivots breechblock back, exposing chamber. Linen cartridge. Over 25,000 purchased by Federal Government.*

**Gallager Percussion Carbine**, *.54 caliber; length, 38 inches. Trigger guard lever cammed barrel forward and let it tip down. Chamber was half in breech, half in barrel, for easy manual extraction. Cartridges—brass, or brass foil and paper. U.S. bought over 22,000.*

**Joslyn Cartridge Carbine**, *.52 caliber; length, 38¾ inches. Hinged breechblock. Fired Spencer .56-52 rimfire cartridge. Over 10,000 purchased.*

**Sharp & Hankins Cartridge Carbine**, *.52 caliber; length, 38⅝ inches. Trigger guard lever slides barrel forward. Chambered for Spencer .56-52. Barrels of some made for Navy, leather-covered against salt and spray.*

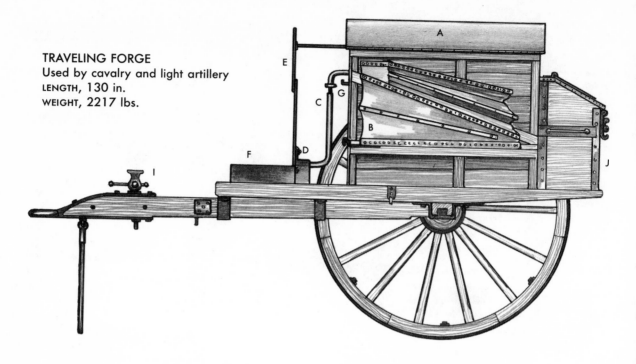

TRAVELING FORGE
Used by cavalry and light artillery
LENGTH, 130 in.
WEIGHT, 2217 lbs.

A. Roof of bellows house (canvas-covered)
B. Bellows
C. Windpipe
D. Air back
E. Sheet-iron fireplace back.

F. Fireplace
G. Fulcrum and support for bellows pole
H. Bellows hook
I. Vise
J. Coal box

At a conservative estimate, at least a million horses were used by the military during the war. Multiply this by four and the answer comes out to a lot of horseshoes. Small wonder that the rolling forges were a vital part of any outfit relying on horse power—cavalry, artillery, quartermaster corps, or what have you. The outfit was compact, consisting of forge and limber. The latter, on which the smiths rode, was similar in appearance to that of the artillery, and contained tools —chisels, hammers, tongs, punches, etc., plus spare hardware and 200 pounds of horseshoes and 50 pounds of nails. The forge part contained the bellows, firebox, coal, anvil, 250 pounds of spare iron, and 100 pounds of shoes. A vise was mounted on the stock.

Cutaway diagram showing how bellows were operated.

# THE ARTILLERY

ARTILLERY was classed partly according to its weight and caliber, and partly by its mobility and the form of its carriage or mounting. "Field" artillery, as the name implies, was ordnance light and mobile enough to move with the army in the field, and to be freely maneuvered in battle. This also included mountain artillery—exceptionally light pieces which could be manhandled if necessary, or transported in pieces on muleback.

Heavy artillery included siege guns and siege mortars, which were mobile, although slow and unwieldly; garrison or fortress artillery; and the great sea coast mortars and pieces like the huge Rodmans, the largest of which weighed 117,000 pounds and fired a 1080-pound projectile 8000 yards.

Ordnance was again divided into types. *Guns* were comparatively heavy, of long range and flat trajectory. *Howitzers* were lighter and shorter, fired a relatively heavy shell with a light charge, and usually had a powder chamber smaller than the bore of the gun. *Mortars* were very short and heavy, and fired large projectiles with a high trajectory. The "workhorse" of the Civil War artillery, the 12-pounder smoothbore "Napoleon," model of 1857, was a *gun-howitzer,* being both shorter and lighter than the older 12-pounder gun, but using the same powder charge.

Guns were either smoothbore or rifled, and

fired solid shot, shell, spherical case (shrapnel), grapeshot, and canister. The last three were all referred to as "case" shot. Howitzers fired shell and "case," while mortars fired only shell and spherical case. The last two pieces were smooth-bores.

The lighter smoothbore ordnance was usually of bronze (often referred to as "brass"). Some rifled pieces were made of bronze, but the rifling wore too rapidly. Most of the rifled field pieces were of wrought iron, or cast iron with wrought iron reinforcing hoops at the breech. The larger smoothbore weapons, those used in fixed positions, were nearly all of cast iron.

Cast iron was easiest and cheapest to produce, but comparatively weak and brittle, and unequal to the strain of firing with heavy charges in a rifled gun. Steel was superior to cast iron but was expensive and difficult to produce and work in large quantities.

Few of the Civil War guns were breechloaders. Field artillery could be loaded "down the spout" just as fast, if not faster, than a crew could operate the relatively clumsy and complicated breech mechanisms then in use.

Guns of that period had no recoil mechanisms. When fired they leaped back in recoil, and had to be run back and reaimed and pointed after each round. Aiming, rather than loading, took the time.

Gun sights were crude, range-finding apparatus nonexistent, and anything approaching modern fire control unknown. Indirect or night firing by field artillery was considered a waste of time and ammunition.

Fuzes were uncertain, and many shells failed to burst at all, or burst prematurely and blew off the muzzles of the guns which fired them.

A Confederate artilleryman wrote of Chancellorsville, "Although the shells were provided with the fuze igniter attachment, but one in fifteen burst."

Even when they did explode, shells of that period were far less destructive than modern projectiles of the same caliber.

The walls of the shells were thick, and bursting charges small, especially so in spherical ammunition. Consequently the missiles broke into a few large pieces, which had little velocity. Elongated projectiles for rifled guns held more powder, and some types were scored internally to insure better fragmentation. However, many of the rifle shells were fitted with impact fuzes. On hitting the

ground, they were likely to bury themselves before exploding, thus reducing their efficiency. The effect of such fire against infantry under cover was so small that long-range cannonading was looked upon by veteran troops with contempt.

The field artilleryman's most lethal load was canister. The tin cylinders filled with iron shot or musket balls turned a cannon into a monster sawed-off shot-gun. Against troops in mass formation it was devastating; and it undoubtedly caused more casualties than all other artillery projectiles combined.

Napoleon had used it with deadly effect, pushing his field artillery well forward and "softening up" the enemy formations before his own columns attacked. But in his day canister, with its effective range of some three hundred yards, outranged the smoothbore musket. The Minié ball and the rifled musket, with its effective range of five hundred yards, changed the picture completely.

To use his most effective weapon, the Civil War gunner had to bring his piece into action well within range of the enemy riflemen. Against sharpshooting veterans this was suicide. Although in many instances batteries were galloped up to close range, to unlimber amid a hail of rifle bullets, it was looked upon as a sacrifice move, to be made only in moments of dire necessity, and at an inevitably high cost in men and horses.

At the Bloody Angle, Spotsylvania, a section of Battery C, 5th U. S. Artillery, was brought into action. ". . . Lieutenant Metcalf gave the command 'Limber the guns,' 'Drivers mount,' 'Cannoneers mount,' 'Caissons rear,' and away we went, up the hill, past our infantry, and into position. . . . We were a considerable distance in front of our infantry, and of course artillery could not live long under such a fire as the enemy were putting through there. Our men went down in short order. The left gun fired nine rounds, I fired fourteen with mine. . . . Our section went into action with 23 men and one officer. The only ones who came out sound were the lieutenant and myself. Every horse was killed, 7 of the men were killed outright, 16 wounded; the gun carriages were so cut with bullets as to be of no further service. . . . 27 balls passed through the lid of the limber chest while number six was getting out ammunition. The sponge bucket on my gun had 39 holes in it being perforated like a sieve."

So from an assault weapon the field gun became mainly a weapon of support, and the infantry, both Union and Confederate, usually made their attacks against an enemy unshaken by effective preliminary bombardment.

In both North and South huge numbers of guns were tied up in permanent fortifications. Most of them never fired a shot at an enemy throughout the entire war. The Washington defenses alone contained 807 guns and 98 mortars.

# FIELD ARTILLERY

Field guns were grouped in batteries. Six guns were considered the ideal number, although four-gun batteries were common, especially in the Confederate service. A six-gun battery, reduced by casualties, might operate as a four-gun unit until replacements enabled it to man six guns once more. The battery commander was usually a captain. Two guns formed a section, under a lieutenant. On the march each gun or "piece" was hooked up behind a limber, which carried an ammunition chest, and was drawn by six horses. Each piece had its caisson, carrying three ammunition chests, and also drawn by a six-horse team. These two units made a platoon, commanded by a sergeant (chief of piece) and two corporals. Each battery was accompanied by a traveling forge, a battery wagon carrying tents and supplies, and usually six more caissons carrying reserve ammunition. Extra wagons for fodder, etc., might be attached as necessary.

Each six-horse team had three drivers, who rode the horses on the left side. The usual gun crew consisted of nine men. If the battery was designated as light artillery, the cannoneers either rode on the ammunition chests or walked beside their piece. If it was horse artillery (sometimes called flying artillery) the cannoneers each rode a horse. Two additional men acted as horse-holders in action.

Another lieutenant usually commanded the line of caissons. In addition there were two staff sergeants (orderly and quartermaster), five artificers, two buglers, and a guidon-bearer.

Organization of the field artillery differed in the two armies and was changed from time to time. In the Army of the Potomac, each field and horse battery contained six pieces. Later, Grant, in the Wilderness campaign, reduced the number of guns to four, feeling that the terrain was unsuited to artillery and wishing to reduce the size of his trains.

Four batteries were assigned to a division, and when several divisions were organized into a corps, at least half the divisional artillery was grouped as corps reserve. There was an army reserve of some one hundred guns. The horse artillery was often attached to the cavalry corps; otherwise it was in the army reserve.

Until 1863 the armies of the Confederacy and the western armies of the Union assigned a battery to each infantry brigade. This was a bad system, dispersing the guns throughout the army, and preventing concentration of fire. The massed batteries of the Federal divisional and reserve artillery gave the North considerable advantage. At Malvern Hill "An almost continuous battery of 60 pieces" directed by General Henry J. Hunt beat down every Confederate attack and smashed one Southern battery after another as they were thrown piece meal into action. So fierce was the fire that a Rebel gunner wrote of the guns of his battery, "In the short time they existed as effective pieces they were several times fired by fragments of Federal shell striking them after the lanyard was stretched, and before it was pulled."

Few of the generals on either side seem to have appreciated the proper tactical use of artillery, and the authority of the chiefs of artillery was often limited and ill-defined. Also, many of the battlefields were in broken country, in some cases so heavily wooded that directions of attack had to be taken by compass. Under these conditions it is understandable that the fullest use of this important arm was seldom made.

On the other hand, the handling of the guns themselves and the conduct of the men who manned them were deserving of the highest praise.

THE composition of the individual batteries differed in both services and there was no set standard for either army. At the outbreak of the war a six-gun battery usually included two howitzers. A 12-pounder battery had four 12-pounder guns and two 24-pounder howitzers. A 6-pounder battery would have four 6-pounder guns and two 12-pounder howitzers. The 6-pounder was used mostly by the South, and was later almost entirely

ACTION POSITIONS. Gun, caisson, and teams drawn to scale, showing regulation spacing

*The above formations, although necessary at times, exposed the teams to heavy casualties. Contemporary sketches show batteries with every horse dead in its traces. Horses grew scarce as the war progressed, especially in the South, where six-horse teams were rare.*

*If no rapid movement was imminent, teams were unhitched and held in readiness close by, but sheltered as much as*

replaced by 3-inch rifles and 12-pounder smoothbores. In December 1862 General Lee recommended that if there were insufficient metal for new guns, the 6-pounders and some of the 12-pounder howitzers be melted down to make 12-pounder Napoleons.

Besides captured material, and what was produced in Southern arsenals, pieces of foreign make reached the Confederacy. Many of their batteries contained a mixture of weapons, which was the despair of the ordnance department. Three different calibers in a four-gun battery was not unusual, and enormously complicated ammunition supply.

There was more uniformity in the Northern artillery. Union batteries were usually armed with the 3-inch rifle, the 10-pounder Parrott (these fired the same ammunition), the 20-pounder Parrott, or the 12-pounder Napoleon. However, there were a few non-standard rifles, and all guns required several types of ammunition.

There was some difference of opinion among artillerists as to the relative merits of smoothbore and rifled cannon. One Confederate Chief of Ordnance said, "We especially valued the 3″ rifles, which became the favorite field piece."

General J. D. Imboden, C.S.A., gave his opinion and also pointed out one disadvantage of the rifled gun. At Bull Run his guns were in action against the six 10-pounder Parrotts of Ricketts, and Griffin's battery of four 10-pounders and two 12-pounder howitzers.

"These last hurt us more than all the rifles of both batteries, since the shot and shell of the rifles, striking the ground at any angle over fifteen or twenty degrees, almost without exception bored their way in several feet and did no harm. It is no exaggeration to say that hundreds of shells from these fine rifleguns exploded in front of and around my battery that day, but so deep in the ground that the fragments never came out. After the action the ground looked as though a drove of hogs had been rooting there for potatoes. I venture the opinion here, after a good deal of observation during four years, that in open ground at 1000 yds. a six pdr battery of smooth guns, or at 1500 to 1800 yds., a similar battery of 12 pdr Napoleons, well handled, will in one hour whip double their number of the best rifles ever put in the field. A smooth-bore gun never buries its projectiles in the ground, as the rifles does invariably when fired against sloping ground."

11 yds.    6 yds.    5 yds.

*possible. In prepared positions, guns and limbers were dug in or protected by earthworks. Ammunition chests could be removed from the caissons and dug in and the caissons moved to the rear with the teams. After the battery's spare horses were used up, the teams on the pieces were replenished at the expense of the caissons.*

Rifled guns were of longer range and far greater accuracy. While there were some remarkable instances of "sharpshooting" with smoothbores (the celebrated Pelham hit a Union standard-bearer at 800 yards with one shot), the large windage and consequent irregular flight and loss of velocity of the spherical missile made accurate shooting at any great distance impossible. On the other hand, in wooded and broken country it was seldom possible to place rifled guns where their long range might be used to advantage. Also, the dense volumes of black powder smoke made gun laying difficult, the direction sometimes being marked only by the tracks made by the wheels in recoil.

AT the outset of the Civil War most of the country's powder mills were in the North. U.S. arsenals in the South had been used mostly as depots, and little ammunition had been made there for some fifty years. Starting almost from scratch, the Confederates rapidly built up some remarkably efficient mills and arsenals. The great

mill at Augusta, Georgia, one of the world's finest, was begun in September 1861 and went into production in April 1862, producing a total of two and three quarter million pounds of fine quality powder. There were other mills, at Nashville and Manchester, Tennessee; New Orleans, Louisiana; Marshall, Texas; and Petersburg, Virginia.

The great Northern manufacturers were the Du Ponts and the Hazard and Oriental mills. A list of U.S. mills in 1864 shows eleven others, although their total output did not equal that of the Du Ponts alone. Working at full capacity, the Northern mills could produce over five hundred barrels a day.

Being an imported article, saltpeter was a problem for both sides, especially the blockaded South. There, when the beds in northern Alabama and Tennessee ran out, artificial beds were started in Columbia, Charlestown, Savannah, Augusta, Mobile, Selma, and Richmond. Considerable use was made of human urine for lixiviation of the earth.

Cottonwood groves on the Savannah River produced excellent charcoal, and sulphur was made in Alabama and Louisiana by reduction of iron pyrites.

[65]

## 12-POUNDER GUN-HOWITZER M1857 (NAPOLEON)

1. Stock
2. Cheek
3. Handspike
4. Prolonge hooks
5. Lunette
6. Cap-square
7. Part of lock chain
8. Sponge chain
9. Hand spike ring
10. Sponge hook
11. Elevating screw
12. Pointing rings

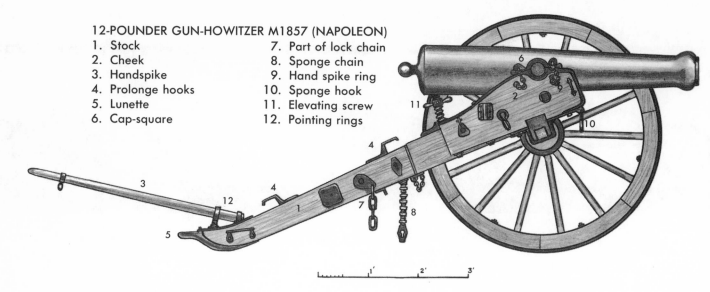

Bronze; Smoothbore; Rate of fire: two aimed or four canister per minute. Effective range 2000 yards. Horizontal deviation at 600 yards, about 3 feet; at 1200 yards, 12 feet

12-pdr. M1857 superimposed on 12-pdr. M.1841–44. Performance about the same. Weight saved 530 lbs.

Below is a front view of the "Napoleon," showing cheeks, handspike rings, and hooks for sponges and worm.

12-pdr. Howitzer

24-pdr. Howitzer

6-pdr. gun

| Type | Model | Cal. | Length of tube (in.) | Wt. of tube (lbs.) | Wt. of carriage (lbs.) | Wt. of Projectile (lbs.) | Wt. of charge (lbs.) | Range (yds.) 5° elevation |
|---|---|---|---|---|---|---|---|---|
| 6-Pounder | 1841–44 | 3.67 | 60 | 884 | 900 | 6.10 | 1.25 | 1523 |
| 12-pdr. gun | 1841–44 | 4.62 | 78 | 1757 | 1175 | 12.30 | 2.50 | 1663 |
| 12-pdr. How. | 1841–44 | 4.62 | 53 | 788 | 900 | 8.90 | 1.00 | 1072 |
| 24-pdr. How. | 1841–44 | 5.82 | 65 | 1318 | 1128 | 18.40 | 2.00 | 1322 |
| 32-pdr. How. | 1841–44 | 6.4 | 75 | 1920 | 1175 | 25.60 | 2.50 | 1504 |
| 12-pdr. Napoleon | 1857 | 4.62 | 66 | 1227 | 1128 | 12.30 | 2.50 | 1619 |

# AMMUNITION FOR SMOOTHBORE ARTILLERY

Solid shot was used for battering, and against masses of troops. It was more accurate than shell or spherical case, and ranged further. A complete round of fixed ammunition for a 12-pounder weighed 15.4 pounds.

Shell was used against buildings, earthworks, and troops under cover. Bursting charges were so small in field artillery ammunition (a 12-pounder shell contained only one-half pound of powder) that their effect was often more moral than physical. Time fuzes were used, ignited by the flash of the gun's discharge.

Spherical case (shrapnel) was used against bodies of troops, usually at ranges from 500 to 1500 yards. The fuzes of the period were so crude that spherical case was seldom used when targets were rapidly closing and opening the range. A round for a 12-pounder contained 78 musket balls and weighed, complete with charge, 13.5 lbs. A round for a 6-pounder held 38 balls with a 2.5-ounce burster. The balls in spherical case were usually imbedded in sulphur. The walls of spherical case projectiles were not as thick as those of shell because of the weaker charge used and because, being timed to burst over or just in front of a target, they did not have to withstand impact.

Canister was used at close range, 350 yards or less. In an emergency, double canister with a single charge was used. The shot was fairly large —almost 1.5 inches in diameter. They were packed in four tiers, in sawdust. In a pinch almost anything could be used for canister, and some Confederate ammunition consisted of canvas bags of scraps of metal, piece of trace chain, etc.

Cartridge bags were of serge, merino, or close-textured flannel.

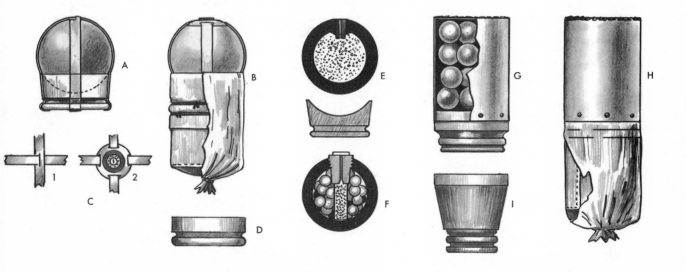

A. Solid shot attached to wooden sabot with tin straps
B. Shell—complete fixed round. Cartridge bag tied to sabot. Paper bag in place
C. Arrangement of straps for 1. shot, 2. shell (opening allowed for fuse)
D. Cartridge block for separate cartridge. Projectile and powder charge for rounds for guns larger than 12-pdrs. were usually loaded separately
E. Shell and sabot
F. Spherical case—12-pdr. contained 4.5-ounce burster and 78 musket balls
G. Canister—12-pdr. contained 27 cast-iron shot, average weight .43 pounds in tin case, nailed to sabot
H. Complete fixed round of canister. Paper bag was torn off before loading
I. Tapered sabot for howitzers (powder chamber in howitzers was smaller than the bore)

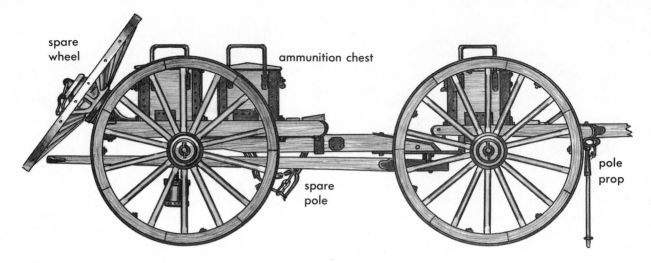

spare wheel

ammunition chest

pole prop

spare pole

CAISSON AND LIMBER

The caisson carried two ammunition chests, and its limber, one. Pick axes, a felling axe, a shovel, and a spare pole and wheel were also carried on the caisson. The weight of the caisson, with ammunition, was just over 3800 pounds. When possible, ammunition was served to the gun from the rear chest of the caisson, number eight of the crew doing same duties as number six at the gun limber. Rounds served out of the gun limber were replaced from the rear chest. When the limber chest of the piece was empty it was exchanged for that of the limber of the caisson; then the empty chest was unkeyed and lifted off, the forward chest of the caisson was loosened and slid forward onto the limber and fastened.

The battery wagon carried equipment needed to keep the battery in running order. It included oil and paint, spare gunners' tools, axes, spare stocks and spokes, over 200 pounds of spare harness, scythes, spades, picks, and forage in the rack at the back. The chest of the battery wagon limber contained carriage makers' tools—planes, saws, chisels, etc., and a set of saddlers' tools. The total weight of a wagon with stores was about 1289 pounds.

A traveling forge was attached to each battery. It carried blacksmiths' tools, 300 pounds of horseshoes, nails, spare hardware and iron, etc. It was similar to the forge used by the cavalry and described on page 60.

BATTERY WAGON

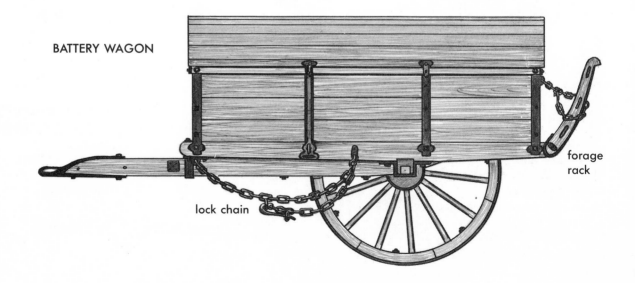

forage rack

lock chain

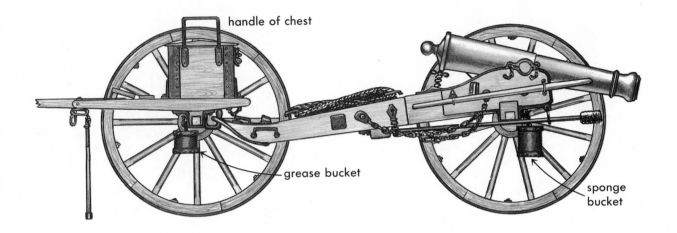

handle of chest

grease bucket

sponge bucket

LIMBER AND SIX-POUNDER GUN

Each limber carried an ammunition chest, a grease bucket slung underneath, a couple of canvas water buckets, and a tarpaulin strapped on top. Without the chest it weighed 695 pounds. The chest weighed 185 pounds empty. For a 6-pounder the chest contained fifty rounds, two spare cartridges, seventy-five friction primers, one and a half yards of slow match, and three portfires. The weight of a loaded chest was just under 560 pounds. The chests for a 12-pounder were the same size but contained 32 rounds.

The carriages for the 6-pounders were the same as for the 3-inch rifles. The 12-pounder and 24-pounder howitzer also used a similar carriage, with

the exception that the cheeks were a little further apart to accommodate the greater diameter of the tubes.

On the carriage were two handspikes, carried in rings on each side; two sponges and a worm, on hooks underneath; a sponge bucket, and the prolonge around the prolonge hooks. The weight of a 6-pounder gun and limber, complete with ammunition and implements, was 3185 pounds. The 12-pounder outfit weighed 3875 pounds.

The pole prop, which supported the limber pole, hooked up out of the way when not in use. Wheels on all field artillery equipment were the same size and interchangeable.

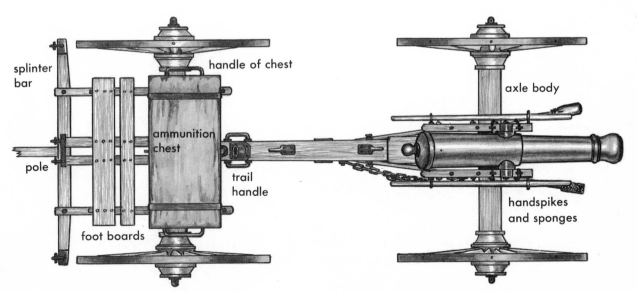

splinter bar

handle of chest

ammunition chest

pole

trail handle

foot boards

axle body

handspikes and sponges

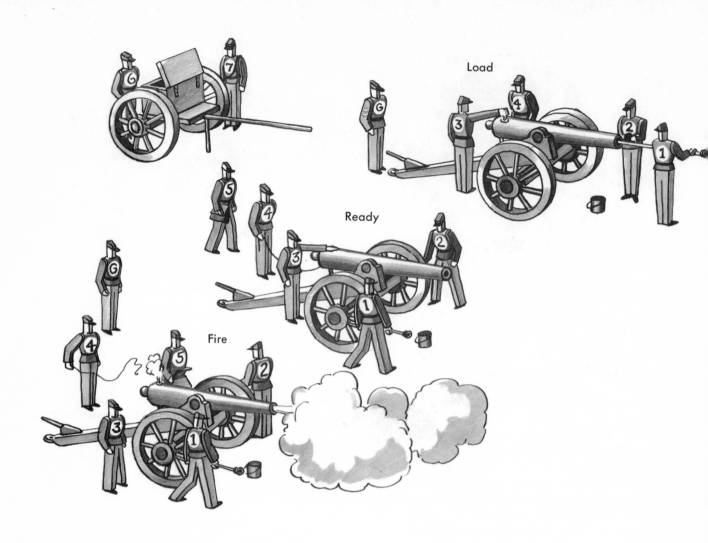

At command "COMMENCE FIRING," **G** orders

### "Load"

**1** *sponges.* **2,** *takes round from* **5,** *puts it in gun.* **1** *rams round home, while* **3** *holds thumb on vent.* **G** *sights gun. When round is in,* **3** *goes to trail, moves it as* **G** *orders "Trail right" or "Trail left."* **5** *gets another round from* **6** *or* **7** *at limber where* **6** *cuts fuses. (When firing case or shell* **5** *shows fuses to* **G** *before giving it to* **2.**) **G** *steps clear to side where he can best observe effect of fire, gives command.*

### "Ready"

**1** *and* **2** *step clear.* **3** *pricks cartridge.* **4** *hooks lanyard to primer, puts primer in vent.* **3** *covers vent with left hand,* **4** *moves to rear, keeping lanyard just slack.*

### "Fire"

**3** *steps clear of wheel.* **4** *pulls lanyard.* **G** *orders gun run up. "Load," etc.*
*(In action, only commands "Commence Firing" and "Cease Firing" were necessary.)*

NOTE. *If fire is rapid,* **7** *may alternate with* **5,** *and* **2** *may change places with* **1.** *Rather ominously, drill instructions provide for firing with diminished crews, ending with "Service by two men." In actual combat, crews were replenished from any nearby units, including, on at least one occasion, by a passing general and his staff.*

When fighting a "rear-guard" action where continuous fire was necessary, the order was given to "fix prolonges to fire while retiring." The prolonges were passed up through the lunettes and held by the toggles, while the rings were hooked over the pintles. The limbers moved to the rear, hauling the guns at the end of the prolonges with the cannoneers marching alongside. The guns could be loaded while in motion, and the teams halted just long enough for the guns to be aimed and fired.

When really hard pressed, the guns were sometimes retired by section or half-battery. One unit remained in position covering the withdrawal of the other, then in turn retired under its protective fire.

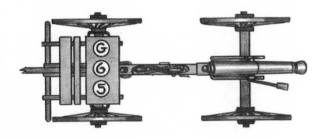 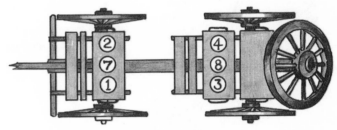

Cannoneers were seated on the ammunition chests in the positions indicated above. Saber belts were worn but the sabers were carried on the ammunition chests. The drivers wore theirs, as did the mounted cannoneers of the horse artillery. As a general rule, the cannoneers rode on the ammunition chests only for a rapid movement. When in range of enemy guns, the drill books recommended that they dismount lest an exploding caisson cause severe casualties. However, as most movements under fire *were* rapid, the cannoneers rode on their powder kegs and took their chances.

Although a folded tarpaulin was strapped to the lid of each chest, a rapid change of position over rough ground was a spine-jolting experience, akin to riding a bucking bronco, and more dangerous. An artilleryman sent flying from his perilous seat was lucky to escape with nothing worse than a broken bone or two. The pounding hoofs and bounding wheels of a battery at the gallop were universally dreaded.

In the field, spacing depended both on the tactical situation and the lay of the land. Regulations called for 14-yard intervals between pieces. Allowing 2 yards per piece, battery front was 82 yards.

Limber                                      Wheel Pair

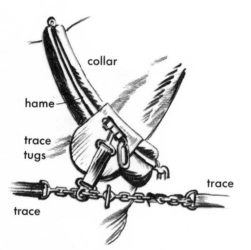

collar

hame

trace
tugs

trace

trace

**TRACE HITCH FOR SWING PAIR**

**SIX-HORSE GUN TEAM** *Harness was designed for quick removal and replacement of dead and injured horses. The wheel pair had breast and breech straps. The breech straps were to take the strain when backing up.*

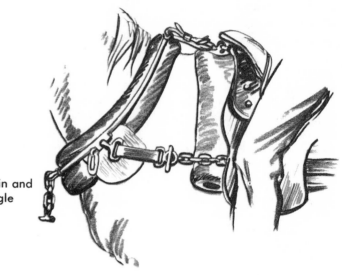

chain and
toggle

**NEAR LEAD HORSE**

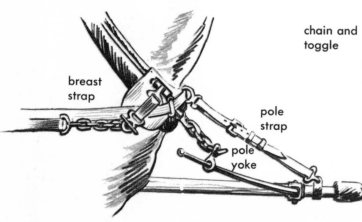

breast
strap

pole
strap

pole
yoke

**TRACE AND POLE HITCH FOR WHEEL PAIR**
Trace from off swing horse not shown

The two movable branches of the
pole yoke prevented the pole from
striking the horses.

Swing Pair                           Lead Pair

A 6-pounder battery—usually four guns and two 12-pounder howitzers—had fourteen 6-horse teams and seven spare horses. A battery of 12-pounders, with two caissons per gun, needed twenty teams plus ten spares. The officers and sergeants were mounted, as were the buglers and guidon-bearer.

The pace of field or horse artillery was the same as that of the cavalry—around five miles an hour over smooth roads and with horses in good condition, but this could not be done for any length of time. When hills were steep the columns were halted, the teams doubled, and the cannoneers and anyone else nearby gave a hand at the wheels.

Batteries usually maneuvered at a trot . . . the gallop was reserved for great emergency. From the command, "Action Front," a battery could come into action and fire one round in twenty-five seconds.

The valises strapped on the valise saddles of the off-horses held the personal effects of the drivers.

The guidon-bearer rode boot to boot with the lead driver—the butt of guidon staff in right stirrup socket. The guidon was once a sergeant's scarlet sash, tied on a rammer staff to mark the line for the battery when it formed front. It was scarlet with crossed cannon, with the regimental number above and the battery letter below in gold, or swallow-tailed, with stars and stripes.

LIGHT-ARTILLERY GUIDONS

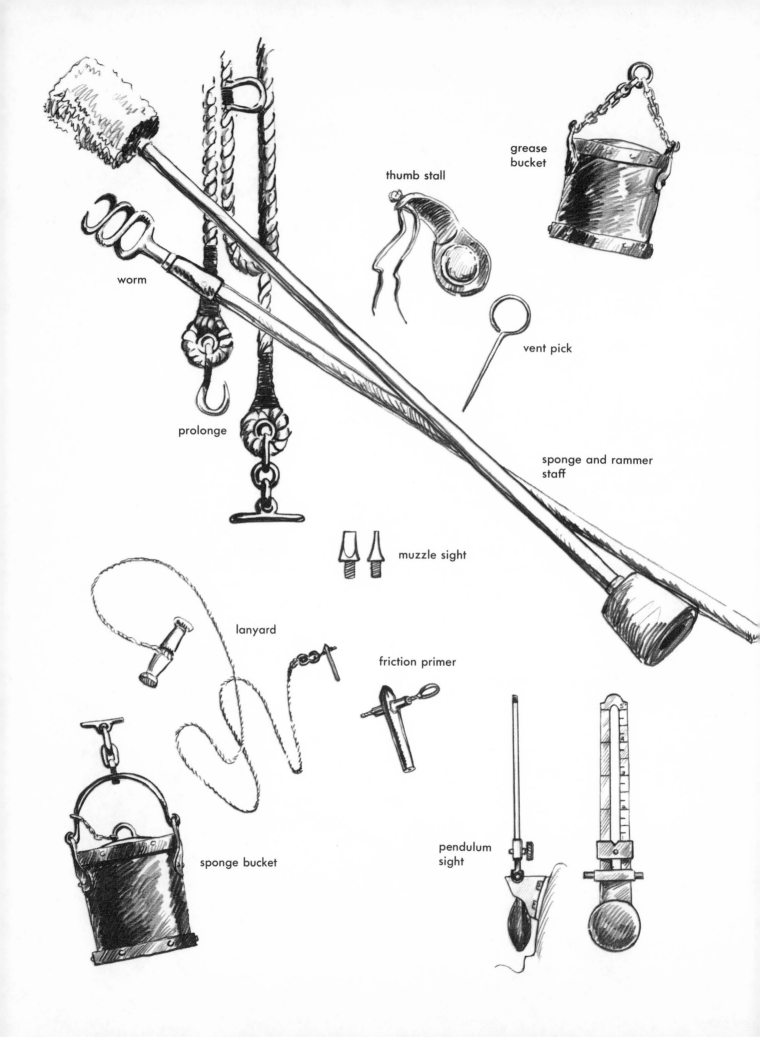

worm

prolonge

thumb stall

grease
bucket

vent pick

sponge and rammer
staff

muzzle sight

lanyard

friction primer

sponge bucket

pendulum
sight

## MOUNTAIN ARTILLERY

The 12-pounder mountain howitzer was a lightweight piece designed to be easily disassembled and transported on muleback. It could be reassembled and one round fired in one minute. The tube was only 32.9 inches long and weighed 220 pounds. The carriage was 61 inches long and weighed 157 pounds. The wheels were 38 inches in diameter and weighed 65 pounds apiece. At a 5° elevation, a half-pound charge threw a shell 900 yards.

Pack horses or mules can carry 250 to 300 pounds 20 miles a day. But on an ordinary road an animal can draw about seven times as much as he can carry; so, when possible, shafts were attached and each gun was pulled by a mule.

There was no limber. The ammunition was carried in narrow boxes holding eight rounds and weighing 112 pounds packed. One of these was strapped to each side of a packsaddle. When packed, one mule carried the tube and the shafts, and the other the carriage, implements, and wheels. A forge and tools were carried in two chests, carriage makers' tools and coal in two more. A complete battery consisted of 6 howitzers, 7 carriages (one spare), 36 boxes of ammunition, and the forge and tools, plus 33 animals.

12-Pdr. Mountain Howitzer and Ammunition Carried on Muleback

12-Pdr. Mountain Howitzer Harnessed to pack mule

1500 yds.　　　650 yds.

7 rounds spherical case—3 min., 32 sec.

*Diagram showing time and pace of cavalry attack on a battery of smoothbores. Also battery's rate of fire and type of ammunition used at different ranges. An attack by infantry from a similar distance is shown below.*

## RIFLED ARTILLERY

Although there were two schools of thought as to the effectiveness of rifled versus smoothbore guns, there was no question as to the greater accuracy of the rifle. There was also a marked increase in efficiency. A 12-pounder James, for instance, weighed less than a 12-pounder Napoleon and attained greater range and accuracy with a much smaller powder charge. Part of this was due to the reduction of windage.

Windage (the difference between the diameter of the shot and that of the bore) was allowed to take care of rust, the straps on the sabot, the expansion of the shot, and for ease in loading in a foul bore. It amounted to one-tenth of an inch in a 12-pounder smoothbore, and resulted in loss of accuracy as well as loss of velocity, since much of the force of the explosion of the charge was wasted.

In wooded country, the 12-pounder smoothbores had an advantage. Their accuracy was of secondary importance, and at close range their larger bores could inflict more damage than the 3-inch rifles. As the Napoleons used fixed ammunition and the rifles, semi-fixed—that is, the projectile and the charge were loaded separately—the smoothbore had a higher rate of fire. The 3-inch canister was fixed, however, with forty-nine .96 caliber iron balls in a tinned iron case, although it was claimed that, being long and thin, the load did not perform as well as that of the 12-pounder.

Of the many types of rifled pieces used in the war, the 3-inch Ordnance and the 10-pounder, 3-inch Parrott were the most popular. Originally the Parrott had been made in 2.9 caliber, but it was later changed so that the same ammunition might be used in both pieces. The Ordnance gun was of wrought iron while the Parrott had a cast-iron tube, reinforced at the breech by a wrought-iron hoop.

1400 yds.

1500 yds.

20 rounds spherical case—9 min., 53 sec.

350 yds.

2 solid shot—48 sec.     2 canister—34 sec.

## RIFLED FIELD PIECES USED BY FEDERAL AND CONFEDERATE ARTILLERY

| Type | Cal. | Length of Tube (in.) | Wt. (lbs.) | Wt. Projectile (lbs.) | Wt. Charge (lbs.) | Range (yds.) 5° Elevation |
|---|---|---|---|---|---|---|
| 10-pdr. Parrott | 3.00 | 74 | 899 | 9.5 | 1.00 | 1900 |
| 3″ Ordnance (Rodman) | 3.00 | 69 | 820 | 9.5 | 1.00 | 1830 |
| 20-pdr. Parrott | 3.67 | 84 | 1750 | 20.00 | 2.00 | 1900 |
| 12-pdr. James | 3.67 | 60 | 875 | 12.00 | .75 | 1700 |
| 24-pdr. James | 4.62 | 78.0 | 1750 | 24.00 | 1.50 | 1800 |
| 6-pdr. Wiard | 2.56 | 56 | 600 | 6.00 | .60 | 1800 |
| 10-pdr. Wiard | 3.00 | 58 | 790 | 10.00 | 1.00 | 1850 |
| 6-pdr. Whitworth | 2.15 | 70 | 700 | 6.00 | 1.00 | 2750 |
| 12-pdr. Whitworth (breech-loading) | 2.75 | 104 | 1092 | 12.00 | 1.75 | 2800 |
| 12-pdr. Whitworth (muzzle-loading) | 2.75 | 84 | 1000 | 12.00 | 2.00 | 3000 |
| 12-pdr. Blakely | 3.40 | 59 | 800 | 10.00 | 1.00 | 1850 |
| Armstrong (breech-loading) | 3.00 | 83 | 918 | 12.00 | 1.25 | 2100 |
| Armstrong (muzzle-loading) | 3.00 | 76 | 996 | 12.00 | 1.25 | 2200 |
| Confederate Mt. Rifle | 2.25 | 44 | 225 | 3.00 | .15 | 1100 |

at quick step     double-quick step and charge

650 yds.     350 yds.     100 yds.

7 solid shot—3 min., 29 sec.     9 canister—2 min., 54 sec.     2 canister—40 sec.

**RIFLED PROJECTILES.** *These are a few of the different types used by both sides, and were chosen to show some of the varied methods used to enable a projectile to be loaded easily at the muzzle and yet take the rifling. Most of the best known ones are represented as are a few oddities. The former came in many calibers, and in most calibers were made as solid shot, shell, or case.*

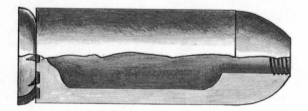

3-in. Parrott Shell

*This type engaged the rifling by expansion of a base ring, or cup, of brass, copper, lead, or wrought iron. These cups were cast into the shell, or attached to it by screws and locked by studs. Space between cup and base was usually filled with tallow.*

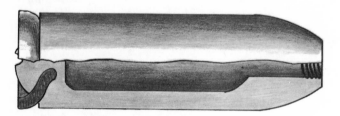

3-in. Reed Shell

3-in. Absterdam Shot

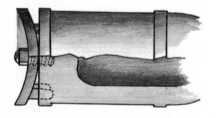

3-inch Confederate Shell
Showing one method of attaching base plate to shell.

12-Pounder Blakely          Whitworth 12-Pounder Shot

*Projectiles of this type were made to fit the rifling by various methods. Several used studs, including the muzzle-loading Armstrong. One Sawyer model had lead-coated flanges.*

Confederate 4.2-in. Flanged Percussion Shell

**3-INCH PARROTT SHELL**—*A brass ring attached to rear of projectile expanded into grooves of the gun. Early model made for 10- and 20-pounders had rings of wrought iron but brass was found to take the rifling better. A very successful type (tests showed 95% took grooves successfully), but sometimes dangerous to fire over forward troops, as the ring was apt to come off and shatter. Over one and a quarter million Parrott projectiles were made for the Northern armies.*

**3-INCH REED SHELL**—*Similar to Parrott (Reed was associated with Parrott before the war). An expanding ring of wrought copper or lead was forced into the rifling by the powder gases.*

**3-INCH CONFEDERATE SHELL**—*One of the many types to use a base plate of copper or wrought iron, fastened to the shell by a screw. Studs on the plate fitted with holes in the shell prevented lateral twisting. Others had the studs on the shell base. Also prone to scatter pieces of the base plate over forward troops.*

**3-INCH ABSTERDAM SHOT**—*This had a hollowed lead base and the two lead rings which rode the lands, allowing a closer fit and causing less wear in the barrel.*

**12-POUNDER BLAKELY**—*Mechanical-fit type. The studs, usually copper or brass, fitted into the grooves of the gun. (Projectiles of this and the two following types could only be fired in the guns for which they were designed.)*

**WHITWORTH 12-POUNDER SHOT**—*hexagonal. Accurate mechanical fit. Used as breech- or muzzle-loading projectile. A few Whitworth guns were used, mostly by the South, where they were noted for their accuracy. For some reason Whitworth shot were always referred to as "bolts."*

**CONFEDERATE 4.2-INCH FLANGED PERCUSSION SHELL**—*6 diagonal ratchet flanges fitted the rifling. Note the cap nipples of the unusual fuse device.*

## TABLE OF FIRE.  LIGHT 12-POUNDER GUN.  MODEL 1857.

| SHOT. Charge 2¼ Pounds. | | SPHERICAL CASE SHOT. Charge 2¼ Pounds. | | | SHELL. Charge 2 Pounds. | | |
|---|---|---|---|---|---|---|---|
| ELEVATION In Degrees. | RANGE In Yards. | ELEVATION In Degrees. | TIME OF FLIGHT. Seconds. | RANGE In Yards. | ELEVATION In Degrees. | TIME OF FLIGHT In Seconds. | RANGE In Yards. |
| 0° | 323 | 0°50′ | 1″ | 300 | 0° | 0‴75 | 300 |
| 1° | 620 | 1° | 1‴75 | 575 | 0°30 | 1″25 | 425 |
| 2° | 875 | 1°30′ | 2″5 | 635 | 1° | 1″75 | 615 |
| 3° | 1200 | 2° | 3″ | 730 | 1°30′ | 2″25 | 700 |
| 4° | 1325 | 3° | 4″ | 960 | 2° | 2″75 | 785 |
| 5° | 1680 | 3°30′ | 4″75 | 1080 | 2°30′ | 3″5 | 925 |
| | | 3°40′ | 5″ | 1135 | 3° | 4″ | 1080 |
| | | | | | 3°45′ | 5″ | 1300 |

Use SHOT at masses of troops, and to batter, from 600 up to 2,000 yards.  Use SHELL for firing buildings, at troops posted in woods, in pursuit, and to produce a moral rather than a physical effect; greatest effective range 1,500 yards.  Use SPHERICAL CASE SHOT at masses of troops, at not less than 500 yards; generally up to 1,500 yards.  CANISTER is not effective at 600 yards; it should not be used beyond 500 yards, and but very seldom and over the most favorable ground at that distance; at short ranges, (less than 200 yards,) in emergency, use double canister, with single charge.  Do not employ RICOCHET at less distance than 1,000 to 1,100 yards.

### CARE OF AMMUNITION CHEST.

1st.  Keep everything out that does not belong in them, except a bunch of cord or wire for breakage; beware of loose tacks, nails, bolts, or scraps.
2d.  Keep friction primers in their papers, tied up.  The pouch containing those for instant service must be closed, and so placed as to be secure.  Take every precaution that primers do not get loose; a single one may cause an explosion.  Use plenty of tow in packing.

(This sheet is to be glued on to the inside of Limber Chest Cover.)

Reproduction of table of fire which was glued to inside of limber chest cover

**4-INCH HOTCHKISS SHELL**—*shown in 2 sections* (LEFT), *cast in two parts. The space between was cast full of lead, covered with a greased canvas band* (TOP SECTION). BOTTOM—*The base was forced by the explosion further up on the cylindrical body, squeezing the lead into the rifling. Close to a million made in calibers from 2.6 inches to 7 inches in various types, 35 in all, of shot, shell, case, and canister, the latter being in the usual tin container. The ragged edge of lead which remained on the shell as it left the gun caused a tremendous scream, noted for its effect on morale.*

**THE JAMES SHELL** *was cast with eight or ten longitudinal slits leading from a central hollow in the base to the outside of the projectile. These slits were filled with lead, which was squeezed outward into the rifling by the explosion. The lead was covered with a thin plate of tin and wrapped with greased canvas for easy loading. Manufacture was abandoned before the end of the war, but not before some 94,000 of these complicated projectiles were made, in the usual assortment of sizes and types.*

**2.4-INCH PATTISON SHOT**—*The Pattison projectile was cast with projections to fit the grooves of the gun. Windage was stopped by the fitted leather band, which acted somewhat in the manner of a washer in a pump.*

**3-INCH SCHENKL SHELL**—*The rear of this projectile was in the form of a truncated cone, with straight projections cast on it. Around this was placed a papier-mâché sabot, grooved to fit the projections, which prevented lateral slipping. The powder gas drove the sabot up the cone and jammed it in the grooves of the gun. It performed well when the sabot was in good condition and as the papier-mâché flew to pieces on leaving the muzzle it was safe to fire over troops. Swelling of the sabot sometimes caused trouble in loading, and if the sabot disintegrated in the barrel the shot tumbled. The North made over 338,000 from 3 inches to 7 inches.*

**2.25-INCH CONFEDERATE SHELL**—*Somewhat similar to the Schenkl design. A copper cup ring was forced up the cone and expanded sufficiently to take the rifling.*

**3.75-INCH SAWYER SHELL**—*These projectiles were lead coated. The lead base was upset into the rifling by the force of the powder gases. Another Sawyer, also lead coated, was a "mechanical-fit type," cast with flanged projections which fitted into the grooves. Over 24,000 made by the North.*

**24-POUND DYER SHELL**—*Lead base cast over base of shell, and prevented from slipping by projections. Head at base upset, as in the Sawyer. Over 168,000 made by the North—some as large as 8 inches.*

**CONFEDERATE 3.5-INCH WINGED SHOT**—*This weird type was a Confederate attempt to get rifle accuracy from a smoothbore gun. The base was cupped and the slitted wings opened by means of springs after leaving the muzzle. The author knows nothing of its efficiency, but it must have made an awe-inspiring racket.*

Top and side view
of lead-coated Sawyer shell
with projections
cast on

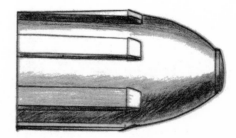

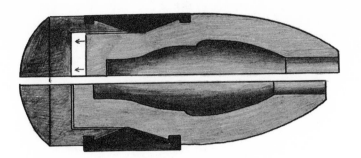

4-inch Hotchkiss Shell

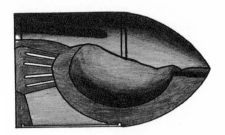

The James Shell

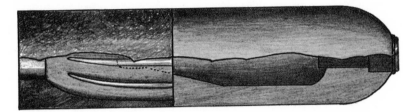

3-inch Schenkl Shell

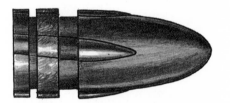

2.4-inch Pattison Shot

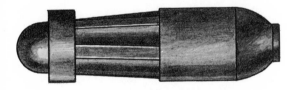

2.25-inch Confederate Shell

*None of the expanding-type projectiles performed as consistently as those relying on mechanical fit. Of the shells on this page, tests showed that a higher percentage of Hotchkiss took the grooves, closely followed by the Schenkl. The Dyer outpointed the lead-coated Sawyer.*

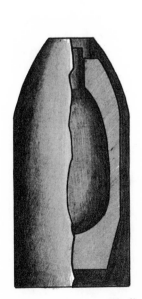

3.75-inch Sawyer Shell

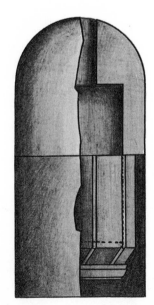

24-Pound Dyer Shell

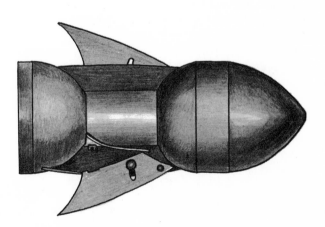

Confederate 3.5-inch Winged Shot

[81]

## FUSES

Fuses were used to explode shell and spherical case shot. They were either ignited by the flash of the discharge and timed to set off the bursting charge on or near the target, or fired by the impact of the projectile striking the target (percussion). As the functioning of most percussion fuses depended on the projectile striking nose-first, the majority of smoothbore shells, being spherical, used the first type of fuse. (There were percussion fuses for spherical ammunition, but they were very complicated.) Shells for the rifled guns used either time or percussion fuses, and sometimes both as a double insurance.

Despite all the care and ingenuity used in their design and construction, fuses frequently failed to function correctly. Some prematures burst at or in the muzzles, while others were "duds" (not unknown in modern ammunition). Spherical case shot, to be effective, should have exploded fifty to seventy-five yards short of its target. This called for finer adjustment than the fuses of the period were capable of, especially if the target was moving. The tendency of some rifled projectiles to "tumble" prevented their percussion fuses from functioning, while others failed to explode when they struck sand or loose earth, the impact being insufficient to detonate them. Time fuses in rifled guns were often unreliable when the expanding-type projectiles cut off the flame in the bore.

The Borman fuse usually used in smoothbore ammunition consisted of a circular disc of pewter or other semisoft metal threaded to screw into the shell. This contained a ring of powder composition, the zero end of which led to some fine powder in the center of the case. The thin cover of the fuse, over the ring, was marked in seconds and quarter-seconds. To set, the cover was cut with a knife or fuse-cutter at the required point, exposing the composition to the flame of the gun's discharge. The composition burned down and set off the center, which blew off a protective tin plate on the bottom of the fuse and ignited the burster in the shell.

Another type of time fuse, used in the Parrott and Dyer projectiles, had a soft metal plug, which screwed into the fuse hole in the nose of the shell. Into this was placed a conical paper-case fuse holding the fuse composition. The cases were of different colors, denoting different burning times. Black fuses burned two seconds per inch, red

three, green four, and yellow five. Each fuse was two inches long and could be adjusted by cutting if necessary.

Mortar shells or "bombs" used a long tapered wooden tube filled with fuse composition and marked in graduations on the outside. The fuse was set by simply cutting or piercing the wooden tube at the required place. They were not put in the shell until ready to fire.

There were several percussion fuses which relied on a movable or "floating" plunger, filled with powder and topped with some kind of cap of fulminate. When the shell hit, the impact caused the plunger, up to this moment held back by inertia, to fly forward and explode the cap against the solid nose plug, which acted as an anvil. In the Hotchkiss, the plunger was held on "safe" by two wires which were in turn held in position by a tapered lead plug in the base of the fuse. When the projectile jerked forward upon discharge, inertia dropped the lead plug into the shell, releasing the wires and the plunger, which was then free to move forward on impact and strike the anvil in the nose plug.

The plunger of the Parrott fuse was surrounded by a soft metal cylinder. Two small projections sheared on impact, releasing the plunger. These projections did not always break and the gunners often removed the cylinder altogether—trusting to inertia to keep the plunger in place until the moment of impact.

In the Schenkl fuse, the plunger was held by a small screw through the side, and in the Absterdam, by a lead cone on the base of the plunger. In another type, the hollow plunger with its fulminate cap was screwed in place and the cap detonated by the nose collapsing upon it.

The Tice fuse used a glass tube of fulminate protected by a movable brass tube. The shock of discharge broke the brass supports holding a plunger, which in turn released a spring sliding the tube away from the glass container, which broke on impact.

In combination fuses, the plunger, actuated by the shock of discharge, ignited a preset time fuse. In some fuses a fulminate detonator was also provided, which went off on impact if the time fuse failed to operate.

The Borman time fuse functioned properly about seventy-five per cent of the time. The Parrott time fuse worked about as well, while the Parrott percussion rated about eighty-five per cent.

BORMAN FUSE—Top view

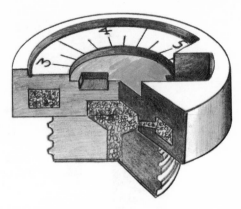

CUTAWAY DIAGRAM OF BORMAN FUSE.
A key for tightening the fuse fitted into the square holes

MORTAR FUSE
with paper cap

IMPACT-TYPE PERCUSSION FUSE. A screw
plug holding a detonator was screwed into
the cap just before firing. Impact flattened
cap, hit detonator on nipple. Explosion
blew out cork and ignited charge

CONICAL
PAPER-CASE FUSE
Wooden plug

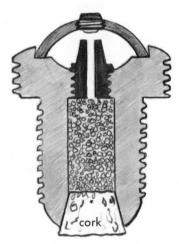

cork

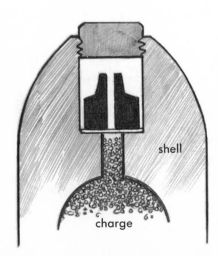

shell

charge

RIGHT—HOTCHKISS FUSE
with safety wires held by
lead plug

LEFT—Before firing, detonating cap was placed over
nipple. Inertia kept plunger
back until moment of impact.
Paper disc kept powder out
of plunger chamber

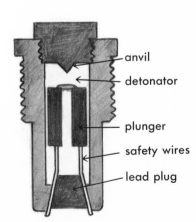

anvil

detonator

plunger

safety wires

lead plug

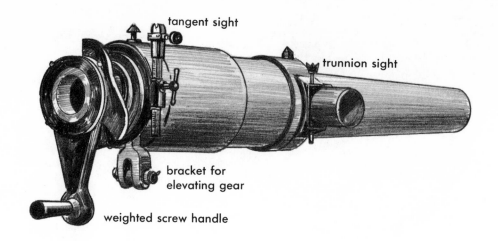

ARMSTRONG BREECHLOADER

*The breechblock or ventpiece was held in place by a powerful screw in the rear of the gun. This screw was hollow, and was a prolongation of the bore. When the screw was turned out, the ventpiece was lifted out by its handle, leaving the bore clear for loading. To ensure the tight turning up of the screw, and also to help in releasing it when getting ready to reload, a weighted, free-swinging handle was attached to the rear of the breech. A half turn on this acted almost like a blow from a sledge and was sufficient to drive the screw well home or to start it from the closed position. Although a spare ventpiece was usually provided with each gun, there was considerable trouble with the ventpieces fracturing, or blowing out, especially in the guns of large caliber. Structurally, the built-up Armstrong gun tubes were very strong, and the multi-grooved system of rifling is in use today.*

ARMSTRONG 12-POUNDER BREECHLOADER—CUTAWAY VIEWS

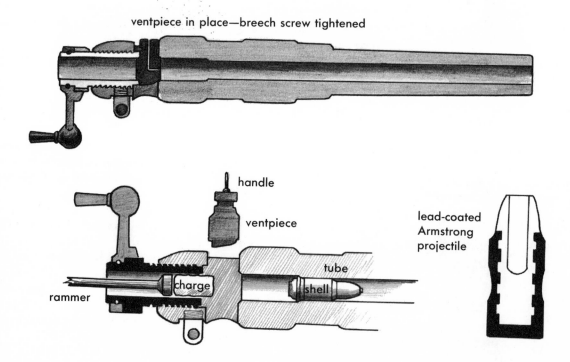

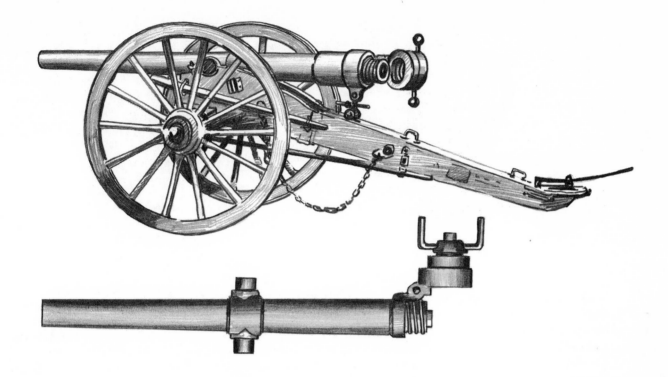

## 12-POUNDER WHITWORTH BREECH- AND MUZZLE-LOADING FIELD GUN

*The Whitworth breechloader, with its peculiar hexagonal bore, used a device resembling a hinged screw cap. The cartridge was in a hexagonally-shaped tin container which assisted in preventing the escape of gas from the breech. A lubricating wad (tallow and wax was used) was inserted behind the projectile.*

*The projectile was a mechanical fit and did not rely on expansion to make a tight fit in the bore. Because of this, and because there was no chamber, by closing the breech and using a copper disc as a gas check, the guns could be (and often were) used as muzzle-loaders. This could not be done in the Armstrong, with its lead-coated shell and powder chamber larger than bore size.*

## BREECHLOADERS

Few breechloaders were used in the Civil War (for their breech mechanisms were relatively clumsy and complicated), but the two that did see service—the Armstrong and the Whitworth—were a great deal more accurate than any of the muzzle-loading smoothbore field pieces. The Armstrong is reported to have been more than fifty times as accurate as the standard British smoothbore field piece at one thousand yards. The Whitworth was every bit as accurate. Both had considerable range with low elevation, which meant a larger "danger space." But long range (the Whitworth 12-pounder could send a bolt nearly six miles) was not of much advantage in the days of imperfect means of observation and poor fire control, and small-caliber shells with comparatively weak bursting charges.

Neither of these breechloaders had any great advantage over muzzle-loaders in rapidity of fire (for one thing, neither used fixed ammunition). A light rifle and shrapnel-proof gun shield, as used in more modern field pieces, might have increased their value, as the gun crews could have been partially protected from musketry. But this did not come into being until the development of a workable recoil mechanism.

# SIEGE AND GARRISON ARTILLERY

The heavy artillery was divided into two classes —(1) siege and garrison, and (2) seacoast. In the former class were pieces which could be moved on carriages by road and which formed the siege train of an army. The seacoast artillery was intended to be used in fixed positions and, as weight did not matter, were heavier than the siege pieces (the largest weighed 117,000 pounds) and were mounted on a variety of specialized carriages.

On several occasions very heavy pieces were laboriously moved into prepared positions and used as siege weapons. At other times, as at Malvern Hill and Shiloh, guns of the siege train took an active part in the action.

The Civil War saw the end of the smoothbore as a siege weapon, and the superior range, accuracy, and penetration of the new rifled pieces made the old type of brick or stone fort obsolete. Fort Pulaski, at the mouth of the Savannah River, was a well-built structure, considered so strong that the U. S. Chief of Engineers said of it, "You might as well bombard the Rocky Mountains." It surrendered after a two-day cannonade, and General Hunter reported to Washington that, "No works of stone or brick can resist the impact of rifled artillery of heavy caliber."

In view of the number of smoothbore guns of early models available, it was natural for both sides to attempt to convert some of them to rifles. (The guns which did the most damage to Fort Pulaski were old model 42-, and 32-, and 24-pounders, rifled and firing James projectiles of 84, 64, and 48 pounds, respectively.)

Cast iron by itself, however, was not strong enough to stand the increased pressures, and even when reinforced with wrought-iron hoops, many such guns burst. The larger Parrotts, although specially designed as rifled pieces, were liable to let go on occasion.

Various types of hooped or built-up guns were used during the war, but even the best of them were none too good, and any cannoneer who pulled the lanyard on a large-caliber rifle did so at some risk.

In connection with this, it must be remembered that the manufacture of steel was in its infancy, and the working and forging of masses big enough for large cannon would have been both technically impossible and prohibitively expensive.

Smoothbore guns of large size were successfully made by an improved method of casting developed by Major Rodman. In this system, which modified the initial strains in the chamber of the gun, the iron was cast around a central hollow core, through which a stream of water passed while the metal was cooling. The larger guns, called Columbiads, after the old-style gun-howitzer monsters of an earlier date, were mounted in forts. The largest, a 20-inch giant, used a 100-pound charge. So well did guns cast under this system withstand the tremendous shock of the large charges that later even the 4.5 siege rifles were hollow-cast.

The terrific gas pressure in the chambers which gave the gunmakers of the period so much trouble was due to a defect inherent in the propellant itself. Unlike the slower-burning high explosives used in charges today, the explosion of black powder was sudden and violent. The whole charge of ordinary cannon powder was consumed before the projectile had barely started up the bore. This was not only inefficient, but also produced enormous strains in the gun. By using larger grains of powder, Major Rodman attempted to slow down combustion and give the projectile more of a slow "push" up the bore. His "mammoth" powder was an improvement, but real progress along these lines had to wait upon the introduction of the nitrocellulose- and nitroglycerin-based propellants later in the century.

## PENETRATION IN BRICK WORK AT FT. PULASKI (WALLS 7½ FEET THICK)

| Kind of Gun | Range—Yards | Projectile | Elevation | Charge—lbs. | Penetration—in. |
|---|---|---|---|---|---|
| Old 42-pdr. rifled | 1650 | James 84-lb. shot | 4½ degrees | 8 | 26 |
| Old 32-pdr. rifled | 1650 | James 64-lb. shot | 4 degrees | 6 | 20 |
| Old 24-pdr. rifled | 1670 | James 48-lb. shot | 4½ degrees | 5 | 19 |
| Parrott 30-pdr. | 1670 | Parrott 30-lb. shot | 4½ degrees | 3½ | 18 |
| 10-in. smoothbore | 1740 | 128-lb. solid shot | 5 degrees | 20 | 13 |
| 8-in. smoothbore | 1740 | 68-lb. solid shot | 5 degrees | 10 | 11 |

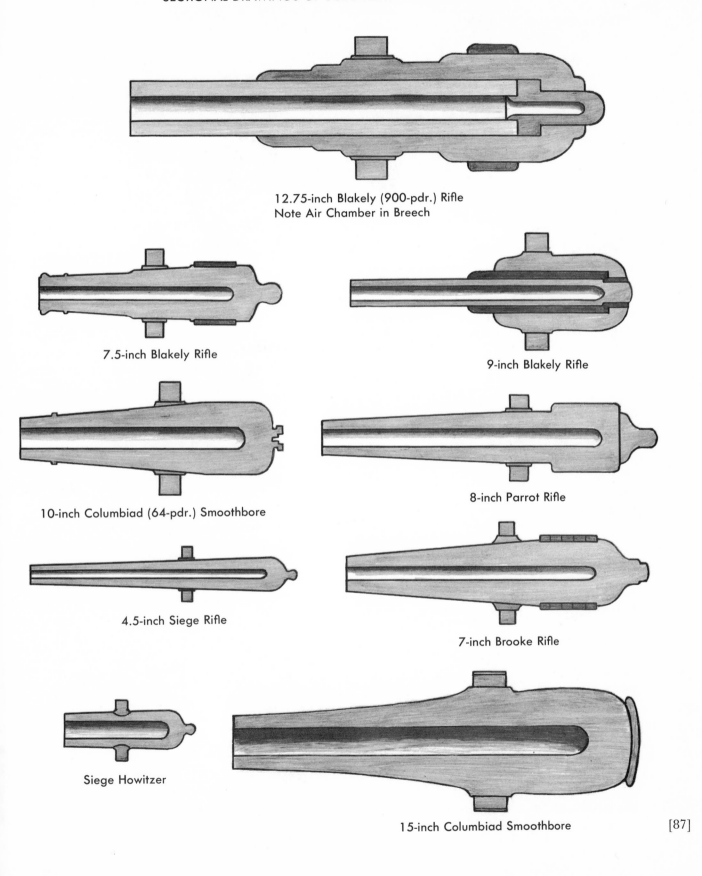

12.75-inch Blakely (900-pdr.) Rifle
Note Air Chamber in Breech

7.5-inch Blakely Rifle

9-inch Blakely Rifle

10-inch Columbiad (64-pdr.) Smoothbore

8-inch Parrot Rifle

4.5-inch Siege Rifle

7-inch Brooke Rifle

Siege Howitzer

15-inch Columbiad Smoothbore

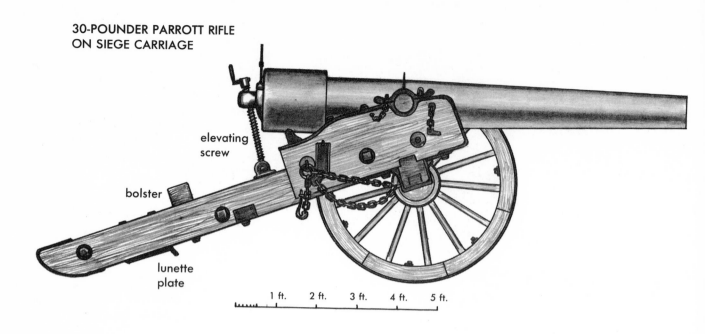

**30-POUNDER PARROTT RIFLE ON SIEGE CARRIAGE**

elevating screw

bolster

lunette plate

1 ft.  2 ft.  3 ft.  4 ft.  5 ft.

## SIEGE AND GARRISON ARTILLERY

| | Bore diameter (in.) | Length of tube (in.) | Weight of tube (lbs.) | Weight of Projectile (lbs.) | Weight of charge (lbs.) | Bursting charge (lbs.) | Range (yds.) | Elevation (degrees) |
|---|---|---|---|---|---|---|---|---|
| 4½-in. M.L.,R. | 4.5 | 133 | 3450 | 33 | 3.5 | | 2078 | 5 |
| 30-pdr. Parrott M.L.,R | 4.2 | 136 | 4200 | 29 | 3.75 | | 2200 | 5 |
| 24-pdr. gun S.B. | 5.82 | 124 | 5790 | 24 | 6 | 1 | 1900 | 5 |
| 18-pdr. gun S.B. | 5.3 | 123.25 | 4680 | 18.5 | 4.5 | | 1592 | 5 |
| 12-pdr. gun S.B. | 4.62 | 116 | 3120 | 12.3 | 4 | | 1834 | 5 |
| 8-in. howitzer S.B. | 8 | 61.5 | 2614 | 50.5 | 4 | | 1241 | 5 |

## SEACOAST ARTILLERY

| | Bore diameter (in.) | Length of tube (in.) | Weight of tube (lbs.) | Weight of Projectile (lbs.) | Weight of charge (lbs.) | Bursting charge (lbs.) | Range (yds.) | Elevation (degrees) |
|---|---|---|---|---|---|---|---|---|
| 32-pdr. gun S.B. | 6.4 | 125.2 | 7200 | 32.6 | 8 | 1.5 | 1922 | 5 |
| 42-pdr. gun S.B. | 7 | 129 | 8465 | 42.7 | 10.5 | | 1955 | 5 |
| 8-in. columbiad S.B. | 8 | 124 | 9240 | 65 | 10 | 1.5 | 1813 | 5 |
| 10-in. columbiad S.B. | 10 | 126 | 15,400 | 128 | 18 | 3 | 1814 | 5 |
| 15-in. columbiad S.B. | 15 | 182 | 50,000 | c./350 | 40 | 17 | 5730 | 28.35 |
| 20-in. Rodman S.B. | 20 | 190 | 117,000 | 1080 | 100 | | c./3.5 mi. | 25 |
| 100-pdr. Parrott M.L.,R | 6.4 | 151 | 9700 | 70–100 | 10 | c./2.5 | 2370 | 5 |
| 200-pdr. Parrott M.L.,R | 8 | 159 | 16,300 | 132–175 | 16 | | 2000 | 5 |
| 300-pdr. Parrott M.L.,R. | 10 | 173 | 26,500 | 230–250 | 25 | | 2500 | 10 |
| 80-pdr. Whitworth M.L.,R. | 5 | 118 | 8582 | 80 | 10 | 3.17 | 13,665 | 10 |
| 70-pdr. Armstrong B.L.,R. | 6.4 | 110 | 6903 | 79.8 | 10 | 5.4 | 2183 | 5.9 |
| 8-in. Blakely M.L.,R. | 8 | 156 Bore | 17,000 | 200 | 20 | | | |
| 150-pdr. Armstrong M.L.,R. | 8.5 | 120 | 15,737 | 150 | 20 | | | |
| 12¾in. Blakely M.L.,R. | 12.75 | 192 | 54,000 | 700 | 50 | | | |

*Key:*

*Smoothbore—S.B.; Rifled—R.; Muzzle-loading—M.L.; Breech-loading—B.L.; Projectile weights and charges varied greatly, solid shot being heavier: .ie., 15-inch S.B. shot weighed 440 pounds, shell, 352 pounds.*

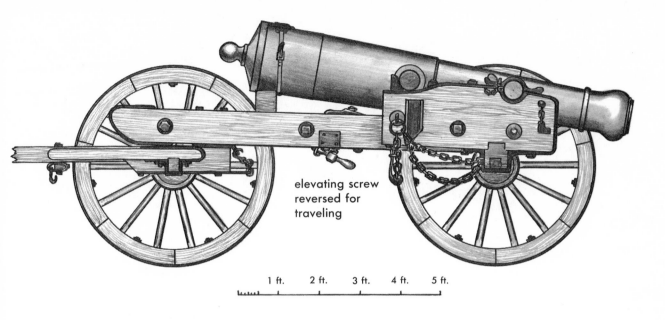

elevating screw
reversed for
traveling

1 ft.  2 ft.  3 ft.  4 ft.  5 ft.

24-POUNDER SMOOTHBORE GUN ON SIEGE CARRIAGE
in traveling position

The 24-pounder smoothbore model 1839 was about the heaviest piece which could be moved by road. At five degrees, with a six-pound charge, it could throw its projectile close to two thousand yards.

Although longer and heavier, the gun carriage was similar in construction to the field carriage but joined to the limber in a different manner. A pintle projecting from the limber fitted into a hole made in the underside of the trail, the two parts fastened with a lashing chain and hook. The weight of the trail resting on the rear of the tongue kept it almost horizontal, thus relieving the horses of its weight.

The splinter bar, to which the traces of the wheel pair were fastened, was stationary, but the traces of the next team were hitched to a movable bar connected to the end of the tongue. The tongue had pole chains but no yoke. The rest of the teams were harnessed as in the field artillery.

The limber weighed 1393 pounds and the whole unit, as shown above, ready to roll, weighed 10,155 pounds. It was drawn by ten horses with five drivers.

For traveling, the trunnion caps were removed and the gun slid back until the breech rested in a hollow in a block on the trail called the bolster. The trunnions rested up against the traveling trunnion bolts, which projected from the rear of the cheek. The elevating screw was reversed and held by a strap. Note the vent cover.

This type of gun was designed in the days before the introduction of the rifled gun and the rifle-musket for close-range battering. Counted a powerful piece in its day, it could, at one hundred yards, penetrate eight feet, six inches of old earth parapet; fifteen feet of new earthwork; close to two feet of stone, and three feet of brick. Its shell held a bursting charge of one pound.

Smoothbore guns could also throw red-hot shot for use against buildings or ships. Furnaces were used which usually held sixty shot or more. A cold furnace took about an hour and a quarter to heat a 24-pounder shot to red hot. The shot was carried to the gun on ladles. A dry wad was put in over the powder, and one or two wet wads on top of that. The manual states that the shot would cool in the gun before it burned through the wads and set off the charge.

Its ammunition was similar to that used in the smoothbore field pieces, but included grapeshot, spherical case, and canister.

## 24-POUNDER GUN ON BARBETTE CARRIAGE

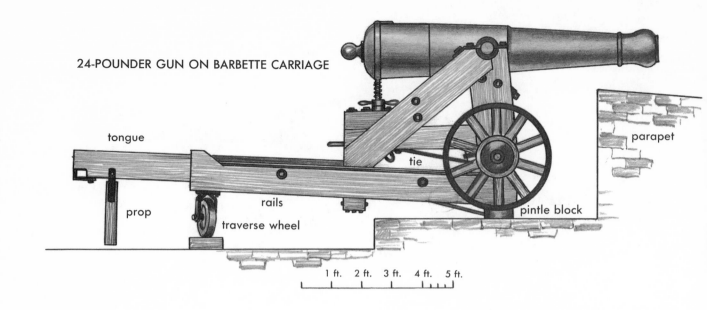

tongue

prop

rails

traverse wheel

tie

parapet

pintle block

1 ft. 2 ft. 3 ft. 4 ft. 5 ft.

## 150-POUNDER ARMSTRONG MUZZLE-LOADING RIFLE

*An Armstrong gun of this type was "built up" of a series of concentric wrought-iron tubes made from spiral coils welded together under a steam hammer.*

*The tubes, or hoops, were then shrunk over one another so that the inner tube, or barrel, was in a state of compression and better able to resist the force of explosion. Each tube was turned on a lathe to a slightly smaller diameter than the one it was to fit over. Then it was expanded by heating and dropped into place.*

## DIAGRAM OF COMPRESSOR

regulating wheel

side plates pivot, clamp slide between them

slide

Enlarged view of compressor

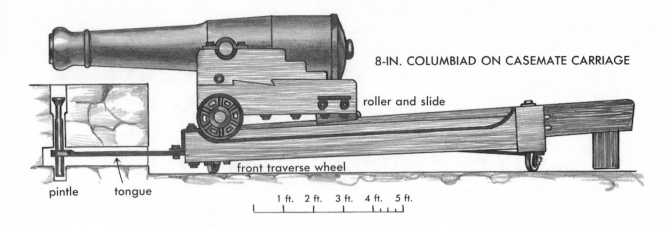

**8-IN. COLUMBIAD ON CASEMATE CARRIAGE**

roller and slide

front traverse wheel

pintle    tongue

1 ft.   2 ft.   3 ft.   4 ft.   5 ft.

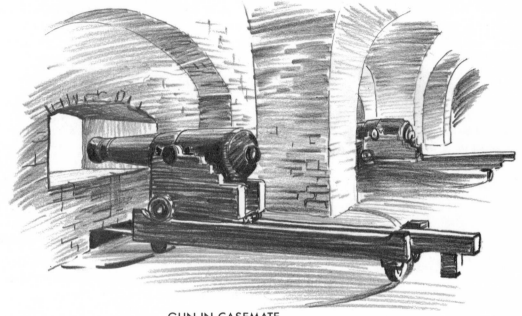

**GUN IN CASEMATE**

Typical permanent fortress installation

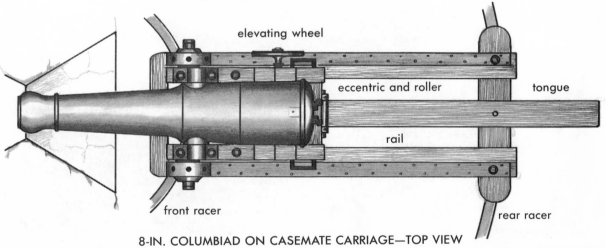

elevating wheel

eccentric and roller    tongue

rail

front racer    rear racer

**8-IN. COLUMBIAD ON CASEMATE CARRIAGE—TOP VIEW**

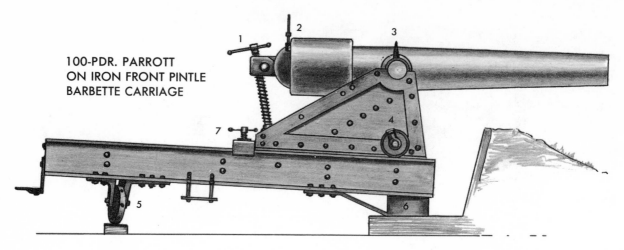

100-PDR. PARROTT
ON IRON FRONT PINTLE
BARBETTE CARRIAGE

1. Elevating screw   2. Rear sight   3. Sight on trunnion ring   4. Truck, with fitting on axle, for handspike, for throwing eccentric.   5. Traversing wheels, with holes for handspikes.   6. Pintle   7. Compressor

In many types of mountings recoil was taken up by friction of the carriage on the slide. To run the gun out, trucks with eccentric axles were used. The trucks were made to bear on the slide by turning the axle with a wrench placed on the hexagonal end. Handspikes were then inserted in holes in the rims of the trucks to work the gun forward.

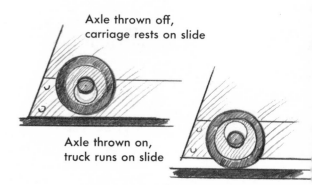

Axle thrown off, carriage rests on slide

Axle thrown on, truck runs on slide

FRICTION RECOIL
Trucks on eccentric axles

8-IN. PARROTT

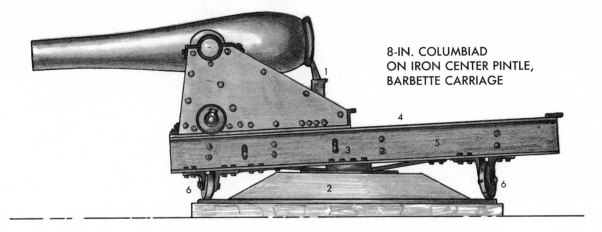

8-IN. COLUMBIAD
ON IRON CENTER PINTLE,
BARBETTE CARRIAGE

1. Elevating mechanism   2. Traversing circle   3. Pintle   4. Slide   5. Rails
6. Traversing wheels

*This type of carriage and elevating mechanism was frequently used. In the South most of the carriages, rails, etc., were of wood. In the North they were usually made of iron, which stood up better under the shock of recoil. All basically the same, they differed in many minor details. All could be traversed by handspikes, although some were trained by block and tackle. Nearly all used the friction of the carriage on the rails to check recoil. A few used compressors. Sights on the muzzle, or trunnion ring, and breech were usually removed when the gun was not in action.*

When pawl in notch, handspike withdrawn.
Fine adjustment then made
with elevating screw

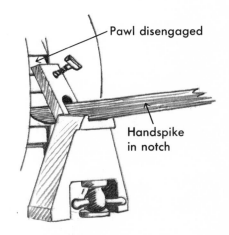

Pawl disengaged

Handspike
in notch

NOTCH AND PAWL
ELEVATING GEAR

Notches
in breech
of gun

movable pawl          lock screw

slot for
handspike

slide

elevating          box
screw

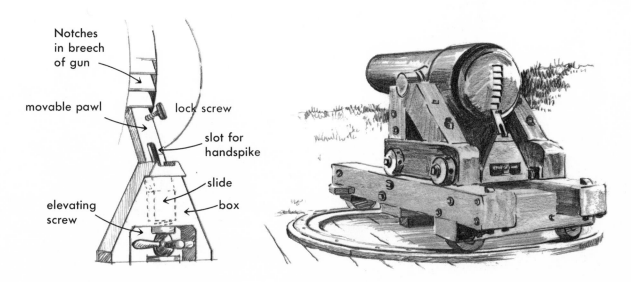

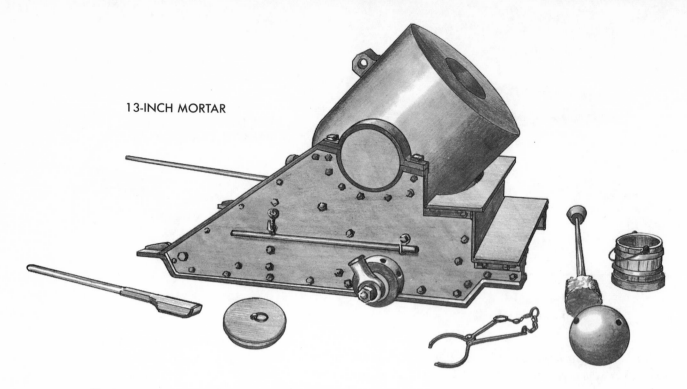

**13-INCH MORTAR**

*Equipment shown: Handspikes (one in elevating lugs on breech), sponge and rammer, shell tongs, shell showing holes for tongs, and wooden tompion which fitted in muzzle when gun was not in use.*

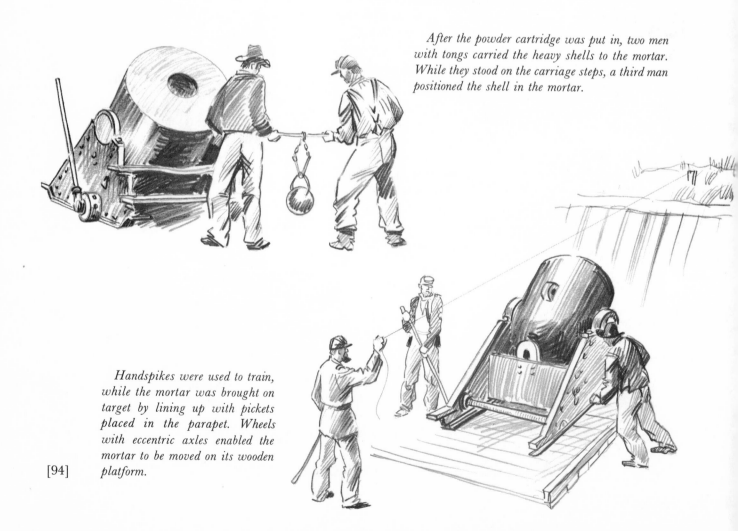

*After the powder cartridge was put in, two men with tongs carried the heavy shells to the mortar. While they stood on the carriage steps, a third man positioned the shell in the mortar.*

*Handspikes were used to train, while the mortar was brought on target by lining up with pickets placed in the parapet. Wheels with eccentric axles enabled the mortar to be moved on its wooden platform.*

[94]

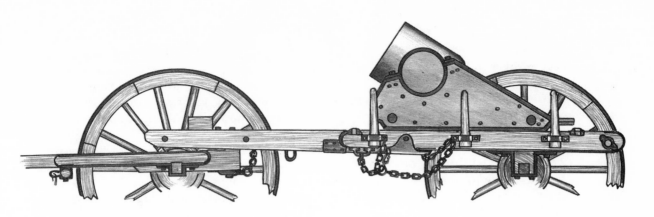

**10-IN. SIEGE MORTAR ON MORTAR WAGON**

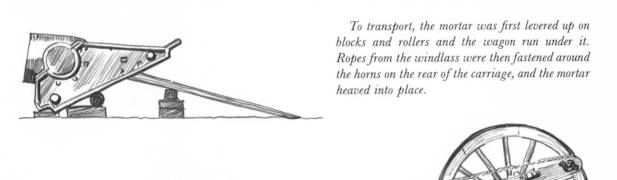

*To transport, the mortar was first levered up on blocks and rollers and the wagon run under it. Ropes from the windlass were then fastened around the horns on the rear of the carriage, and the mortar heaved into place.*

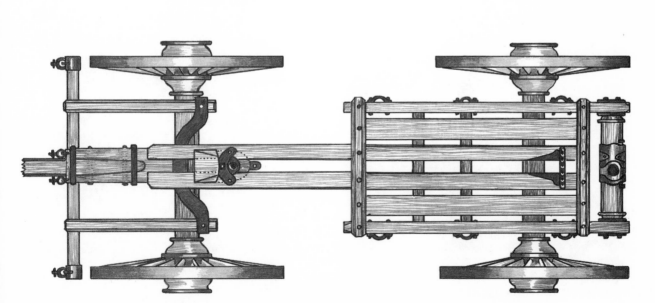

Mortar wagon, top view. Note windlass

# MORTARS

Like heavy artillery, mortars were classed as "siege" or "seacoast." Siege mortars, the 8-inch and the light model 10-inch, although cumbersome, could accompany the siege train on mortar wagons. Also classed as a siege weapon was the coehorn. This was a small bronze mortar, light enough (296 pounds with bed) to be carried by four men. It was useful in trench warfare—such as Petersburg—and mobile enough to appear at a battle like Cold Harbor.

The longer and far heavier models of the 10-inch and the giant 13-inch were of the "seacoast" variety. They could be moved only with great difficulty, and over long distances were carried by rail or ship. To transport a large mortar from railhead or dock to its emplacement, it was dismounted and slung under a sling carriage, while its bed was carried under another.

While prolonged mortar bombardments fre-quently did remarkably little actual damage, the moral effect of the screeching shells and noisy bursts was very great, and often drove enemy gunners from their guns and kept them pinned in the bombproofs.

Mortars usually fired spherical shells, with two holes for the lifting tongs, and were much like a bowling ball in appearance. In 1863, experiments at Fort Scott near Washington were made with mortar shells containing canister shot and 2.5 pounds of bursting powder, and timed to explode over the target. Ten-inch shells of this description were used at Petersburg and at the battle in the crater there, where they silenced a Confederate battery, the men being unable to remain at their guns under the showers of balls.

Fuses were time—touched off by the explosion of the charge, or percussion. There was the usual percentage of premature bursts and duds.

## SIEGE AND GARRISON MORTARS

| | Bore diameter (in.) | Length of tube (in.) | Weight of tube (lbs.) | Weight of projectile (lbs.) | Weight of charge (lbs.) | Bursting charge (lbs.) | Range (yds.) 45° elevation |
|---|---|---|---|---|---|---|---|
| 8-in. mortar | 8 | 22.50 | 930 | 44.5 | 3.75 | 2.0 | 1200 |
| 10-in. mortar | 10 | 28.00 | 1852 | 87.5 | 4.00 | 5.0 | 2100 |
| 24-pdr. Coehorn | 5.82 | 16.32 | 164 | 17.0 | .50 | 1.0 | 1200 |
| 10-in. mortar | 10.00 | 46.00 | 5775 | 87.5 | 10.00 | 5.0 | 4250 |
| 13-in. mortar | 13.00 | 53 | 17,120 | 220 | 20 | 11 | 4325 |

Above—24-pdr. Coehorn
Left—10-in. mortar with iron carriage showing elevating screw, lifting lug, and handspike

Rocket used in the United States service was Hale's. Two sizes were listed, 2¼ inch (outside diameter), weight 6 pounds, and 3¼ inch, weight 16 pounds. Ranges: at 5° elevation, 500 to 600 yards; at 47°, 2¼ inch, 1760 yards, and 3¼ inch, 2200 yards. Light iron case. War heads solid, explosive, or incendiary.

Usually fired from tubes or light carriages. Modern-looking launcher shown has adjustable front legs and sight. It was five feet long. The Hale was an improvement on the Congreve, being spin stabilized by rotation caused by three metal vanes inserted in the exhaust nozzle. The Congreve was stabilized by a long stick. Propellant was slow-burning mixture of niter, charcoal, and sulphur, forced into case under great pressure. Fissuring of packed propellant often caused irregular burning or explosion. Flight was erratic (sometimes endangering the rocket crews), and consequently weapons saw little service.

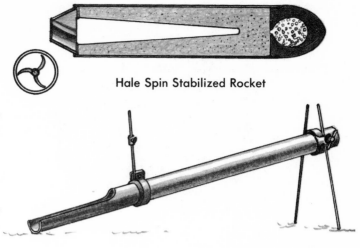

**Hale Spin Stabilized Rocket**

**Launcher for Hale's Rocket**

**Congreve Stick Rocket**

From War Years with Jeb Stuart, *by Lieutenant Colonel W. W. Blackford, C.S.A.*

"Stuart opened on them with a Congreve rocket battery, the first and last time the latter ever appeared in action with us. It had been gotten up by some foreign chap who managed it on this occasion. They were huge rockets, fired from a sort of a gun carriage, with a shell at the end which exploded in due time, scattering "liquid damnation," as the men called it. Their course was erratic; they went straight enough in their first flight, but after striking, the flight might be continued in any other course, even directly back towards where it came from. Great consternation was occasioned among the camps of the enemy as these unearthly serpents went zigzagging about among them. . . . A few tents were fired but the rockets proved to be of little practical value . . ."

**Ketcham's Grenade, made in several weights: 1, 2, 3, and 5 lbs.**

*This percussion grenade had to land point first on the plunger, which was kept from striking the cap on the nipple prematurely by a friction spring in the side of the plunger hole. To ensure this, a wooden tail with cardboard fins was plugged into a hole in the upper end.*

Hand grenades are almost as old as gunpowder itself and the name of the weapon is immortalized in the titles of many famous European regiments. Technical deficiencies, mainly in the weakness of the bursting charge and the means of ignition, kept it from becoming the popular and effective weapon it is today, but the perfection of the percussion cap in the mid-nineteenth century gave the grenade a new lease on life. Thousands were used during the Civil War, over 90,000 of Ketcham's grenades being purchased by the U.S. government. There were other types: the Adams, and the ingenious but dangerous "Excelsior." In addition, many thousands of rounds of 6-pdr. spherical case were used as grenades, either thrown or rolled down inclines after the fuse had been lit.

HAYNES "EXCELSIOR" PERCUSSION GRENADE

# FREAK GUNS

Among the numerous weird and wonderful inventions with which the Union, or the Confederacy, were to be saved, were several attempts to make repeating cannon on the revolver principle. Most of these never got beyond the testing stage and none ever saw action. The *Scientific American* illustrated many such during the first few months of the war. (Later the magazine, like many of its readers, became disenchanted with the seemingly endless struggle, and pictures of warlike gear gave way to woodcuts of cultivators and thrashing machines.) The majority of the rapid-fire cannon appear as unwieldly monstrosities, overdecorated with wheels and gears.

One relied on steam as a propellant; the "Justly celebrated Winans steam-gun which . . . was expected to revolutionize the then existing system of warfare," was captured by Union General Ben Butler's men in May of '61. The wood engraving shows it as a fascinating-look contraption, part fire engine, part snowplow. It was obviously not up to revolutionizing warfare, or anything else, or the astute and unconventional Ben Butler, who would try anything if he thought it would work, would have made some use of it.

One of a pair of revolving cannons cast by Tappey & Lumsden of Petersburg, Virginia for H. C. Pate (the other burst during its test firing and killed three of the crew) still can be seen outside a Petersburg museum. It is really not much more than a large revolver on wheels, with a crank at the back to force the cylinder forward against the barrel, to cut down leakage of gas.

Another "freak" gun still to be seen (this one at Athens, Georgia) is the famous double-barrel cannon. The device, which consists of two 6-pounder cannon cast in one piece so that they diverge slightly, is only the last of a long line of such pieces, designed to mow down the enemy like ripe grain, by two cannon balls connected by a chain. There is only one thing wrong with this delightful conception, as other enterprising artillerists have found out through the ages—it won't work. No matter that the vents are drilled so as to give fire simultaneously to both barrels. No matter that the powder charges and balls are carefully weighed and that the chain is cunningly arranged. It is physically impossible to give both projectiles exactly the same momentum at exactly the same time. The results, as might have been foreseen, were spectacular, to say the least. A contemporary account says:

"It had a kind of circular motion, plowed up an acre of ground, tore up a cornfield, mowed down saplings, and the chain broke, the two balls going in opposite directions. One of the balls killed a cow in a distant field, while the other knocked down the chimney from a log cabin."

ENGINEERS BUILDING A CORDUROY ROAD

# THE ENGINEERS

IN 1861 the engineers of the Union army were organized in two small but highly professional bodies—the Corps of Engineers, and the Corps of Topographical Engineers. In 1863 these were merged and were known as the Corps of Engineers. As its name implies, the Topographical Engineers were principally map makers, but the duties of the two overlapped to such an extent that they can be considered as one unit from the war's beginning.

The duties of the corps were many. It was in charge of planning and superintending the construction of all fortifications, permanent or otherwise, and all siege operations. It also had charge of all bridging equipment and the surveying and making of roads and pontoon trains. The corps also had to furnish maps (the country over which most of the war was fought was largely unmapped) and detailed descriptions of terrain, sufficient for the planning of troop movements. Engineer officers were attached to the various staffs, and reconnoitered the enemy's positions and chose routes and camp sites.

In short, there was very little an engineer was not expected to do or could not do if ordered. The small body of regular enlisted men was greatly expanded and numerous engineer regiments raised. These were officered either by regulars or by men with engineering training, of which the North had a good supply. Americans in those days were no strangers to the pick, shovel, and ax. The amount of work accomplished by manual labor was stupendous, and if necessary they could fight as well as they could dig.

Very few of the officers of the Confederate Engineers had had any experience as military engineers. For the most part they were men with technical training as civil engineers, some of whom had attended one or another of the military academies. These officers performed the same duties—reconnaissance, map making, fortifications, etc.—as their enemies in blue. However, until 1863 there was no provision for engineer troops. Up to that time the duties of such troops had been performed by the Pioneer Corps, which consisted merely of men detailed from the different divisions, and directed by the engineers assigned to those divisions. That such troops were not readily available is shown by the fact that an engineer officer assigned to build a bridge of boats above Drury's Bluff on the James had to enlist civilian aid and had to order the provost marshal to round up five hundred men and march them under guard to the job.

In 1863 two regiments were formed. The following is an excerpt from a description by a lieutenant colonel of his unit, The First Regiment of Engineers (the unit was made up of ten companies of one hundred men each):

"The conscript laws was just then being enforced . . . . men from twenty-five to thirty-five, mostly married, and skilled in the use of tools in some way or other, mechanics of all sorts, and farmers, etc. . . . The field and company officers were civil engineers by profession, also most of the lieutenants, . . ."

Considering the chronic shortage of men and materials, the Southern engineers performed

[99]

Cross section of permanent fort mounting two tiers of guns

*The diagram at right shows the cross section in perspective. The masonry at* **A** *is a platform for one of the center-pintle guns, mounted* en barbette *on the grass-covered terreplein. The parapet gave some protection to guns and gunners. Temporary bombproofs were sometimes built on the terreplein as added protection. Note how guns behind 5-feet thick walls could sweep the glacis. Fresh water was provided by rain which seeped through earth on the terreplein. When it penetrated to the lead-covered roof it was carried off in pipes to huge underground cisterns* **B**.

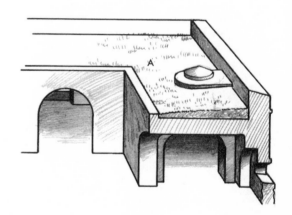

Bastions projected from walls
so guns could cover "dead space"
at foot. Built in many shapes.

*Bird's-eye view below shows layout of a typical one-story fort (some, like Sumter, had two stories). The outlying earthwork was called a demilune. A drawbridge gave access to the fort through the sally port, which was built in the gorge wall (usually the rear of the fort). This section held living quarters and often the magazines, which had interior walls twelve to fifteen feet thick. Bastions on the gorge wall enabled guns to sweep the approach to the sally port. Casemates were often fully enclosed to provide extra living space for the garrison.*

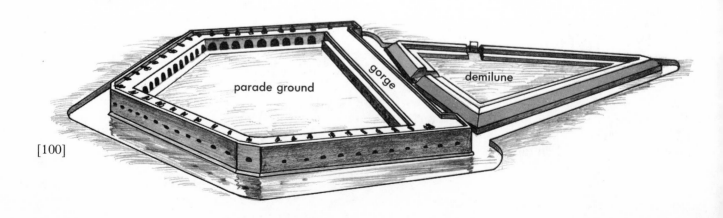

parade ground    gorge    demilune

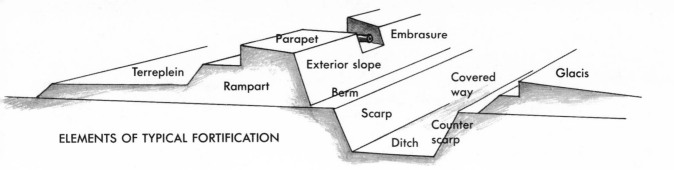

ELEMENTS OF TYPICAL FORTIFICATION

miracles, and their endeavors did much to stave off the defeat which they, of all men, must have known was inevitable.

## FORTS AND FORTIFICATIONS

The permanent fortifications existing at the outbreak of war were massive structures of bricks or stone, carrying cannon in casemates (covered gun positions in which the guns were fixed through openings in the walls of the fort) or mounted *"en barbette,"* that is, mounted in the open and firing over the top of the walls. These structures were frequently surrounded by moats, and enclosed officers' quarters, barracks, and all things necessary for permanent garrisons. They were built as coast defenses and were located at or near the entrances to most of the major harbors and river mouths.

They were constructed before the days of rifled artillery and were considered more than a match for any fleets of wooden vessels which could have been brought against them. Sumter, the most famous of them, was unfinished at the time the Civil War began, as was Pulaski, off Savannah, and only a small proportion of their intended armament had been mounted. But, although Sumter held out to the very end, defying Federal naval guns and shore batteries alike, the old-style masonry forts, with their high walls pierced for tiers of cannon, were no match for the new heavy-rifled artillery.

Far more effective were the earthwork type of fort. For one thing these were low-lying and offered little in the way of a target, and missiles burying themselves in the earth or sand did little harm. Exploding shells threw up clouds of earth and dust, but the damage could be easily repaired, and about the only way to silence such a work was to dismount its guns with direct hits. This called for better shooting than most of the artillery of the time was capable of, unless the siege batteries were pushed up almost to within rifle range. Intensive bombardment usually sent the fortress gun crews scampering for their bomb-proofs, only to return to their pieces when the fire slackened.

Field works of earth, sandbags, and logs were constructed in great numbers. Axes, shovels, and wheelbarrows in the hands of husky pioneer battalions could transform the most peaceful site into an impregnable redoubt in a very short time. Gabions (cylindrical baskets without a bottom, placed upright and filled with earth) could be easily made. Sand bags were used by the hundreds of thousands, and simple earth banks, if they were thick enough (fifteen feet), would stop most artillery.

Wire entanglements were strung in many places (plain wire—to trip and thus slow down the advance; barbed wire did not make its appearance until 1874). *Chevaux-de-frise* (logs pierced by sharpened stakes) were also much in evidence, as were picket fences with sharp points, or simpler still, tree limbs or heavy brush laid with the boughs pointing toward the enemy.

Trench warfare developed as the war went on, running all the way from simple gouges in the earth made by tin cups, bayonets, or fingers, to elaborate trench systems, with zigzags, revetments, fire steps, and mortar-bomb-proof dugouts. Mining and countermining were resorted to, and the pick and shovel became almost as important to a soldier's survival as his cartridge box and rifle.

The two capitals, in particular, ringed themselves with complicated earthworks—Washington had sixty-eight separate forts and many blockhouses connected by twenty miles of trenches. The entire circuit of the defenses was thirty-seven miles. The final Richmond-Petersburg defense lines were longer than that. Although the original inner Richmond defenses were only some twelve miles in circumference, there also were two outer rings. To ensure clear fields of fire, obstructions such as buildings and trees were cleared away. Great care was taken to site earthworks so as to afford supporting fire from neighboring positions.

[101]

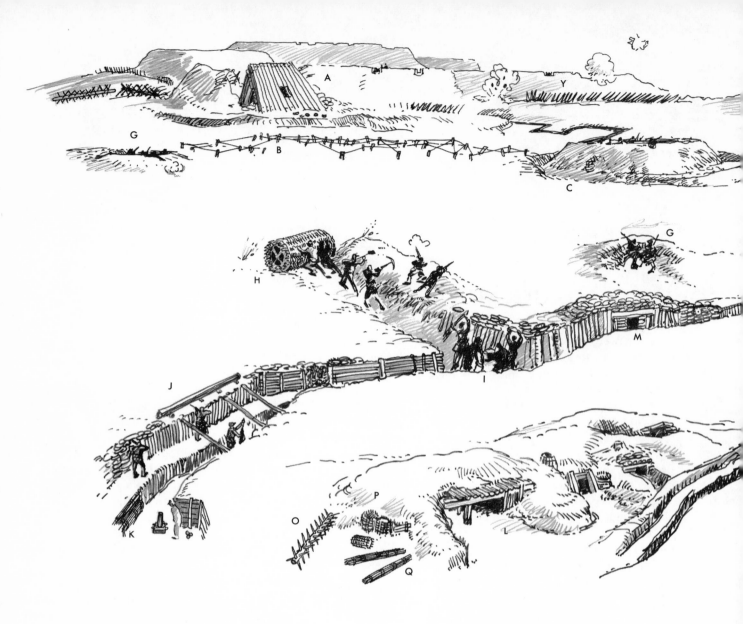

## DIAGRAM OF SIEGE OPERATIONS

A. Heavy timber casemate faced with railroad iron. B. Wire about 18 inches above ground. Mines with sensitive fuses often buried in front of works. C. Advanced redoubt flanked attackers, sappers. D. Berm kept earth from parapet from filling ditch. E. Crest of glacis protected foot of ramparts. F. Redoubt protects parallel, flanks counterattack. G. Rifle pits of both sides cover for pickets, listening posts to detect mining operations. H. Basket-type sap roller, 4 feet in diameter, 9 feet long, weighing about 1 ton when filled, protected sappers from raking fire. I. Engineers fill sandbags, shore sides of sap. Parallels were dug from end of zigzagged sap. Much digging done at night. Fires and calcium lights used to spot enemy working parties. J. Man on fire step aims under head log. Crossbars keep log from falling in trench if hit. K. Coehorn mortar fires from bay in trench. L. Men lived in dugouts and bombproof shelters. M. Bombproofs sheltered men in trench from mortar bombs, served as command and first-aid posts. N. Sap widened, becomes communication trench, covered over if in dangerous spot. O. Chevaux-de-frise were logs about 12 feet long and 10 inches thick, drilled through every foot at right angles for sharpened stakes which projected 3 feet. P. Gabions were cylindrical baskets, no top or bottom, 3 feet high, 2 feet in diameter. Weight 50–60 pounds empty. Were also made of planks and iron hoops. Q. Fascines were long bundles of thin saplings used mostly for sides of trenches (revetments). R. Heavy siege tube hung under sling cart. S. Siege battery. T. Platform of field piece sloped at back; gun run back out of sight to load. U. Splinterproof traverse localized damage. V. Heavily protected magazine. W. Siege mortar battery (no embrasures necessary). X. Shells filled from magazine and fused. Y. Defense of sharp stakes, often hidden in ditch. Z. Redoubt protecting batteries.

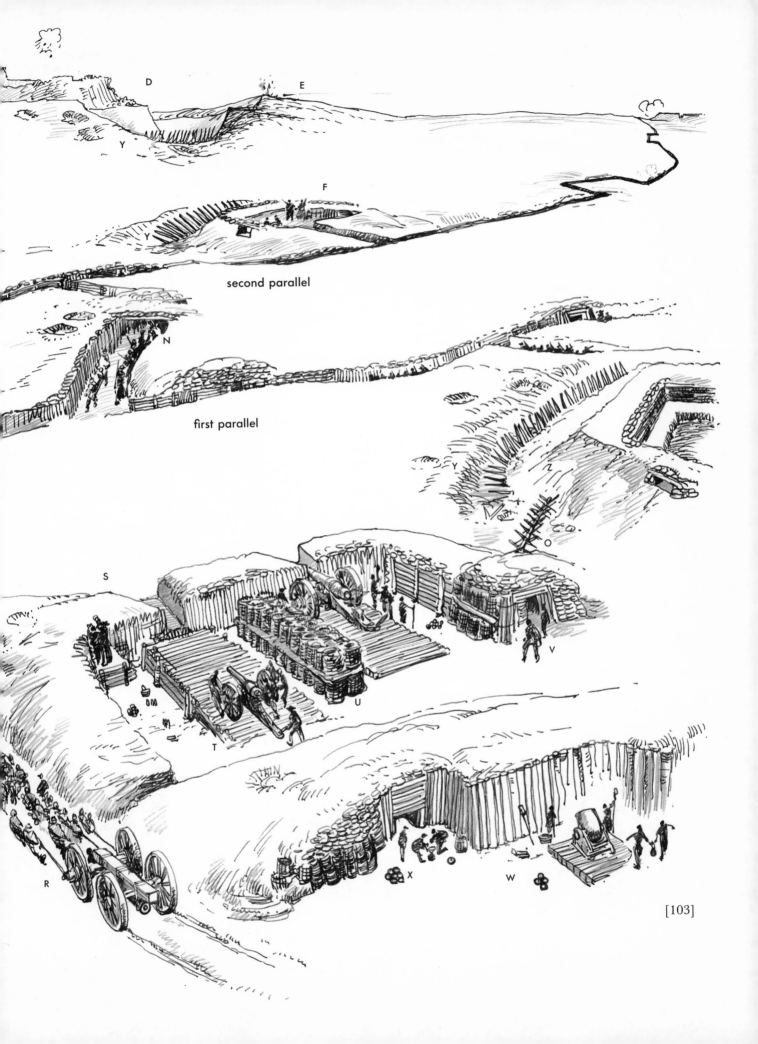

D

E

Y

F

Y

second parallel

N

first parallel

Y

O

S

V

U

T

R

X

W

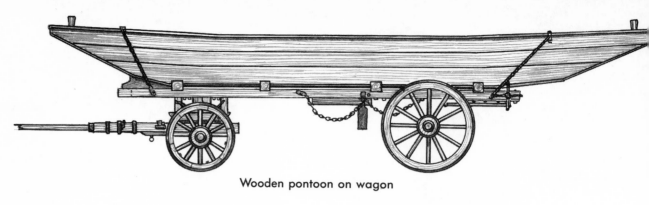

Wooden pontoon on wagon

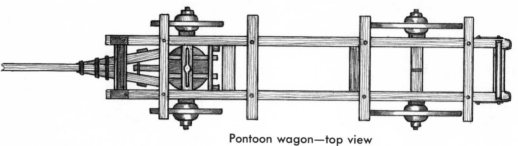

Pontoon wagon—top view

# PONTOON BRIDGES

In a country veined with numerous streams and rivers, bridging trains played a very important part in the strategy and tactics of every campaign. Bridges were among the primary objectives. Permanent bridges were among the first victims of the war. Even a small river could prove an insurmountable obstacle to an army if unaccompanied by sufficient portable bridging material and an efficient corps trained in its use. In country cut by rivers and streams, a bridging train was as vital as food and ammunition. A typical train, one or more of which might be attached to a command as needed, consisted of some thirty-four pontoon wagons such as that above. Each pontoon contained ropes, oars, rowlocks, boat hooks, and an anchor, sometimes lashed under a rear axle.

The timbers upon which the bridge was laid were conveyed on other wagons, which also carried chains, cables, etc., and the cross planks (chesses) were carried on twenty-two chess wagons, each of which also carried two cables.

Four tool wagons carried entrenching and carpenter's tools, spare cordage, etc., while two traveling-forges with ironworking tools, spare iron, etc., completed the working part of the train (it would, of course, have its own supply wagons).

Besides the heavy wooden pontoons, much use was made of pontoons with collapsible wooden frames, over which was stretched a canvas cover. Dismantled, these boats took up little space, and so increased the capacity of a bridging train.

In constructing a pontoon bridge, the first boat was rowed upstream, its anchor let go, and the rope played out to drop the boat into place. The second boat was positioned next to the first in

Loaded chess wagon, front elevation

Loaded chess wagon

*Chesses were usually 12 inches wide and 1½ inches thick. Lengths varied, 13 feet for the large canvas and wooden pontoons and 11 feet for the small ones. The reach **A** was adjustable.*

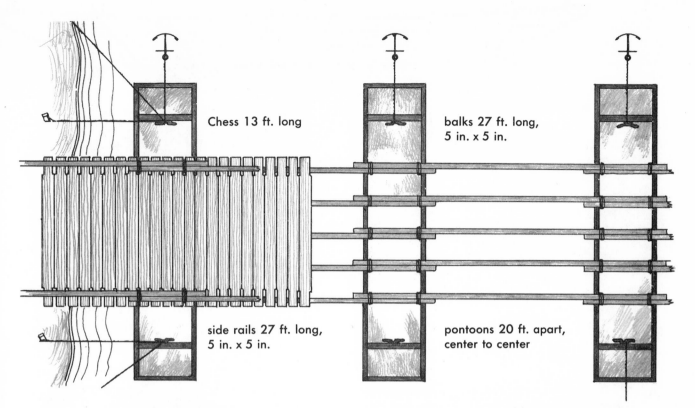

Chess 13 ft. long

balks 27 ft. long,
5 in. x 5 in.

side rails 27 ft. long,
5 in. x 5 in.

pontoons 20 ft. apart,
center to center

same way. Balks were then laid across the gunwale (they had cleats to hold them in place), and the second boat was shoved out by pushing on the ends of the balks. Chesses were laid next, then side rails were laid and lashed to the balks through slits in the chesses. This stiffened the bridge and held the chesses in place. Each pontoon was anchored upstream, and every other one, downstream. If the current was very strong, boats were tied to heavy cable stretched across river above the bridge. Straw or earth protected the chesses and deadened the sound. Construction was speeded by having whole sections made up at the bank and then floated into position. Federals built a 2200-foot bridge like this across the James in five and one-half hours.

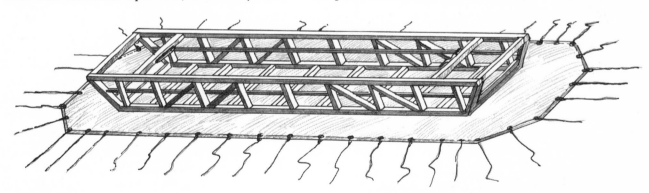

**CANVAS PONTOON BOAT**—*Canvas was laid out, bottom pieces of frame put in place, tenons of braces and uprights fitted in corresponding mortises, gunwales and endpieces put on top, and canvas brought over sides and lashed. The corners were wrapped around bow and stern and fastened and the ends brought up over them and lashed. Boat was then soaked to make canvas watertight.*

Canvas pontoon boat, 26 feet long, 5-foot 6-inch beam, 2 feet, 4 inches deep. Small size 21 feet long, same beam and depth

[105]

# THE SIGNAL CORPS

## MILITARY TELEGRAPHY

IN THE extent and character of its battle area, the Civil War was unique. Never in modern times had such great armies marched and fought over such a vast and, in great part, primitive area. The immediate need of both sides for a comprehensive system of long-distance communication became apparent very early in the conflict. First in the field were the Confederates, who organized a corps of signalers under E. P. Alexander, later Chief of Artillery. This corps was attached to the Adjutant General's Department and handled signaling, telegraphy, and secret-service work. The Union signalers were formed with

Major A. J. Meyer, inventor of the U. S. Army's signal system, at its head. There was considerable opposition at first, and all through its early existence the Signal Corps suffered severely from departmental jealousies and strife in Washington. It was not until August 1864 that it was finally organized as a separate corps, although it had long since proved its worth in the field.

In spite of this, the corps, which at the outbreak of the war consisted of Major Meyer alone, eventually grew to some three hundred officers and twenty-five hundred men, and performed a vital service to the Union.

Signaling on both sides was done with flags, torches, rockets, and flares. Signal guns are often mentioned as being used on the battlefield to ensure concerted action in a prearranged attack, but these were purely local arrangements, not involving the signal services.

High points of land or, if these were not available, wooden towers were used as vantage points —and chains of such points relayed messages with rapidity and accuracy, subject to interruption by such weather conditions as rain, snow, or fog.

Messages were sent by waving a signal flag, torch, or light from up to the right to left and back (one) or down to the right and up (two). Combinations of these numbers stood for letters, phrases, or numerals. The flags were white, with a red square; black, which could be seen better against snow; or red with a white square, which showed up well against varied backgrounds.

Colored lights, or rockets were used in combinations for prearranged sets of signals. The flags or torches were worked by enlisted men, signaling the numbers read off by the officer in charge. A constant station-to-station watch was kept by alert men with powerful telescopes, ready to receive a message at any hour of the day or night.

The signal service was a dangerous one. Any group of signalers near the battlefield was a favorite target for rifle or artillery fire—and many signalmen were picked off their exposed perches by enemy snipers in blue or gray.

Navy signals were different from those used ashore, so if co-operation between the two services was required, army signal officers were carried aboard ship. This was particularly useful in directing naval gunfire on shore targets.

Besides the mechanical means employed by the signal corps of both armies, there was still much use of the whip and spur, as well-mounted couriers and staff officers plied between nearby headquarters.

Because wigwag flags and waving torches could be seen by the enemy, messages were seldom sent in "clear," and codes or ciphers of various types and complexities were resorted to. One quick way of enciphering a message was by use of a cipher disc. This consisted of two concentric discs, one smaller than the other. Letters, word pauses, and so forth marked around the edge of one disc corresponded with signal numbers on the circumference of the other. Revolving the disc changed the cipher.

In cipher, every letter of the "clear" stands for another letter, symbol, or an entire message. In code, a code word represents a phrase, sentence, or an entire message. Codes are thus limited in scope and can only be decoded by use of a code book. Any message, however complicated, can be sent in cipher, and the receiver only has to know the key to be able to decipher it, no code books or code dictionaries being necessary.

These codes and ciphers were changed constantly because cryptographers on each side worked hard to interpret the messages sent by their opponents. In this the Federals were more successful than the Confederates. Although the latter used a relatively complicated system, while the Federals used a simple word-transposition cipher, the Union experts had no difficulty in breaking down the Southerners' communications, while the Confederates never succeeded in breaking down a single Federal message.

Such codes and ciphers were particularly useful in telegraphic communication, which was much subject to "wire tapping."

This is the alphabet, numerals, and code signals adopted late in the war:

| | |
|---|---|
| A = 11 | O = 12 |
| B = 1221 | P = 2121 |
| C = 212 | Q = 2122 |
| D = 111 | R = 122 |
| E = 21 | S = 121 |
| F = 1112 | T = 1 |
| G = 1122 | U = 221 |
| H = 211 | V = 2111 |
| I = 2 | W = 2212 |
| J = 2211 | X = 1211 |
| K = 1212 | Y = 222 |
| L = 112 | Z = 1111 |
| M = 2112 | & = 2222 |
| N = 22 | |

tion = 2221; ing = 1121; ed = 1222.

Wait a moment = 12221; Are you ready? = 21112; I am ready = 11211; Use short pole and small flag = 11121; Use long pole and large flag = 11112; Work faster = 21111; Did you understand? = 22111; Use white flag = 22221; Use black flag = 22122; Use red flag = 11111.

End of word = 3 (dip in front); end of sentence = 33; end of message = 333; error = 121212; message received & cease signaling = 11, 11, 11, 3; attention, look for signals = constant waving.

*Large wire used during first years required a great amount of work. Later flexible insulated wire was adopted which could be unreeled from moving mule and strung on fences and bushes.*

THE telegraph was of paramount importance to both armies, and it seems strange that both services relied on civilian personnel and, in the case of the South, on the co-operation of private companies.

In the Confederate service, it was at least under some control of the Signal Corps, but in the North it operated as a separate bureau, the United States Military-Telegraph Corps, attached to the Quartermaster's Department, in which a few of its members held commissions.

The operators and technicians were employees, not too well paid, with no system of pensions—although the work was hazardous enough (one out of twelve operators were killed, wounded, captured, or died in prison), and with no definite status.

The whole setup was rigidly controlled from the War Department, the commissioned officers being responsible only to the Secretary of War. Even the operators in the various theaters were completely independent of the general commanding. Not only that, but under a War Department order:

"The cipher books issued by the Superintendent of Military Telegraphs be entrusted only to the care of telegraph experts, . . . the ciphers furnished . . . . are not to be imparted to any one. . . . They will neither be copied or used by any other person without special permission of the Secretary of War."

This order caused heart-burning among several generals, including Grant, who got involved in a spat with the War Department on account of it. This cumbersome and inefficient system made for endless friction between the military and the Telegraph Corps. The Signal Corps attempted to gain control of at least the field telegraph, and there was more trouble about that. It is one of the wonders of the war that the military telegraph functioned as well as it did.

The lines around Washington had been taken over by the Government in April 1861, and early in 1862, by Act of Congress, the military took over all private telegraph lines and offices in the United States. The South preferred to rely on the co-operation of the private telegraph companies and the railroad telegraphs.

Major General Frémont formed three companies of field telegraphers in the West at the very start of the war, but pressure on the Secretary of War by the private companies, who while freely putting their personnel and equipment at the disposal of the Government, objected strongly to any rival organization, even military, forced their disbandment.

Where possible, the field telegraph linked headquarters of the army in the field with the capital, and with the headquarters of the corps commanders. The construction crews kept the main line up with the troops as they advanced, running loops to corps headquarters. Cable, which was strong enough to resist being cut by heavy artillery traffic, was strung on short poles or on trees. The reels were carried in wagons. Insulation was poor and there was much power loss due to escape, so high-resistance relays and the strongest nitric acid batteries available were used.

Thousands of miles of field cable were strung, often under enemy fire. During the last year of the war over one and three-quarter million messages were transmitted over the Federal System.

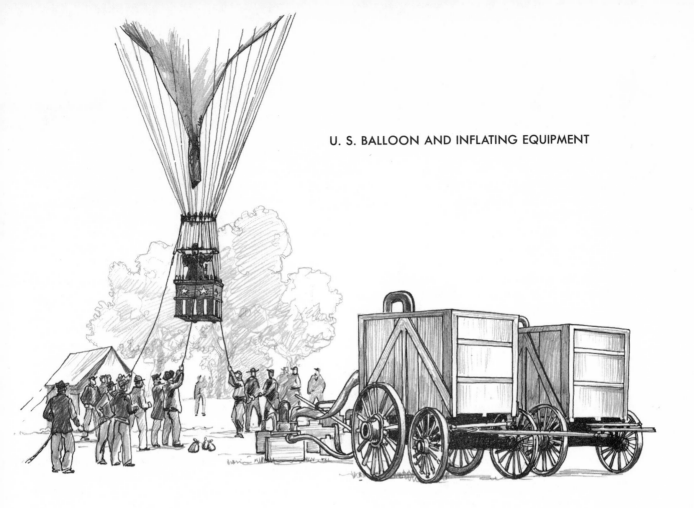

# MILITARY BALLOONS

Since men banded together with the idea of committing collective mayhem on a like gathering of their opponents, one of the most pressing needs of a general in the field has been to find out what is going on "on the other side of the hill." This is as true today as it was in Caesar's time, and the necessity for information is the same whether it is gathered by a legion's auxiliary of barbarian cavalry or by a U-2.

Naturally, when man learned to conquer gravity by means of a balloon, it took only five days from the first ascension for an article to appear pointing out the advantages of such an invention to the military. Here at last, seemed the means of answering the age-old question. Balloons were used for a short time by the French during the wars of the revolution, where they accomplished little beyond shaking enemy morale. They made subsequent sporadic appearances in combat, but their use proved a disappointment. As the Federals were to discover, it was one thing to

see, and another to interpret what was seen in terms of strategy and tactics.

The celebrated balloonist Thaddeus Lowe organized a balloon corps for the Union armies, and he and his assistants made hundreds of ascensions during McClellan's Peninsular campaign in 1862 and in the spring of 1863. A light telegraph wire was carried aloft and information transmitted to the ground. Sketches were also made aloft, and the Confederate lines around Richmond observed through telescopes.

Hydrogen was manufactured in the field from portable, though bulky, equipment.

The Confederates also had a balloon, made out of silk dresses, contributed by the patriotic ladies of the South. As gas could only be made in the city, the inflated balloon was tied to a locomotive and run down the York River Railroad. It was also used fastened to a steamer which, running aground one day, was captured along with the precious balloon.

[109]

Artillery was used in vain by both sides in attempts to down the aerial spies, but insufficient elevation and tricky fuses made any form of successful antiaircraft fire impossible.

Balloons were used by Burnside and also by Hooker at Chancellorsville.

Lowe's little balloon corps had, at one time, a balloon boat, on which were gas generators; a tug; and an attached gunboat.

The balloon corps operated under difficulties, being first under the Corps of Topographical Engineers and relying for its telegraphic communication on the Military-Telegraph Corps. Then it was allowed its own telegraph train. It then came under the Quartermaster's Department and later under the Corps of Engineers. Later still, Hooker transferred it to the Signal Corps, who claimed they had neither men nor money to run it, and it was then disbanded. There is no doubt that the equipment was unwieldy and that the results had not lived up to expectations. Still, if there had been someone in authority with faith enough in the idea, it could have rendered valuable service. As it was, it would seem that military conservatism and interdepartmental difficulties robbed the Union of a valuable unit. The Rebels went to considerable trouble to conceal their movements whenever a balloon was in evidence, and the Confederate General Alexander commented that it would have been worth keeping for its nuisance value alone.

The following excerpts from dispatches, from the Official Records, give some idea of the scope of the operations which extended from June 1861 to May 1863.

"Sir: Upon the recommendation of Major-General McClellan, the Secretary of War has directed that four additional balloons be constructed at once under your direction, together with such inflating apparatus as may be necessary for them and the one now in use. . . ."

" . . . The whole amount to be paid being about the sum . . . for the two largest [balloons] $1500 and for the smallest $1200 each."

" . . . This is the third of the new inflating apparatus which had been sent out, and three more are now ready. . . . I commenced inflation . . . and in three hours generated gas sufficient to lift 1200 pounds. . . ."

" . . . One set of gas generators to go in two army wagon running-gears, same dimension as wagon body and five feet high, weighing about 1,000 pounds each. Material to keep one balloon inflated day and night for two months will consist of 100 carboys of sulphuric acid, weighing about 16,000 pounds and 20 barrels of iron turnings weighing about 10,000 pounds . . . cost of above amount of gas material, as now purchased is about $350.00—less than $6.00 per day."

"The commanding general directs that upon application of Professor Lowe, balloonist, you furnish him with a detail of one officer, one sergeant and thirty-five men to assist him in making an ascension. . . ."

"Confidence in this new means of observation soon began to be manifested and many officers made ascensions, among whom were Generals McDowell, Porter and Martindale. On the 7th of September, Major-General McClellan ascended. . . ."

(From a carnival event, the balloon was becoming a useful military machine.)

"Have you been able to ascend this morning? Your balloon should be in connection by telegraph and messages should be sent constantly —at least every fifteen minutes. The balloon must be up all day. The balloon at Mechanicsville should likewise be sent up at once and remain all day. . . ."

"At about 8:30 tomorrow morning I wish to fire from here at Falls Church. Will you please send the balloon up from Fort Corcoran and have note taken of the position reached by the shell, and telegraph each observation at once. . . . During the time of fire it is very important to know how much the shot or shell fall short, if any at all. . . . If we fire to the right of Falls Church, let a white flag be raised in the balloon; if to the left, let it be lowered; if over, let it be shown stationary; if under, let it be waved occasionally."

" . . . The numbers upon the map are for the purpose of explaining the various points better when telegraphing from the balloon. Please preserve it for that purpose."

" . . . while up with the balloon made a very fine map of the enemy's works and surrounding country. . . ."

"I ascended at noon and remained at an elevation of 1000 feet for an hour. Could see the Rebel line of works and camps from York to James rivers. . . ."

" . . . directing the commanders of the batteries where to fire, as they could not see the objects fired at. . . ."

*Wooden trestles were easily destroyed, so blockhouses were built to protect bridges and vulnerable stretches of track. All were loopholed for musketry, and some had stockades, and embrasures for light field pieces.*

# RAILROADS

In the Civil War, for the first time in history, railroads played a major role in warfare. Campaign strategy was often based on the availability and capacity of a railway line, and the construction, maintenance, and defense of these vital links involved large numbers of men and much equipment. Throughout the war the railroads bore an ever-increasing load, carrying tens of thousands of men and hundreds of thousands of tons of urgently-needed supplies.

Sherman said in his memoirs that the Atlanta campaign would have been an impossibility but for the single track road, much of its 473 miles subject to sudden raids, which carried supplies for 100,000 men and 35,000 animals for 196 days. For that matter the whole series of battles around Atlanta centered around the railroads, and the bloody fighting around Petersburg in 1865 was in great part dictated by the Federal threats to the railroads linking Richmond with the South, and Lee's desperate attempts to keep that line of communications intact.

As far back as 1837, the United States government had adopted the policy of loaning technically-trained officers to the growing railroad industry, both sides profiting by the experience. By coincidence, both Cameron and Scott of the War Department were ex-railroaders, and McClellan himself had been a railroad executive. There was at all times during the war an awareness by the Federal authorities of the necessity of keeping the railroads in a state of high efficiency, and a determination to see it done at all costs.

Of the 30,000-odd miles of railroad in operation in the United States at the outbreak of the war, less than 9000 miles lay in the seceding states. This system or systems, for they were not all connected, had been dependent, to a great extent, on the North for locomotives, rolling stock, and railroad iron. Once this supply was cut off, the Southern railroads began to deteriorate, a process hastened by the inroads of the Federal armies. As early as January 1862 the Confederate Quartermaster General complained that some of the railroads on which the government was depending for transportation were only operating two trains a day, and those at an average six miles per hour!

A Confederate staff officer wrote of a troop movement:

"Never before were so many troops moved over such worn-out railways, none first-class from the beginning. Never before were such crazy cars—passenger, baggage, mail, coal, box, platform, all and every sort wobbling on the jumping strap-iron—used for hauling good soldiers." (from *Recollections of a Confederate Staff Officer,* by General G. Moxley Sorrel)

Certainly the South had the advantage of interior lines of communication, but when the lines were only "two streaks of rust and a right of way," much of that advantage was lost. However, bad as the Southern railways were, they played an important part in the maneuvers by which the Confederates switched their outnumbered troops from one theater to another. By such a movement, Longstreet rushed a whole corps of 18,000 from the Army of Virginia to Georgia, by various routes and railroads, in time for the decisive second day's fight at Chickamauga.

In the war's early days, the Northern railroad companies met with the government and agreed on fixed rates for hauling supplies and troops. This was adhered to throughout the war, although other prices soared. It was cheaper, the government found, to transport 1000 men a distance of 100 miles for the price of $2000.00 than to march them the same distance by road. When space was at a premium, as in Pope's campaign in Virginia in '62, priorities were awarded in the following order: Rations, forage, ammunition, hospital stores, veteran infantry regiments, and, lastly, "green" regiments. Batteries marched, except in emergencies, and cavalry marched and wagons were driven.

There were very few actual military railroads during the war, but both sides occasionally took over privately-owned lines and ran them when the situation demanded.

THE work of maintenance of the United States Military Railroads fell on the Construction Corps. This corps, which at its peak numbered over 24,000 men, performed prodigies, building trestles, repairing bridges, and laying track, often under fire from guerrillas and enemy scouting patrols. They were civilians and were well paid—$2.00 a day and double for overtime. While the mileage of the United States Military Railroads did not run much above 2000 miles, there were over 6000 cars in operation and more than 400 locomotives.

The bridge-building feats of the Construction Corps were fantastic. Operating in many cases with unskilled labor, they could build a one hundred and fifty-foot span with a thirty-foot elevation across a creek in fifteen hours. Some of them looked flimsy enough, but they held. Speaking of Herman Haupt, the engineering genius who headed the railway and transportation service, Lincoln said:

"That man, Haupt, has built a bridge across Potomac Creek, about four hundred feet long and nearly a hundred feet high, over which loaded trains are running every hour, and, upon my word. . . . There is nothing in it but bean-poles and corn-stalks."

The Chattahoochie bridge, eight hundred feet long and nearly one hundred feet high, was rebuilt, starting with unfelled timber, in four and a half days. Trusses were designed with interchangeable parts, adapted to any span. Timber was plentiful in most of the war theaters and was usually available at the building sites, where it was cut and trimmed on the spot. Where necessary, prefabricated trusses were brought in on flatcars. Toward the close of the war, the Union engineers were rebuilding bridges and repairing

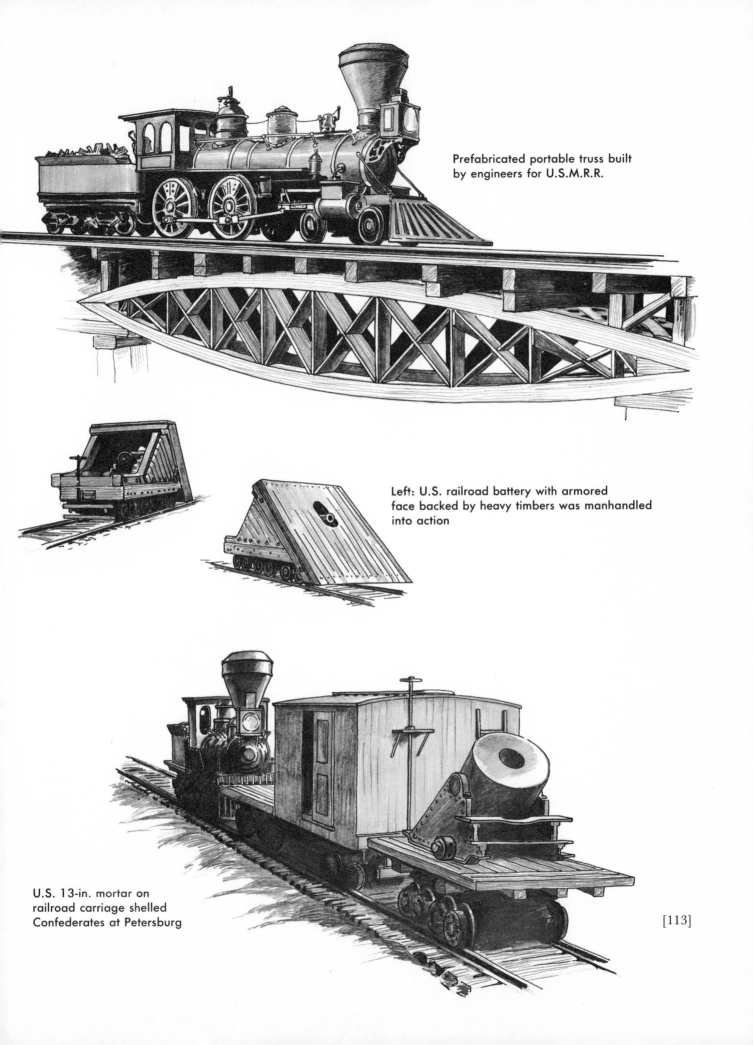

Prefabricated portable truss built by engineers for U.S.M.R.R.

Left: U.S. railroad battery with armored face backed by heavy timbers was manhandled into action

U.S. 13-in. mortar on railroad carriage shelled Confederates at Petersburg

tracks almost as fast as the Confederates could destroy them.

When Hood cut Sherman's rail communications at Big Shanty and Resaca, he destroyed over thirty-five miles of track as well as burning bridges. Although a number of construction men had been killed, repair work began before Hood had left the railroad. One twenty-five mile stretch was laid in seven and a half days. New ties had to be cut, and the rails brought forward almost two hundred miles.

The Federal cavalry raiders found that the Southerners, too, could repair track at a great rate, even when the business of railroad destruction had become almost a science. Although one lone saboteur and a loosened rail could add up to a lot of trouble, the following method was used when time permitted a thorough job to be done.

The men were divided into parties, and the men of the first party distributed along the track, one man to each tie. At a signal the whole section of track was raised on edge and tipped over, ties on top. The ties were pried loose from the rails and the first party moved on to another section, while the second party stacked the ties and laid the rails over them. The ties were then set alight and when the rails were red-hot the third party, using pinchers or "railroad hooks," bent them around trees and also twisted them. The twist was important, for both the Southern and Northern repair crews became as adept at straightening rails as the soldiers were at bending them. Rails which were not bent in too small a **U** could be straightened, but a scientifically twisted one had to go back to the rolling mill.

No tracks laid down in as great a hurry as these military railroads and subject to the above treatment were any joy to ride on. Contemporary photographs reveal stretches of track which any self-respecting railroader would hesitate to travel in a handcar. But they did the job, and that was all that mattered.

The wrecking of a railroad might delay a whole campaign or turn a victory into defeat. The wild ride of the "General" under Andrews and his desperate crew had its inception in Gen. O. M. Mitchell's campaign for Chattanooga, and its purpose was to isolate that city by destroying bridges on the Georgia State railroad and one on the East Tennessee. The attempt failed and Mitchell abandoned his drive on the city.

By the war's end most of the railroads in the South had been destroyed by the invading Fed-

erals or crippled by continued use without repair. The only Northern road to suffer much damage was the Baltimore and Ohio, some of whose tracks ran through the battleground of northern Virginia.

Besides transporting men and supplies to the theaters of war, these railroads also brought back many whose fighting days were over, at least for the time. Trainloads of wounded were carried back from the fronts, at first in any makeshift car or coach and later in specially-designed hospital trains. These were marked by bright red stacks, and at night by three red lanterns hung in a row beneath the head lamp.

Early in the war cars had been armed and even armored. An armored (bulletproof) car patrolled the Philadelphia and Baltimore Central, and a Confederate field gun on a flatcar shelled the enemy at the Battle of Seven Pines. A heavily-armored siege gun was used by Grant during the fighting around Petersburg, as was a 13-inch mortar, complete with ammunition cars and locomotive.

To combat repeated raids on stations and bridges, Major General Dodge, foremost railroad builder of the Western armies, developed a system of blockhouses and stockades. These little forts worked well against attacks by cavalry alone, but when accompanied by horse artillery, the raiders usually had it all their own way. No method of assuring one hundred per cent protection for the miles of railroad was ever found. The only answer was to keep the repair crews well supplied and in constant readiness.

Loading and unloading, and the prompt return of empty cars, became at times a major problem. Quartermasters in the field were prone to use rolling stock as portable warehouses and considerable effort was, at times, required to keep the empties moving. Train schedules were almost impossible to keep and the telegraph was usually tied up by the military. There was also much interference by subordinates, in the Quartermaster's Department and officers in the field. In the Federal service this resulted in positive orders from the Chief of Staff forbidding all orders, except through the chief of the Construction Corps.

Despite these difficulties, which were increased by the fact that many of the lines were single-tracked and that there was no uniformity of rail gauge throughout the nation's railroads, the railroaders, Union and Confederate, lived up to the tradition of their calling, and, where humanly possible, "kept 'em rolling."

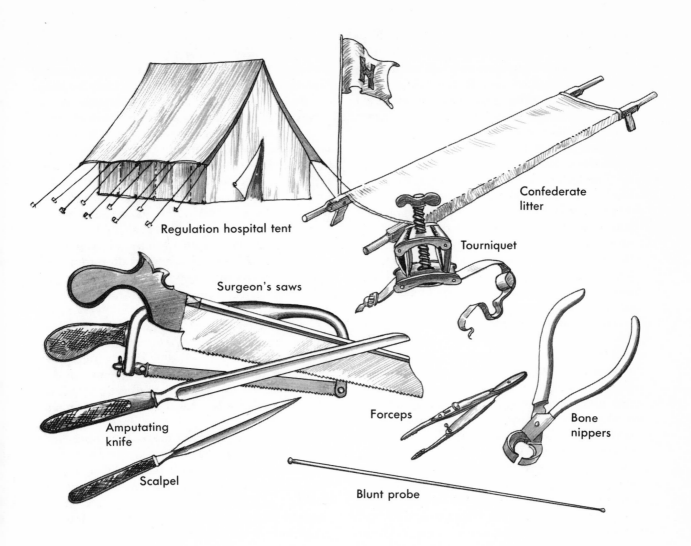

Regulation hospital tent

Confederate litter

Surgeon's saws

Tourniquet

Amputating knife

Scalpel

Forceps

Bone nippers

Blunt probe

# THE MEDICAL DEPARTMENTS

NO ONE will ever know how many men died in the Civil War. It was probably over 600,000, and of these more than twice as many died of disease as from enemy bullets. These are shocking figures, but too often the blame is laid solely on the medical profession. Actually they did the best that could be done with imperfect knowledge, equipment, and techniques, at a time when stethoscopes were a novelty, when there were probably not more than twenty clinical thermometers in the whole Union army, and when such diseases as lockjaw, septicemia, malaria, and gangrene were attributed, among other things, to the "evening dews and damps."

In studying statistics on sickness and death from wounds it must be remembered that, to begin with, facts relating to personal hygiene and public health were all but unknown. The unsanitary and unhealthful conditions of normal civilian life of the period were multiplied by the gathering together in close quarters of huge numbers of men, many of whom looked on army life as an escape from the restrictions of society and "either from apathy or from laziness neither washed their persons nor the clothes they carried with them." Cold, damp, unsuitable or inadequate clothing, atrocious food, and contaminated water all took their toll. Also, many recruits were young boys from isolated areas, particularly susceptible to such common ailments as mumps, measles, and scarlet fever. Men unaccustomed to wet and exposure were subject to bad colds, which in turn often led to bronchitis and pneumonia. That ever-present scourge of all armies, dysentery, laid many low, and under the necessarily crowded conditions, communicable diseases of all kinds spread like wildfire.

To make matters worse, the physical examinations given recruits were, in most cases, a joke, and the rolls included a high percentage of those with pre-service disabilities: epileptics, syphilitics, and so forth.

However, attempts were rapidly made to better conditions, at least as far as hygiene and public health were concerned. Booklets on hygiene were distributed and efforts made to clean up the camps and provide proper latrines and toilet facilities.

The better the discipline of the unit, the better the health was likely to be, and in those regiments where the officers were intelligent enough to issue and enforce orders relating to sanitation, drinking water, etc., the sickness rate was much lower than in those units in which the officers were too ignorant or too lazy to care.

As the war progressed the men became better able to take care of themselves and a veteran regiment in the field would show a far smaller sick list than a "green" regiment under canvas.

A major problem during the first part of the war was the collection and transportation of the wounded. There was no system and no central control. The collection was bad enough—the men detailed for this job were usually the ones the company commanders could best spare—that is, the skulkers and shirkers, and the bandsmen, who were expected to "double in brass"—or blood, when the occasion arose. In consequence, many men were left lying on the battlefields unattended—sometimes for days.

But even more unnecessary death and suffering were caused by the failure of the medical service to provide for moving the wounded from the regimental aid stations to the large general hospitals in the rear. (It is stated that after the First Battle of Bull Run, no casualties reached Washington in ambulances—although some wounded walked the twenty-seven miles.)

Transport was largely in the hands of the Quartermaster Corps. The ambulances, what there were of them, were usually driven by civilians —a drunken, good-for-nothing lot, by all accounts, who were likely to take off for the rear at the shriek of the first shell. At Ball's Bluff it was reported that one surgeon had to fire on the ambulance attendants to make them do their job.

Care of the wounded was far down the priority list, and there were cases where the ambulance horses were taken for mounts by the cavalry. The Government—or at least the War Department— seems to have turned a blind eye to these appalling conditions, while the Medical Department, which at the outbreak of the war was geared to meet the needs of an army of some 16,000 regulars, was utterly unable to cope, physically or mentally, with its sudden expansion into a vast and completely untrained citizen army.

Meantime, in August 1862, McClellan had issued an order setting up a much-improved system, which later became standard with all Union armies. Among other things, this insured that ambulances and hospital supply wagons, etc., were no longer operated at the convenience of the Quartermaster Corps. Eventually the Federal Ambulance Corps became a model organization.

The original system of regimental hospitals, both Federal and Confederate, was cumbersome and inefficient. One criticism was that one regimental surgical staff might be overwhelmed by a rush of casualties, while another nearby might be inactive. There also seems to have been a reluctance on the part of some regimental surgeons to treat the wounded of other regiments. In addition, when brigaded with other regiments, there was duplication of equipment, and unnecessary enlargement of the hospital train.

In the system as finally adopted, the wounded first walked, or were carried to a forward dressing station, established by the regimental medical officers as close to the firing line as possible. After hasty first aid they were loaded on ambulances and sent to the divisional field hospital, which was usually set up just out of artillery range. There the worst cases were operated on, and from there all who could be moved were sent to the base or general hospitals, of which there were, at one time, two hundred and five on the Federal side alone.

The average Federal divisional hospital train consisted of fourteen army wagons and four medical wagons, carrying twenty-two hospital tents and medical and surgical supplies and equipment sufficient to care for seven thousand to eight thousand men.

The Confederate setup was similar, except that most of the wounded were conveyed in ordinary wagons, drawn by two mules and without springs. There were a few spring vehicles used at first, but when they wore out they were not able to be replaced, except by captured Federal ambulances. Because of transportation difficulties, the Confederate wounded were sometimes held in field hospitals for several weeks. Field hospitals were often under canvas, but where suitable buildings were available, they were requisitioned.

THE general hospitals on both sides grew in capacity and efficiency as the war progressed. Some were very large, even by modern standards. The great Chimborazo Hospital, at Richmond, then the largest in the world, treated in all some 76,000 patients. It could handle 4800 patients in 150 one-story buildings, each 100 feet by 30 feet. A bakery with a capacity of 10,000 loaves a day, ice house, and soup kitchens were included in the 125-acre grounds, as well as a farm with 200 cows and a large goat herd.

The Union's City Point Hospital was a merger of five corps hospitals. Partly under canvas, it had a huge capacity—6000 to 10,000 in warm weather. It also boasted a steam laundry.

Hospitals were generally well laid out, and much thought was given to ventilation. Fresh air was considered a "must" partly because bad smells (miasmas) were believed to cause or spread disease. Flies and mosquitoes were considered a nuisance and an irritation, and attempts were made to keep them from bothering the patients, but they were not suspected of being disease-spreaders. Plumbing was often conspicuous by its absence (and nothing can be more so than plumbing), and many otherwise modern-seeming hospitals had open latrines. However, there was widespread use of disinfectants and deodorants, chlorine and Dakin's solution (sodium hypochlorite) being much in favor.

Hospital ships were used on the western rivers and in the east. At first, these were run by the Quartermaster Corps, which, of course, gave priority to its own duties. Some were freighters returning empty to their bases, others were fast steamers, completely remodeled as hospital ships. At first some, and then all, were put under complete charge of the Medical Department, either for the return runs or full time. There were also hospital ships run by some of the states, and by the Sanitary Commission.

Railroad hospital trains might be nothing more than a string of empty cattle trucks well bedded with straw—or specially-fitted coaches with cars fitted as kitchens, dispensaries, and surgeries.

Surgery was more advanced than most people realize. Unfortunately, in those days, a doctor might be skillful with the knife without realizing that it should be kept clean. The need for the sterilization of instruments and for even the simplest preventive measures against the spread of infection was unknown. Happy in his ignorance, the Civil War surgeon wiped his knife on his dripping apron while waiting for the next patient, and the nurse rinsed out the blood-stained sponges in the same filthy water which had stood by the operating table all day.

Lister and Pasteur's theories about germs had not yet been advanced, and any form of asepsis was accidental. A Confederate surgeon, Dr. C. H. Tebault, wrote after the war:

"One blessing we enjoyed, due to the blockade, was the absence of sponges, clean rags being substituted for them with telling advantage. These rags could be washed, as was done and used over and over again. It is next to impossible, easily, if possible at all, to wash an infected sponge."

Amputations were frequent. In excuse of the excessive use of the saw, it must be remembered that the vast majority of wounds were caused by heavy bullets from rifled muskets, and many of the operations were performed in the most primitive surroundings, often on a kitchen table in an open shed by surgeons half-dead from overwork. Confederate Army surgeon D. J. Roberts wrote:

"The shattering, splintering, and splitting of a long bone by the impact of the Minié or Enfield ball were, in many instances, both remarkable and frightful, and early experience taught surgeons that amputation was the only means of saving life."

Wounds were supposed to suppurate ("laudable pus" was the term), and that they could heal without inflammation was unthinkable. The use of maggots as cleansers had been discovered years before, but apparently forgotten. A few surgeons rediscovered them, probably by accident—but the majority looked on them as the worst kind of infection. Water dressings were usually used for large wounds, amputations, etc.

Chloroform was used as an anesthetic, and morphine or opium to relieve pain. Despite harrowing tales to the contrary, many Confederate surgeons reported that they never ran short of quinine, morphine or chloroform.

Whiskey was administered to combat the effects of shock—a sizable amount being carried by the hospital orderlies in the field. (Stiff doses of alcohol seem to have been prescribed for practically everything. One man was kept alive (?) by thirty-six ounces of brandy a day.)

THE Medical Department of the Regular Army at the start of the war numbered one hundred and fifteen. Of those, twenty-seven resigned—twenty-four of whom went South and formed the nucleus of the Medical Department of the Confederacy. These regulars acted in a staff or administrative capacity, and, while additional appointments were made during the war, the regular establishment was always small.

In contrast was the vast number of Regimental Surgeons and Assistant Surgeons who entered the service with the formation of the volunteer regiments. These men were appointed by the governors of the states. While some were well known physicians, and gave up lucrative practices to serve their country, others were country doctors of varying degrees of proficiency, while still others could best be described as quacks. State examining boards passed many who were unfit to practice surgery, but by tighter supervision from the Medical Department this evil was remedied, though naturally, in such an emergency, the supply of competent physicians ran far behind demand.

To staff the growing number of base and general hospitals, civilian surgeons were hired. These signed a contract approved by the Surgeon General's office. Many of these "contract surgeons" were young men from medical schools without previous experience.

The Confederate Medical Department differed only in minor details from that of the Union.

There were some female nurses, assigned to the general hospitals. They frequently had to contend with the outspoken antagonism of high-ranking medical men, who resented their invasion of man's domain. But Florence Nightingale's work in the Crimea had created a great impression in this country, and many devoted women were willing to endure the slights and snubs of officialdom to bring a little extra comfort and care to the wounded. Their work seems to have been universally appreciated by their patients,

who were likely to get only the scantiest attention from the enlisted men and convalescents who made up most of the nursing staff.

There were numerous relief agencies run by civilians with the aim of doing for the soldiers what the Government should have done, but in many cases, failed to do. Of these the U. S. Sanitary Commission was the most powerful. It was formed in 1861, in spite of opposition from the Medical Corps and the War Department. It included many influential people and wielded considerable power through public opinion, sufficient enough to force passage of a bill partially doing away with promotion by senority and allowing the promotion in April 1862 of the brilliant, young (35) William A. Hammond as Surgeon General.

Besides inspecting camps, their locations, drainage, food, etc., and recommending improvements, the Commission distributed food, clothing, and medical supplies (after the Second Battle of Bull Run the Commission's supplies replaced those of the Medical Department's, which had been captured).

Even though, later in the war, the increased efficiency of the Medical Department made some of the Commission's work supplementary, right down to the war's end a Sanitary Commission wagon was with every corps, with such things as beef stock, chloroform, bandages, writing paper, and chewing tobacco.

The Commission's hospital ships transported thousands of wounded while its "homes" fed and sheltered soldiers on leave, recruits on their way to their regiments, and men recently discharged. In all, the Commission distributed some $15,000,000 worth of supplies. Its work was supported by contributions, and money raised by various ladies' aids, etc. Gifts to the soldiers, from blankets to butter, were packaged and sent. The women's relief organizations ran into a snag here. Some communities, at first, objected to sending relief to other than their own locally-raised companies or regiments, but because of frequent troop movements, thousands of boxes went undistributed, and gradually gift parcels became part of a general relief program and were given out impartially.

Supplementing the work of the committees and commissions, there were several one-woman relief organizations, such as that run by Clara Barton, who in later years formed the American Red Cross.

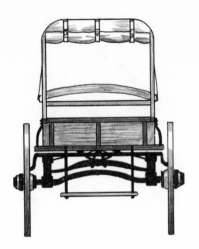

Rocker ambulance—rear view

Rocker ambulance—side view

 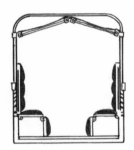

Arranged for
four stretcher cases

Arranged for
ordinary use

*Most successful of various types of four-wheeled ambulances. Drawn by two horses (mules were too uncertain and liable to bolt under fire). Crew was driver and two stretcher-bearers (privates). Besides water casks, cans of beef stock, bread, cooking and mess gear and bed sacks were carried under the driver's seat. In 1863, Army of Potomac had forty such vehicles per division under a first lieutenant. Each brigade had also one medicine wagon and one army wagon for hospital stores.*

*Two-wheeled ambulances bounced, jolted, and rocked sufferers unmercifully. Adopted without testing, they were much disliked, were later superseded by the heavier but more comfortable four-wheeler.*

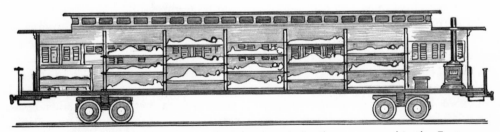

Cross section of thirty-stretcher U. S. Army hospital railway car used in the East.
Stretchers were suspended on rubber rings

# THE QUARTERMASTER CORPS
## SUBSISTENCE DEPARTMENTS

ON THE Quartermaster's Department fell the task of supplying and clothing the armies, providing shelter for them in the form of tents or barracks, and transporting them by land or water. It furnished vehicles and the horses and mules to haul them, found mounts for the cavalry, built ships and docks, roads and bridges. While not operating the railroads (the United States Military Railroads functioned almost independently), it provided all supplies for their construction and operation and paid for their maintenance.

It built and purchased wagons by the tens of thousands. Its huge wagon trains were to be found on almost every road in the war zones, and its repair shops alone employed thousands. The appropriations for this department of the Federal service totaled more than a billion dollars.

The Confederate department served the same function, with the difference that, despite valiant attempts to set up manufacturing of its own, it still had to rely on imports run through the blockade. To offset this somewhat, the Southern armies were fighting almost exclusively on their own soil, and there was not the need for the vast and vulnerable wagon trains which followed the invading Federal columns.

To some extent the Confederates were able to equip themselves from captured Union supplies. Bad Federal generalship, culminating in several defeats, and insufficiently guarded trains and depots all contributed to this. But even the fine

materials so unwillingly supplied by the U. S. Quartermaster's Department wore out after a while, and as the war went on, disastrous Union defeats became less frequent—and so did the chances of capturing supplies. For the blockade was growing tighter; Union troops could take dumps and wagon trains, too, and more and more often the captured material could not be replaced.

And so the boys in gray tightened their belts, if they were lucky enough to have any, and fought on; a little leaner and a little more ragged, until at the end, many had nothing left but their tattered clothes and their ever-bright rifles.

In contrast, the Union soldier fared better as the war progressed. Better supervision over purchasing of supplies meant better materials. More efficient distribution meant fewer shortages (these, while at times acute, never were of long duration in the Union Army). Today's citizen-soldier would have found the conditions under which his counterpart of one hundred years ago lived and fought intolerable: his clothing unsuitable; his boots and equipment uncomfortable; and his food uneatable. Yet, never before in history had any army been so well equipped, nor had so much been done for its comfort and well-being.

The field organization in the Union Army called for a Regimental Quartermaster for each regiment (lieutenant); a Quartermaster for each Brigade, with the rank of captain; a Divisional Quartermaster for each division (major); a lieutenant colonel was Chief Quartermaster of each army corps, and a colonel, Chief Quartermaster of an army. These, of course, had their staffs and assistants.

The work was demanding, the responsibilities heavy, and the rewards small, as far as chances of glory went. (Those who succumbed to the numerous temptations and opportunities the Department offered for rewarding themselves were, in most cases, speedily weeded out.)

The wagon trains of the Federal armies were enormous. Twenty-five wagons per thousand men was not considered too great a number. McClellan's trains in the Peninsula campaign contained some five thousand wagons, as did Sherman's during the Atlanta campaign. All of these had to be carefully routed, and the traffic problems and timetables involved in moving these thousands of vehicles, going up loaded and returning empty, was extremely difficult. It was further complicated by narrow roads and by the fact that troop and artillery movements had priority. Ammunition wagons had precedence over all other supply vehicles.

A large proportion of transport was involved in the feeding of the armies—which leads to the second great supply department, that of the Commissary General of Subsistence. This department and its Confederate counterpart had the gargantuan task of feeding hundreds of thousands of hungry men, many of them far distant from the supply bases and only connected with them, if at all, by miles of rickety rails or inferior roads. Rations for five, six, even ten days were sometimes carried by the men themselves, but the wagons had to get through eventually, and often the state of the roads was as important as the dispositions of the enemy troops. Rains and thaw might make movement all but impossible. Triple teams failed to budge Burnside's supply wagons on the famous "mud march," and even one hundred fifty men tailing on to drag ropes could not move them. Result—campaign abandoned. This was an extreme case—but the difficulties of supply limited all commanders—even the Southern generals. For if the Union supply trains sometimes lagged behind the grumbling troops, the Southern wagon trains were, at times, almost nonexistent. Few troops in any war have marched and fought as prodigiously on as skimpy and intermittent a diet as did those of the Confederacy. But even they had to eat and replenish their cartridge pouches once in a while. And if their

fighting on friendly, although impoverished, soil meant that they were reasonably sure of a little to eat, the increasing difficulties of procuring transport and horses more than offset the advantage.

NOT all food was transported by wagon. "Beef on the hoof" followed most armies, and even contract beeves, underfed and overdriven, were a gourmet's dream compared to raw pork and weevily hardtack.

The commissary stores were obtained through contracts. They were then apportioned by the Commissary General to the commissaries of the armies, the corps, divisions, brigades, and finally to those of the regiments, who distributed the rations to the men.

The Confederacy found early in the war that meat and grain were scarce, and efforts were made to remedy this by ordering grain crops to be raised instead of cotton, and by government-run enterprises, including a pork-packing plant. The state governments did much to raise supplies, but poor transportation was responsible for many of the shortages. The food was usually to be had —but not often where it was most wanted.

Meat, if not driven to the cook pot on the hoof, was shipped in barrels, pickled in brine. This was supposed to insure its keeping for a minimum of two years. However, despite its sojourn in a solution so briny that it was often anchored in a stream overnight to soak out a little of the salt, the meat was often found to be tainted. There were some canned goods available, but they were expensive luxuries and there was nothing comparable to the tins of government "bully beef" and "Spam" of modern times. There were attempts to supply the chronic lack of vegetables with "dessicated vegetables." Assorted varieties were scalded, dried, and pressed into cakes. These "desecrated vegetables," as the men called them, were universally disliked. Floating around in a soup kettle, they reminded one officer of dead leaves in a dirty brook. Fresh vegetables were procured where possible but the supply depended to a great extent on the locality and shipping facilities.

The staples were pork (cured ham and bacon), beef (salted or fresh), beans, flour, salt, sugar, and coffee. Hard bread (hardtack) in the form of crackers about three inches square by one-half inch thick were issued—nine or ten constituting

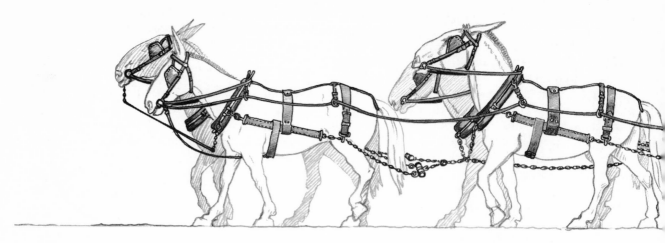

*Six-mule team hitched to army wagon. Driver rode near pole mule; guided near leader with single rein, from whose collar an iron rod fastened to the bit of the off leader. A steady pull headed the team to the left, short jerks to the right, accompanied by shouts of "Haw" (left), "Gee" (right), and "Yay" (straight ahead). Mule skinners were also known to shout other things on occasion. A good team could be guided by voice alone. The standard wagon body was ten feet long and had a box in front for tools and a feed box hung at back which was usually set up on a pole, to which the mules were hitched, three on a side. A spare pole was slung on the right side of the wagon body, and grease and water buckets under the rear axle. The canvas top, which could be drawn close at each end, usually bore the insignia of the*

a ration. Soft bread was issued occasionally, government bakeries being established near the large permanent camps, and late in the war the Union Army had mobile, horse-drawn bake ovens.

The daily allowance for the Federal soldier in camp was: three-quarters of a pound of pork *or* one and a quarter pounds of salted or fresh beef; one pound of hard bread; less than one-third of a cup of dried peas or beans (about a cupful when soaked and cooked); less than one-quarter of a cup of rice or hominy; one and a quarter ounces of ground and roasted coffee (if issued green the ration was a little larger) *or* enough tea to make about three cups; just over one-quarter of a cup of sugar; a little vinegar; about a tablespoon of salt; a pinch of pepper; a swallow of molasses; and, if lucky, one-quarter of a pound of potatoes.

This amounted to some twenty-three hundred calories a day, but was exceedingly low in vitamins. Also, this was what the regulations said a soldier *should* get. War conditions might and often did drastically reduce it.

The Southern ration was less—and even more likely to be cut. As early as the summer of 1861, one Confederate wrote that the camp fare in his regiment consisted of bacon, flour, salt, and a poor coffee-substitute, with the addition occa-

sionally of some tough and stringy horse meat.

At the opening of the Gettysburg campaign, the daily Confederate ration was one-half pound of bacon, one and an eighth pounds flour, just over one-quarter of a cup of peas, less than one ounce of sugar, and a little salt.

The Federal rations might on occasion be augmented by dried fruits, fresh vegetables, and pickled cabbage as anti-scorbutics, but this was rare. However, various states and the Sanitary Commission tried to supply the lack—shipping barrels of potatoes, onions, and apples and, of course, the ever-welcome food parcels.

Of the many letters that have survived, most had hard things to say about the army food—but it is possible that the more literary-minded, whose families were most likely to preserve the letters, were those for whom army fare would have the least appeal. There were many, some of whom probably could not write at all, who "never had it so good," and thought the army a fine provider.

Coffee was consumed in huge quantities, with meals, between meals, and at every halt long enough for a few twigs to be coaxed into a blaze. Condensed milk was sometimes to be had (Gail Borden had patented the process in 1856), but it was usually drunk black and scalding hot.

*corps and the number or name of the outfit to which it was attached, along with the nature of its contents. The brake could be worked from the saddle, and on extra-steep hills a log dragged on a chain was sometimes used. Mules were used in preference to horses as being able to stand rough roads, poor or scanty fodder, and hard treatment generally. Besides being used in the train, mules were utilized as pack animals, carrying supplies where the wagons could not go. Though of uncertain temperament and not as steady under fire as his half-brother, the horse, the pack mule with a case of small-arms ammunition strapped on each side was a familiar sight on many battlefields.*

IN CAMP or winter quarters the cooking was usually done by cooks chosen sometimes by a rotation process. They were more often likely to be men too dirty and lazy to make presentable soldiers. As in more modern times, it was perhaps not so much that the quality of the food the army provided was poor, as what the cooks did with it. Many, especially in winter quarters, when a few buddies messed and lived together, preferred to cook in their own little cabins.

The marching ration was one pound of hard bread, three-quarters of a pound of salt pork *or* one and one-quarter pounds of fresh meat, sugar, coffee, and salt. This was carried in the haversack, and the meat and coffee cooked by the individual soldier over his campfire. (If for one reason or another fires could not be lit, the pork was eaten raw—a favorite sandwich being slices of raw pork sprinkled with brown sugar, between two pieces of hardtack.)

If a fire and a skillet were to be had—and among the light-traveling Southerners, cooking utensils were often few and far between—the bacon was fried and then the hardtack crumbled in the fat.

There was, at times, more nourishment in the hard bread than the commissary bakers intended.

Some disgusted soldiers commented that all the fresh meat came in the hardtack, and another wrote of finding thirty-seven worms in one cracker. However, "we eat them without looking." Soups and stews were popular, as practically any edible object could be used, and its flavor disguised or imparted to the other ingredients.

To eke out the marching rations, which were often just a memory by the time the supply wagons could come up, a certain amount of foraging was resorted to. In friendly territory this might amount to little more than house-to-house scrounging for handouts, plus a few apples and ears of corn, and perhaps a stray chicken. In enemy territory foraging might be strictly forbidden, merely overlooked, or openly encouraged. In the latter case, the local inhabitants might expect to be left with little more than their eyes to weep with.

Foraging should not be confused with looting, however. Soldiers of the Civil War made a nice distinction, and, while feeding oneself at the enemy's expense was considered a legitimate part of war, looting and the senseless destruction that often accompanied it was frowned on as the work of the very lowest characters.

## THE SUTLERS

The other source of supply for the Union soldier was the sutler. The sutler was a civilian, a sort of peripatetic P.X. One was allowed to each regiment, and was appointed either by the governor of the state from which the regiment came or by regimental or brigade officers. His prices were supposed to be set by a board of officers, and the Inspector Generals Department listed the articles he could sell, checked his merchandise, and watched his prices. Despite these precautions many sutlers were accused of outrageous profiteering—made easier by the fact that he had a virtual monopoly. Either the men dealt with him, or went without. A further cause of resentment on the part of some was that the sutler could attach the money of a man, officer or enlisted, up to one-sixth of his monthly pay.

Sometimes the men's annoyance resulted in a "raid" on the establishment—tent, wagon, stall, or booth. Perhaps a tent rope might be cut or the sutler's wagon get into "difficulties"—in which case there were many "helping hands," most of whom would be helping themselves. The relationship between the sutler and the soldier, always a delicate one, seems to have depended to a great extent on the personality of the sutler. If he was reasonably honest and was a good public relations man, then he had little to fear. In excuse for the high prices, the sutler could argue that his profits had to be great to compensate for the risks he ran. In addition to the usual hazards of fire, theft, etc., his wagons often followed the regiment in the field, and in case of enemy raid or sudden retreat was a prime target for the ragged and always half-starved enemy.

Among the many articles to be found on the sutler's shelves were tobacco, fruit, candy, canned goods, fish, soft drinks (the sale of liquor in camp was forbidden, and the sutlers caught selling it lost their permits), cutlery, loaf sugar, paper, clothing, books, razors, paper collars, and cheese.

Another interesting item carried by some sutlers in the war's first months was body armor. Many recruits provided themselves with iron vests, supposedly bulletproof. Most of such cumbersome haberdashery was discarded before reaching the battlefield by hot and weary wearers. Needless to say, the protective vests proved worthless in actual combat.

*Inside a monitor's turret. Sweating guncrews heave 400-pound solid shot up to muzzle of 15-inch smoothbore. Massive port stoppers cover gun ports. Shot are racked around turret, cartridges, holding 35-pound charges, come up from magazines below through grating-covered hatches. Recoil of huge 42,000-pound gun was checked by plates on carriage being squeezed between compressor plates running parallel to iron carriage slide. Solid shot from gun such as this smashed through* Tennessee's *5-inch armor backed by two feet of solid wood. Despite iron gratings on top, interiors of turrets in action were dark, smoky and very hot. Lieutenant Commander Jeffers complained that the temperature in* Monitor's *turret rose to 140°. Sponge and rammer staffs were jointed for use in confined space.*

# THE NAVIES

THE story of the Southern defeat is in part a story of continuous and growing harassment and encroachment from the sea—of seaports blockaded, fortresses reduced, river barriers forced, and the great inland water highways taken and used by the enemy. It is hard to understand how the leaders of the Confederacy could have so fatally underrated the effects of sea power. Perhaps they counted on foreign intervention. They certainly counted on the powerful forts and batteries which guarded harbors and inlets. But forts and batteries were not enough. Warships were needed. And not individual ships, to be risked and lost in gallant but ineffectual single encounters, but a fleet of ships, capable of acting together and with but one end in view, the defeat of the widely-dispersed Federal squadrons.

Mahan wrote in his great work *The Influence of Sea Power upon History:* "Geographical and physical conditions being the same, extent of seacoast is a source of strength or weakness according as the population is large or small. . . . The blockade . . . could not have been carried out in the face of a real navy. Scattered unsupported along the coast, the U.S. ships kept their places . . . in face of an extensive network of inland water communications which favored secret concentration of the enemy. . . . Had there been a Southern Navy . . . the latter could not have been distributed as they were; . . . But as the Southern coast from its extent and many inlets might have been a source of strength, so, from these very characteristics it became a fruitful source of injury. . . . At every breach of the sea frontier, warships were entering. These streams that had carried the wealth and supported the trade of the seceding States turned against them and admitted the enemy to their hearts. . . .

[125]

Never did seapower play a greater or more decisive part...."

But it was not the Federal warships alone, nor the blockade, which spelled defeat for the South. It was the troop transports, safely convoyed to Hatteras and Port Royal, down the Potomac and up the Mississippi, to New Orleans and Fort Fisher and a score of other places. It was the storeships in the hundreds, loaded with ammunition and hardtack, boots and bandages, horses and field guns. It was merchantmen rolling safely in from Europe, and the tow of barges splashing up the James. Federal frigates might splinter and sink in Hampton Roads, and Yankee whalers burn under an Arctic sky, but the steady and relentless pressure went on until the final victory.

But at the outbreak of war these warships, transports, and supply ships, as well as the guns to arm them and the sailors to man them, did not exist.

OF ALL the bolts from the blue which fell upon the various government departments and bureaus in the frantic days of dissolution, none fell with a louder or more devastating smash than the one which struck the Navy. The indecision of the Buchanan administration, the treachery of many of the bureau heads, the defection of some one-fifth of the officers, was coupled with the blunders to be expected of a new administration taking over in times of treason and bloodshed. It led directly to the surrender at Sumter, the seizure of Pensacola, and the criminal folly at Norfolk, where ten warships were burned, the vast yard and its buildings and stores destroyed, and many hundreds of cannon, including three hundred Dahlgrens, abandoned to the Confederacy. These last, far more than the resurrected *Merrimack,* were to cause much grief to the Union in days to come. They were the backbone of the Confederate defenses, from the Virginia capes to the Red River. They were finally won back, but at the cost of much blood, sweat, and tears.

Few officials have ever had to begin a life and death struggle faced with the problems that beset Gideon Welles, Lincoln's Secretary of the Navy. His ships were scattered all over the globe, many of his best officers had gone South, and a blockade of more than thirty-five hundred miles of coast line had been declared.

This last was a mistake and Welles knew it. Under international law nations *close* insurrec-

tionary ports, and only *blockade* those of enemy nations—so Lincoln's proclamation was tantamount to a recognition of the Confederacy as a nation with belligerent's rights. Welles knew, too, that on the day the blockade was declared he had just three available steamers.

So throughout the Northern ports went men to buy or charter "everything afloat that could be made of service." Everything and anything—ocean traders, harbor tugs, and inland-water steamers (an ex-ferryboat captured a blockade-runner off Havana worth $300,000).

Orders went to the government shipyards—lay down eight sloops of war; and to the private yards—twenty-three screw gunboats, to stand the weight of a heavy armament, and we want them fast! And so the great build-up of Gideon Welles' new Navy began. For among all the misfits and incompetents that cluttered the departments and bureaus in those early days, Welles was the right man in the right job. And it was due in great measure to his energy and foresight, ably seconded by Assistant Secretary of the Navy Gustavus V. Fox, that at the war's end over five hundred armed vessels flew the Stars and Stripes.

But if Gideon Welles started the war with a hopelessly inadequate navy, his opposite number in the Confederacy started with no navy at all! Not only no ships, but in the entire South there was only one manufacturer capable of building marine engines powerful enough for a warship. There was a scarcity of iron, and lack of mills to roll it into plates. The navy yard at Norfolk was a wreck, while the only other, at Pensacola, was intended solely for shelter and repair.

Yet the Confederate Navy Department, under the resourceful Stephen R. Mallory, aided by state and private enterprise, performed miracles of improvisation. The countryside might have to be scoured for scrap iron, and railway road tracks ripped up for armor, but by the war's end, thirty-seven ironclads of varying types had been built or were being built. Engine, boiler, and machine shops were constructed, and several factories established for the making and repair of ordnance. Any ships that could serve a useful purpose in the war were purchased, and efforts made to buy vessels abroad. Even a Naval Academy, complete with training ship, was founded.

There were plenty of recruits. There was no period when the number was not more than sufficient to man the ships. The trouble was that few of them were seamen. The crews of most of the ships built abroad were largely made up of foreigners, mostly British, but were always officered by Southerners with Confederate commissions.

MANNING the increasing number of Federal ships become a major problem. At the outbreak of the war Navy personnel numbered less than eight thousand, while at its close the numbers had risen to over fifty thousand. Of these the great majority were landsmen and few were seamen of the blue-water variety. With the sailing warship on the way out, this was not as vital as it might have otherwise been. What was more serious was the lack of trained officers.

The three upper classes at the Naval Academy were put on active duty, but this was only a drop in the bucket. Here the great advantage of the North in possessing a large merchant fleet made itself felt. Volunteers from the merchant marine, captains and mates, filled many subordinate posts, while the regular officers occupied the more important positions.

One great fault lay in the system of promotion by seniority. With no provision for retirement for reasons of age, this filled the higher grades with elderly men who had little incentive to do anything but follow the old and safe routine. Initiative and enterprise were frowned upon, and lack of promotion in the lower grades resulted in subordinates who were not used to responsibility. Following many years of peace, a situation had arisen where many of the senior grades were filled by men who had become unfit for command, while those in the lower echelons were not accustomed to it. A law requiring retirement at sixty-two, or after forty-five years of service, helped ease this situation, as did the institution of examining boards, who passed on the fitness for promotion of all officers below the rank of commodore.

Most Americans preferred the many and varied opportunities ashore to the rough life and low pay of the ordinary seaman; consequently, many of the sailors who found their way into the Federal service were of foreign birth. Negroes were enlisted as early as September 1861. Bounties attracted some seamen into the army. Later this was remedied and bounties also were paid to sailors. The crews of some of the river flotillas were brought up to strength by drafts from the army. "Volunteers" were requested, but some officers availed themselves of such opportunities to unburden their commands of undesirable elements.

Naval discipline was necessarily strict—although flogging was not permitted. Marine detachments aboard the larger ships provided sentries for such places as the door of the captain's cabin, the spirit room, and the "brig." Because the hardships and monotony of a blockader's life prompted many to desert, marines in port guarded decks and gangways to prevent unauthorized personnel from leaving the ship.

In addition to these duties, the marines occasionally manned some of the guns. They also took part in landing operations, such as the attack on Fort Fisher. But the small size of the corps (less than four thousand officers and men at the most) precluded its taking any decisive part in the struggle.

In accordance with standard naval practice, the crew of a warship was divided into two watches port and starboard. These in turn were broken up into divisions and subdivisions, in accordance with their duties.

Conditions varied from ship to ship and from captain to captain. As always, discipline of the spit and polish variety tended to lessen as the size of the ship and, as a general rule, the commanding officer's age and seniority, decreased.

Living conditions for the seamen were pretty miserable in any ship in those days, merchantman or man-of-war. In reading of them, one must recognize that, as far as the foreign seamen went, at any rate, conditions were better than those they had been accustomed to.

Ships were usually crowded, and a poor and monotonous diet, consisting in the main of salt meat and hardtack, did little for either health or morale. Fresh meat and vegetables were seldom obtainable, and then only in quantities barely sufficient to ward off the dreaded scurvy. Those over twenty-one were eligible for a daily half-pint of wine or a quarter of a pint of spirits. Soon even this small comfort was denied the enlisted men, for in September 1862 Congress issued an order that "The spirit ration in the Navy of the United States shall forever cease."

As the Confederate States had no vessels organized into a fleet in the accepted sense of the word, the Federal Navy was able to devote most of its attention to the work of strangling the rebellion by blockade. Because of the great extent of coast line to be watched, the fleet was divided into squadrons and still smaller flotillas.

The North Atlantic Squadron took care of the

coasts of Virginia and North Carolina. The South Atlantic Squadron guarded the coast down to Florida. The East Gulf Squadron patrolled southern and western Florida as far as Pensacola. Later it included the Bahamas, Cuba, and the territory of the West Indian Squadron, which was broken up toward the end of 1864. The West Gulf Squadron's area included Pensacola and extended west to the Rio Grande. The Mississippi Squadron fought to take and hold that vast and vital river system, while the small Pacific Squadron kept watch in the West.

The Potomac Flotilla had the thankless job of patrolling that river, often in ships and cutters, sniped at from the banks and frequently aground on the numerous flats and shoals. Foote's Mississippi Flotilla, which later became the nucleus of the Mississippi Squadron, took part in the early operations around Forts Henry and Donelson.

There were also ships on detached duty in pursuit of the Confederate privateers and cruisers, and on routine foreign service. The crews of these were picked men, and probably contained a higher percentage of veteran sailors.

ALTHOUGH some sailing sloops and frigates still survived, the typical U.S. warship at the be-

ginning of the war was steam-driven, screw or paddle, the former being the more modern and efficient. In accordance with American naval policy they were exceptionally well armed for their size. The standard gun was the nine-inch Dahlgren smoothbore. Unfortunately they were deepwater ships, and their draught limited their use somewhat.

The changes in naval design and armament which were exciting the admiralties of the Old World had their repercussions on this side of the Atlantic. The appeal "For God's sake! Keep out the shell" had resulted in many experiments with armor and was given added impetus by the success of the ironclad gunboats against the Russian forts at Kinburn. Already the French "Gloire" and her sister ships had made the old wooden walls obsolete, while the English boasted of their huge "Warrior"—not only armored with iron, but built of it. By 1862 nearly one hundred armored ships were built or were being built in Europe.

The British admiralty was testing Captain Cowper Coles' revolving turret (and before the news of Hampton Roads arrived in London, had approved the plans for a multi-turreted vessel), and all navies were demanding heavier guns to pierce the new armor.

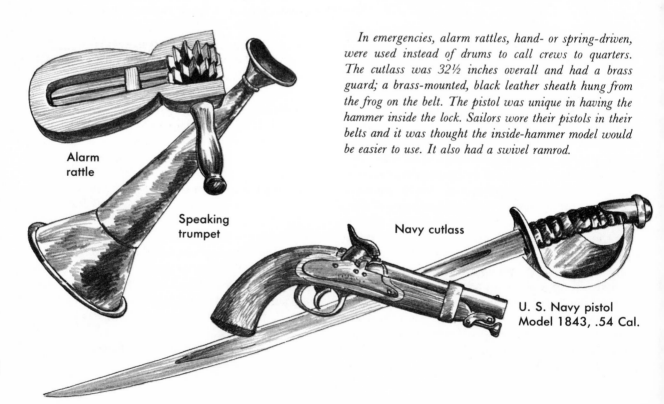

*In emergencies, alarm rattles, hand- or spring-driven, were used instead of drums to call crews to quarters. The cutlass was 32½ inches overall and had a brass guard; a brass-mounted, black leather sheath hung from the frog on the belt. The pistol was unique in having the hammer inside the lock. Sailors wore their pistols in their belts and it was thought the inside-hammer model would be easier to use. It also had a swivel ramrod.*

Alarm rattle

Speaking trumpet

Navy cutlass

U. S. Navy pistol Model 1843, .54 Cal.

LEFT: *Lieutenant commander in summer rig, white straw hat, and white drill trousers. Frock coats were usually worn, frequently unbuttoned to show the vest, although a shorter jacket was allowed as service dress. In full dress, with epaulettes, cocked hat, and sword, the coat was to be kept fully buttoned.*

*The marine sentry is in full dress—shako, white crossbelts, epaulettes and all. The fighting rig was plainer, regulation blue forage cap and blouse; cap device was bugle, with "M" inside the ring. Marine officer's undress uniform was forage cap and blue frock coat with a white sword belt. The Confederate marine officer's uniform was essentially the same as that for the C. S. Army; sky-blue pants and gray, double-breasted tunic with high collar but with the old U.S. marine buttons.*

*The captain in the center is in undress blue, but wearing sword belt and peaked cap. Confederate naval officers wore steel-gray coats and gray or white trousers with gray or white vests. Otherwise the uniforms were very similar, although sleeve and shoulder straps differed.*

*The seaman in whites is a petty officer, as denoted by the eagle device with anchor and star on his left sleeve. Boatswain's mates and those with higher ratings wore theirs on the right sleeve. The seaman at right is wearing blues, although different color combinations of pants, blouses (frocks), and caps were worn at the commanding officer's discretion. Confederates wore gray cloth jackets and trousers or gray woolen frocks with white duck collars and cuffs, black hats, and black handkerchiefs. In both navies chief petty officers wore jackets instead of frocks. C.S. petty officers wore a black fouled anchor in place of the eagle-anchor-star badge.*

[129]

**U.S.S. Hartford**—*Wooden steam sloop, 2900 tons; overall length, 310 feet; beam, 44 feet; draft, 16 feet, 3 inches.*

*A direct-acting two-cylinder engine with a 34-inch stroke turned a two-bladed propeller. Speed under steam, about 9 knots; under full sail and steam, 13 knots. Originally armed with sixteen 9-inch Dahlgren smoothbore shell guns. Later six more of the 9-inch guns were added, and one 30-pdr. rifle was mounted on the forecastle and one on the poop. Later a 30-pdr. Sawyer rifle was also mounted on the forecastle. Two rifled swivel guns and two small howitzers were also carried. The ship is shown above fully rigged. Before battle she was stripped for action and the upper masts and yards sent down.*

*Stern view—showing after rifled 30-pdr. on pivot, and quarter gallery.*

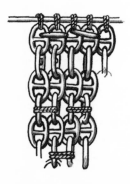

*Extemporized chain "armor" made by suspending chain cable from iron rod fixed about eight feet above the water line and lashing the strands together so that they overlapped. It extended some two feet underwater.*

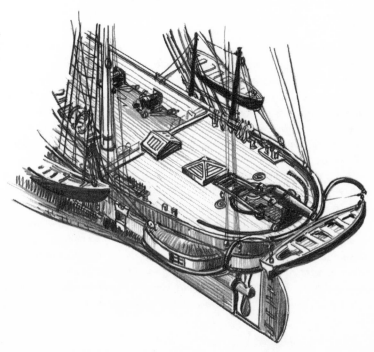

Sails were useless in river warfare. Most of the spars were removed when going into battle. U.S.S. Mississippi is shown stripped for action; even her topmasts have been struck, and all yards sent down except the foreyard. Her tops have been armed with 12-pdr. howitzers and riflemen have been posted. Pilots sometimes conned ships from the mizzentop, communicating with the helmsmen by a speaking tube. To make them more difficult to see at night, the Federal ships were plastered with mud or painted mud-gray.

Sketch below shows deck of warship of the type of the Federal sloops of war (the term "sloop" had nothing to do with size or rig; it meant a vessel carrying the main broadside battery on the upper, or spar, deck). Ship's "bridge" **A** in those days was little more than raised gangway running athwartship. The bulwarks were heightened by wooden troughs **B** with canvas covers. In these the crew's hammocks were stowed. These hammock rails gave some protection against musketry and canister. The stanchions above the bulwarks were for rigging the boarding nets. Semicircular piece at left **C** was cutlass rack. Guns show heavy ropes (breechings) rove through cascabels to check recoil. Windlass on funnel **D** was for raising or lowering telescoping stack. Spare stands of grapeshot surround the base of the stack.

Before going into action decks were sanded (so crew would not slip on blood) and nettings rigged over deck to catch falling spars, blocks, etc. For night action battle lanterns were strung and sometimes decks and gun carriages were whitewashed for greater visibility. By Civil War times most standing rigging (shrouds and stays) were of wire and turnbuckles had replaced old-time "dead-eyes."

A variety of ship's boats were carried—from 36-foot launches pulling 18 oars down to four-oared, 16-foot dinghys. Launches and cutters were for heavy work and could carry 12-pdr. boat howitzers in bows. They were usually stored inboard. Gigs were usually reserved for commanding officers. Barges and whaleboats were double-ended. The latter were used for light work and lifeboats. Lighter boats hung at davits.

**Federal gunboat of the Sacassus class.** *These were shallow-draft, wooden paddle steamers. They were double-enders (pointed at both ends, like a canoe), had rudders at bow and stern, and could steam with equal ease in either direction and so did not have to turn around, a great advantage in narrow waters. They were 240 feet long and 35 feet in beam and were variously armed—two 100-pdr. rifles and four 9-inch Dahlgrens being usual; 12- and 24-pdr. howitzers were also carried and some had 20-pdr. rifles. They were powered with single-cylinder, direct-acting inclined engines. Draft for the fires was forced by blower. These ships (there were 27) were a larger version of a class of 12 double-enders laid down in 1861.*

*There were two pilothouses, armored against musketry, and the masthead lookouts were usually similarly protected. Despite boiler plate, sandbags, etc., many serving in the inshore or river fleets fell victim to the sharpshooter's bullets. But besides the dangers of fire from concealed riflemen or field guns, or the cunningly planted torpedo, there was always risk of attack by boarding parties. So nettings were strung at vulnerable points, cutlass and pistol were always close at hand, and the engine room force ready with hosefuls of scalding water.*

*All sorts of unlikely craft, like this ferryboat, were pressed into service as gunboats. Broad beam made her a steady platform for her armament of heavy guns, and her shallow draft enabled her to operate in creeks and streams inaccessible to deeper vessels. Propelling machinery was usually protected by heavy timbers, coal, etc., while light iron plating was hinged up to shield the gunners from rifle fire. Like many ships of the time, her engine drove the side-wheels by an overhead working beam (known generally but erroneously as a "walking beam").*

[132]

**Confederate Ram, Manassas, First Civil War Ironclad.** *Convex frame of 12-inch oak sheathed with 1½-inch iron (some accounts give ½-inch), built on hull of 387-ton tugboat* Enoch Train. *One 32-pdr. gun fired forward through hooded port; 20 feet of bow solid wood; 143 feet long, beam 32 feet, draft 17 feet; crew of 37.*

NECESSITY is the mother of invention—and during the Civil War she had some ugly children. Squat and grim-looking, they were enough to horrify the conservative sailor used to holystoned decks and towering clouds of canvas. But they did the jobs they were designed for—and no man-of-war, however impressive, can do more than that.

Because of lack of time (and often materials), inadequate building facilities, and the limitations imposed by the shallowness of the coastal and river waters, most of the new types were highly specialized—built to cope only with the immediate local emergency.

But if the eyes of the naval world were focused on the performance of the new ironclads, ships of the older type still won enough glory to delight the heart of the saltiest old sea dog. The *Cumberland* firing 'till the waters closed over the guns; the *Hartford* passing the forts at New Orleans and Mobile in a hail of shot and shell; The *Kearsarge* circling the doomed *Alabama* for the kill—this was in the old tradition and fought by ships that looked like ships and not floating hen houses or cheese boxes on rafts.

IN AMERICA, the War of 1812 had seen several proposals for shotproof batteries propelled by steam. One of these, a steam vessel with inclined sides plated with iron, was under construction, paid for by private funds, when the war ended.

In 1842, Congress made an appropriation for the building of a heavily-gunned ironclad ram. This ram, designed by the Stevens brothers of New Jersey, was to have inclined sides, airtight firerooms for forced draught, and her engines were to be below the water line. Construction lagged, the designs were changed to meet the threat of heavier artillery, and finally, after much heavy expenditure and much litigation, the government relinquished all interest in her in 1862.

Of more interest than the Stevens battery itself is the fact that during much of the time she was

*Floating battery built at Charlestown for attack on Federals at Fort Sumter. About 100 feet long by 25 feet wide. Angled pine face braced with palmetto logs and armored with double layer of railroad iron. Heavy guns (two 42-pdrs. and two 32-pdrs.) were balanced by projection carrying load of sandbags. Struck several times by fort's guns but was undamaged.*

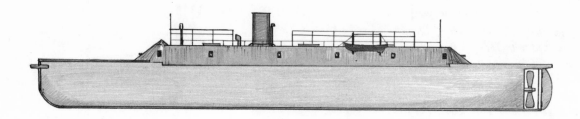

C.S.S. *VIRGINIA*

*Built on the burned-out hull of the frigate* Merrimack. *Armored citadel 170 feet long, sloping sides of wood 24 inches thick covered with four inches of iron. The top of the superstructure was covered with a grating made of two-inch iron bars and had four hatches. The projecting bow and stern (about 100 feet) were unarmored and were just underwater when the ship was trimmed for action. A false bow forward prevented the water from banking up on the casemate. A cast-iron wedge was bolted to the stem two feet underwater and projected two feet for use as a ram. Two 7-inch Brooke rifles were mounted on pivots at bow and stern. A 6.4-inch rifle and three 9-inch smoothbores were carried on each broadside. Iron port shutters were unfinished when she fought the* Monitor. *The original engines and boilers, condemned before the ship was sunk, gave a speed of some five knots. Her length (about 270 feet) made her hard to steer. She had one big stack some eight feet in diameter. Awning stanchions, railings, davits, boats, even the flagstaff, were shot to pieces in the historic fight.*

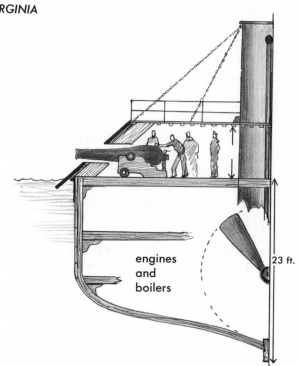

engines and boilers

23 ft.

*The* Virginia *had two horizontal engines. Cylinders were 72 inches in diameter; four vertical watertube boilers; funnel eight feet in diameter. Two-blade, seventeen-foot adjustable pitch propeller. Horsepower was 1294.*

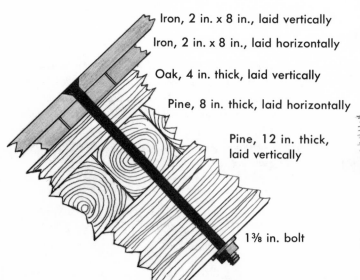

Iron, 2 in. x 8 in., laid vertically

Iron, 2 in. x 8 in., laid horizontally

Oak, 4 in. thick, laid vertically

Pine, 8 in. thick, laid horizontally

Pine, 12 in. thick, laid vertically

1⅜ in. bolt

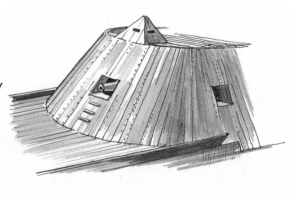

*Forward end of casemate, showing iron pilothouse and false bow.*

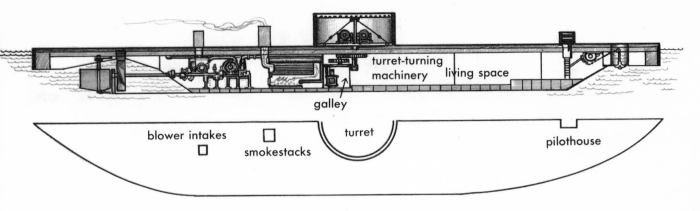

## U.S.S. MONITOR

*Hull: length, 172 feet; beam, 41 feet 6 inches; draft, 11 feet; freeboard (distance from water line to deck), one foot.*
*Turret: 20 feet (inside diameter); height, 9 feet; thickness, 8 inches (8 layers of one inch wrought-iron plates bolted together); revolved on central spindle by small steam engine; turret top, heavy iron grating, with sliding hatches. Armored pilothouse forward.*
*Armament: two 11-inch smoothbores firing solid shot weighing 180 pounds.*
*Engine: single, horizontal, driving one four-bladed propeller nine feet in diameter—speed about five knots; two return-tube boilers, forced draft by blowers; two rectangular smokestacks six feet high; two blower pipes, four and a half feet high (stacks and blower intake pipes taken apart and laid flat when cleared for action).*

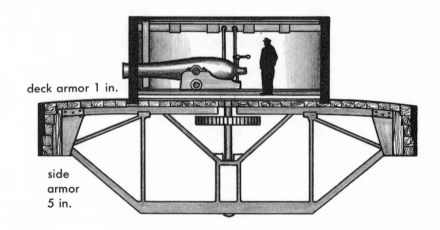

*Guns could each be fired about once every two and a half minutes. Swinging pendulum-type shutters closed ports when guns were run in for loading. Manhandling the port shutters took efforts of whole gun crew so usually turret was revolved, turning guns away from enemy. Due to small gun ports and dense powder smoke, Monitor's turret captain had difficulty sighting target.*

*Pilothouse: length, 3 feet, 6 inches; width, 2 feet, 8 inches; height, 3 feet, 10 inches.*
*Built up of solid iron blocks, 12 inches deep, 9 inches thick, with 3-inch bolts at corners. Eye slits formed by spacers in corners between first and second blocks.*

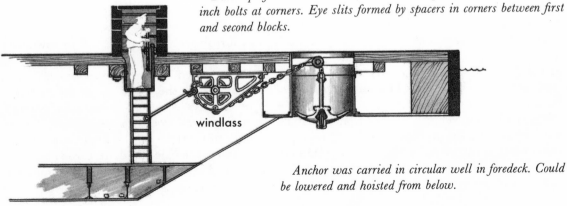

*Anchor was carried in circular well in foredeck. Could be lowered and hoisted from below.*

[135]

Double-turret Seagoing Monitor, Onondaga: *length, 230 feet; beam, 51 feet 2 inches; draft, 12 feet 7 inches; displacement, 3100 tons; turret armor, 12¾ inches; speed, 6.46 knots; armament, two 15-inch smoothbores, two 150-pdr. Parrott rifles.*

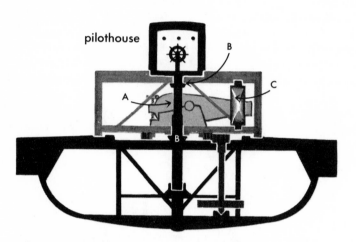

pilothouse

A. spindle
B. collars
C. port stopper

Diagram showing turret, pilothouse, and port stopper

*In most later ships of the* Monitor *type the pilothouse was on top of the turret, and remained stationary while the turret revolved. The spindle which supported the house also took the weight of the turret on two collars. To allow the heavy turret to turn freely the spindle was keyed up, taking the weight off the bronze ring at the base of the turret. The port stopper was of heavy wrought iron, turning on a pivot, and easily worked by two men.*

under construction, Stephen R. Mallory was serving as Chairman of the Committee of Naval Affairs. Upon becoming Secretary of the Confederate Navy, he at once pressed for an ironclad program.

"Inequality of numbers may be compensated by invulnerability," Mallory wrote. While negotiating for purchases abroad (he even had hopes of buying the *Gloire* or one of her sisterships) he ordered plans for an armored ram. Thus was born the famous *Merrimack* (or *Virginia*—take your choice). There is some question as to her designer. This distinction was claimed by John M. Brooke, C.S.N., E. C. Murrat, builder of the *Louisiana,* and naval constructor John L. Porter. There is no question as to her success, however, as the destruction of the heavily-armed *Cumberland* and *Congress* testified. The tiny *Manassas,* of New Orleans fame, was of even earlier date, but she was a private venture, altered from a tugboat to serve as a tinclad privateer. Certainly no reputable naval constructor would have expected her one and one-half-inch plates to stand up to Farragut's Dahlgrens.

The Confederate ironclads generally followed the pattern of the *Merrimack*—a sloping-sided armored structure, pierced for guns which were carried on a hull, the bow and stern of which projected some distance beyond the casemate, and having either a very low freeboard or being submerged altogether. This pattern was also used, with variations, in the ironclad gunboats which James B. Eads built for the Federals for use on the Mississippi.

With the exception of the river boats, most Northern ironclads were of the type which received its name from the first of its kind, the *Monitor.* This class of vessel carried its armament in a revolving armored tower or towers mounted on a hull with very little freeboard; the deck was also armored. An armored pilothouse was usually mounted on the top of one of the turrets, but did not revolve with it. Smokestacks, partially armored, as well as davits, ventilators, etc., were the only projections on the deck—the anchors were usually concealed and were worked from below deck. Surprisingly enough, the monitors as a class were good sea boats, although with their exceptionally low freeboard they could not have fought in a heavy sea. The Ericsson turret, with its central spindle, had many drawbacks, one being that to revolve the turret, the sides of which normally rested on a brass ring let into the deck, the whole structure had to be keyed up. The Coles turret, which became the prototype of the modern gun turret, was supported and turned on rollers or ball bearings, turned more easily, and was not so subject to jamming by enemy shot hitting the base of the tower.

Armor was of wrought iron bolted onto heavy wooden backing. Turret armor on the Federal ships was usually some eight inches thick. The casemates of the Confederate batteries were protected by an average of four to five inches of armor. This was impervious to shell, usually shattered cast-iron shot, but could be penetrated by large-caliber shot of wrought iron fired with battering charges. The *Monitor's* 11-inch Dahlgrens were limited to 15-pound charges (later this was doubled without injury to the guns), and had full charges been used against the *Merrimack*, the bat-

tle would have ended differently. Damage and casualties were often caused by shot which failed to penetrate, but which drove in splinters from the backing and sheared off rivets and nuts on the inside of turrets and casemates.

One objection to the monitors as a class was that while they were practically invulnerable, their offensive power was very limited. As Du Pont said of the monitors at Charleston: "Ability to endure is not a sufficient element wherewith to gain victories. . . ."

Their rate of fire was slow as the loading space was comparatively small and the guns of large size. Also, although provided with port-stoppers, the usual practice was to turn the turret away from the enemy while loading.

Although the new French and British ironclads were designed with ramming in mind, and a strong reinforced spur incorporated in their stems, the actual sinking of the *Cumberland* in Hampton Roads by the *Merrimack's* ram made a great impression in naval circles abroad. Strangely enough, while the ramming of the anchored

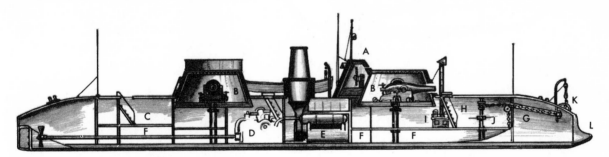

**U.S.S. KEOKUK:** *length, 153 feet, 6 inches; beam, 36 feet; draft, 8 feet, 6 inches; twin screws; two 11-inch guns in two fixed towers, each with three gun ports.*

*The modern-looking but ill-fated* Keokuk *had a career somewhat resembling that of Solomon Gundy—born on Monday and buried on Sunday. Delivered on February 24, 1863, she joined the fleet on March 26, went into action at Charleston April 7, and sank April 8. She was in position some thirty minutes, during which time she was hit ninety times in the hull and turrets, nineteen of which pierced her at or below the water line. Her light 2-inch armor was no match for the Confederate cannon, some of which sent projectiles right through her. She was kept afloat with difficulty during the night and sank in shallow water the next morning. Needless to say, this experiment in ironclad building was not repeated. It is worth noting that although, in the words of her captain, she was "completely riddled," only sixteen of her crew were wounded.*

A. pilothouse
B. gun towers
C. officers' quarters
D. engine room
E. boilers, fireroom
F. storage, magazines, etc.

G. hawsepipe
H. crew's quarters
I. galley
J. windlass
K. anchor davit
L. ram

cross section at J

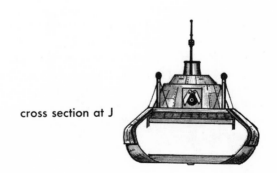

*Cumberland* attracted great attention, the ineffectual attempts of the two ironclads to ram each other *while under way* seems to have passed almost unnoticed.

Generally speaking, the Confederate vessels were underpowered, and most suffered from defective engines. As was to be expected, Northern engineering was far superior, but none of the new ships were capable of any great speed. Six knots was about average for the monitors, and the river ironclads could not do much better.

As the war progressed it became evident that forts could not stop the passage of an ironclad fleet unless aided by formidable obstacles, such as sunken ships and mine fields. On the other hand forts, particularly earthworks, had little to fear from attack by ships alone.

The river gunboats were in a class by themselves. They were strictly shoal-water boats, and were almost exclusively side- or stern-wheelers. Screws were not well adapted for shallow water;

losing power and being more subject to damage.

Some were especially designed and built. Others were existing craft, armed and sometimes armored. The powerful *Benton* was a converted snagboat. The gunboats built by Eads carried only two and one-half-inch armor (Porter says they could have carried more), and that not over the whole casemate. Others carried so little that they were called the "tinclads." Many of the Confederate steamers and rams were protected with wood and cotton bales.

Steam pressures were usually low, but even the so-called high-pressure boilers of these days could not stand much. Engines were of the single expansion type—either vertical, inclined, or horizontal. If the side wheels were on divided shafting with an engine driving each wheel, maneuvering was made easy. The stern-wheelers either had the wheels right aft, or recessed into the hull. Speeds varied—the Eads boats were designed to make nine miles an hour.

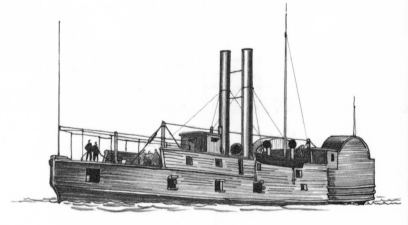

**U. S. GUNBOAT CONESTOGA.** *One of the three side-wheelers converted by lowering engines and boilers into the hold and piercing sides for guns. Armor was five-inch oak. Kept out musket balls but nothing else. Average length, 180 feet; beam 42 feet, draft, 6 feet at full load. Single cylinder high-pressure engines gave them 7-10 knots. Guns:* Lexington, *two 32-pdrs. four 8-inch.* Tyler, *one 32-pdr. six 8-inch.* Conestoga, *four 32-pdrs. and at least one 12-pdr. rifle. Like most gunboats, they carried riflemen.*

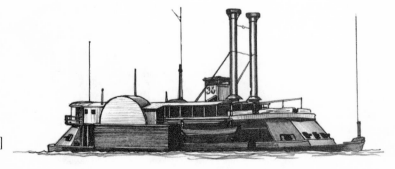

**U. S. GUNBOAT CRICKET.** *One of many converted side- or stern-wheelers. Armor so thin (less than one inch) that they were called "tinclads." Size and armament varied. Six 12-pdr. or 24-pdr. howitzers was average. Crew about fifty men. Very light draft (less than two feet in some). Exposed engines and boilers protected by coal, wood, or anything available.*

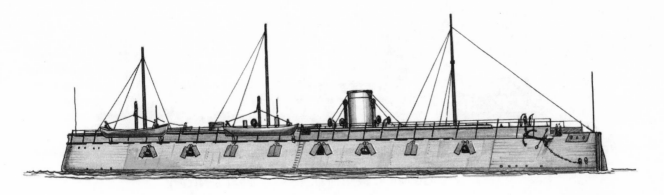

## U.S.S. NEW IRONSIDES

*Wooden ironclad, screw propeller. Length, 232 feet; beam, 57 feet, 6 inches; draft, 15 feet, 6 inches; 3480 tons; speed, 6–7 knots. Armor, 4½ inches; armament, seven 11-inch smoothbores, one 8-inch rifle on each broadside. Crew about 440 men.*

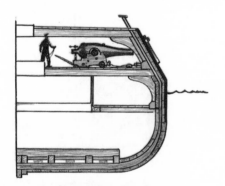

*A broadside ironclad of the type of the* Warrior *and* Gloire. *Armored belt extended along water line and for 170 feet amidships. Armored bulkheads closed in both ends of side armor. As extra protection against plunging fire her decks were covered with sandbags before going into action. Could fire her 11-inchers once every 1.74 minutes. In one operation fired 4439 (11-inch and 15-inch) projectiles. Fire by eight Monitors in same action totaled 3587. Bark rigged, but masts, etc., replaced by light spars before joining fleet off Charleston. One of the most powerful ships then afloat. Took more hits than any other U.S. warship.*

## CONFEDERATE IRONCLAD ATLANTA

*Length, 204 feet; beam, 41 feet; draft, 15 feet, 9 inches. Built on the iron hull of merchant steamer* Fingal, *with sloping casemate typical of Southern ironclads. Protected by two layers of 2-inch iron, 7 inches wide bolted to 3 inches of oak on 15 inches of pine. A wooden pole, lowered and raised by an iron lever, carried a percussion torpedo at the bow. Armed with two 7-inch and two 6.4-inch Brooke rifles.*

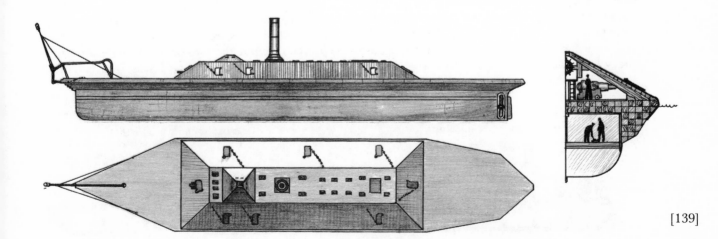

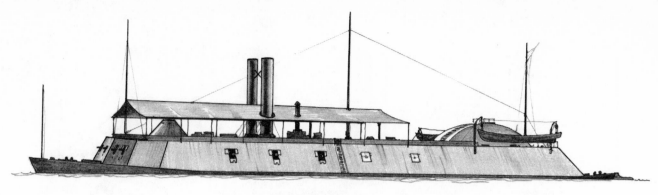

## U. S. GUNBOAT BENTON (EX-SNAG BOAT BENTON)

*Two hulls about 20 feet apart, joined to make one boat, except for 50 feet at stern where wheel was placed. Length, 202 feet; beam, 72 feet; draft, 9 feet. Armor: side and bow, 3½ inches; wheelhouse and stern, 2½ inches; twin engines; speed, 5 knots; armament, two 9-inch Dahlgrens, seven 42-pdr. rifles, seven 32-pdrs.*

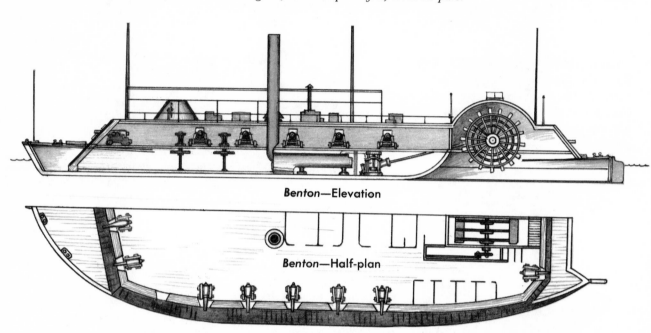

*Benton—Elevation*

*Benton—Half-plan*

The *Benton* was fairly typical of the Federal river gunboats. She was more heavily armed and armored, but her general arrangements were the same. A considerable proportion of their guns could fire dead ahead, an advantage when attacking forts and in fighting other vessels in waters usually too narrow to permit the customary broadside-to-broadside, line-ahead formation. Their shallow draft meant that the engines

and boilers were dangerously exposed, and in several instances, both in the Federal and Confederate river navies, vessels were put out of action, with grave loss of life, by enemy projectiles piercing their boilers. Logs, cables, sandbags, hay, and cotton bales were all used as supplementary protection, but the two or three inches of armor customary on these vessels was insufficient to keep out large-caliber shot at close range.

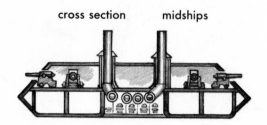

cross section    midships

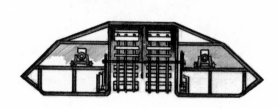

cross section    aft

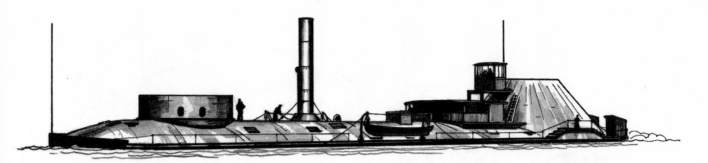

OSAGE—*Federal stern-wheel river monitor. Base of turret was below turtle deck, which rose four feet at center; Deck plated with one-inch iron. Sides sloped outward to gunwale, which was six inches above water. Side armor, 2½ inches, extending 2½ feet under water. Turret held two 11-inch Dahlgrens; armor, 6–8 inches. Draft, 3½ feet fully loaded. Speed, about seven knots.*

*Confederate ram* **GENERAL PRICE.** *Both sides strengthened bows and hulls of fast (about 12-knot) steamers for use as rams. Guns, few or none (U.S. rams at Memphis had only carbines and revolvers). Shapes and sizes varied. All were stern- or side-wheelers except screw propelled* Little Rebel.

*Mortar schooner, showing 13-inch weapon. Vessels were towed into position, anchored bow and stern. If firing from shelter of riverbank, masts were concealed with tree branches. Observers at mastheads corrected aim. Rate of fire, about once in ten minutes.*

*Mortar boats carried one heavy mortar each. They were flat-bottomed, very heavily built to withstand the shock of recoil. Sides of boiler plate about seven feet high protected the crews from sharpshooters' bullets and shrapnel. When not in action, the men and armament were protected from the weather by awnings. Boats were towed into position or could be moved by sweeps (long oars).*

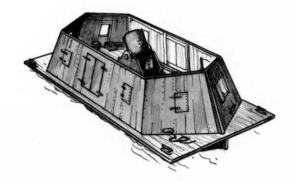

[141]

Old-style wooden gun carriage

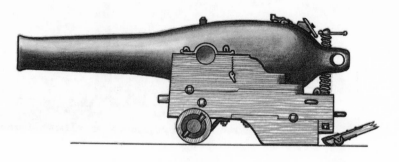

*Nine-inch Dahlgren on two-wheel Marsilly carriage. Rear of carriage slid on deck, checking recoil. Was moved on roller in end of handspike. Gun was trained by train-tackle and handspike.*

# NAVAL ORDNANCE

Naval weapons were as varied as the ships themselves. The standard broadside gun in the Federal Navy was the 9-inch Dahlgren. It was supplemented by heavier guns mounted on pivots which could be brought to bear on either beam and which, if located on poop or forecastle, gave a wide arc of fire. Smaller vessels often carried the 32-pounders, 6.4-inch, in various weights, as a broadside gun. The *New Ironsides,* on the other hand, mounted 11-inch guns on the broadside.

The heaviest gun in use was the 15-inch, mounted in some of the monitors. The smallest was the 12-pounder boat howitzer. (This could be mounted on wheels and used ashore.)

While rifles had more range and accuracy than smoothbores, much of the advantage was lost because of the difficulty of aiming from a heaving rolling deck.

The crude elevating mechanisms did not permit the gun captain to keep the target always in his sight, regardless of the vessel's motion, and the gun was fired at the instant the roll of the ship brought the target into line. Consequently, ranges were kept as short as possible, and much reliance was placed on ricochet fire (the principle was the same as skimming a stone across a pond). Water caps over the fuses helped prevent the extinguishing of the fuse as the shell skipped along the surface. Here the projectile from a rifle was at a disadvantage, as it was more likely to deflect on striking the water and take a new direction altogether.

Ricochet firing was quite accurate up to about a mile in smooth water, but a rough sea made this kind of shooting impossible. Many rifled guns were used, however. Most of those in the Federal service were Parrotts, ranging from the 8-inch, 150-pounder down to 20-pounders. The Confederates used many Brooke rifles. They were generally heavier than the Parrotts of corresponding caliber, for where the Parrott had but one reinforcing hoop at the breech, the Brooke had several. There were also assorted British imports, but a great deal of the Confederate armament was U.S. naval material seized at Norfolk or other yards at the beginning of the war.

For close work, grapeshot and canister were used. Canister was not used much beyond three hundred yards. Grapeshot was heavy enough to be used effectively against ships up to four hundred yards and up to one thousand yards at exposed personnel, small boats, etc. Both grapeshot and canister were used in running past forts and earthworks, as, while incapable of injuring structures, the rapid and continuous fire of case shot from a vessel's broadside usually drove and kept the enemy's gunners from their embrasures.

Solid shot was used for battering, smashing walls of forts, or shattering or penetrating armor. Shells were used against unarmored vessels (the shells of the period invariably broke up on striking all but the thinnest armor), earthworks, personnel, etc.

Carriages used were the old four-wheel truck carriage, the newer two-wheel Marsilly, and pivots of various types. The turret guns of the monitors were on fixed slide-mounts, which revolved with the turret.

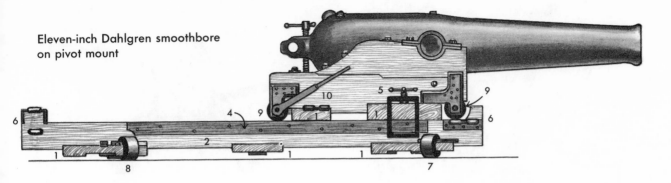

Eleven-inch Dahlgren smoothbore
on pivot mount

1. Transoms
2. Rails
3. Rail plates
4. Compressor battens

5. Compressor
6. Hurters
7. Shifting trucks
8. Training trucks

9. Carriage trucks (rollers)
10. Wrench for throwing eccentrics
11. Rear-pivot plate
12. Eyes for tackles

13. Racers
14. Battens and slats
15. Preventer breeching
16. Breeching

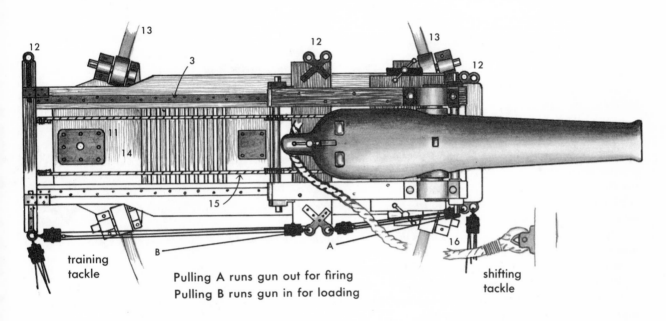

training
tackle

Pulling A runs gun out for firing
Pulling B runs gun in for loading

shifting
tackle

*Length of bore, 132 inches; weight, 16,000 pounds; service charge, 15 pounds; weight of shell, 136 pounds; range at 5°, 1700 yards (one turn of elevating screw equaled 1°). Rate of fire, rapid, one every 1.74 minutes; sustained, one every 2.86 minutes. Dahlgrens had two vents, one kept plugged but which could be opened up when other became too enlarged for safety. Compressors of screw-clamp type, hooked under compressor rails, were loosened to run gun out. Notched and graduated sight-bar worked in box on breech. Blade-front sight on tube between trunnions.*

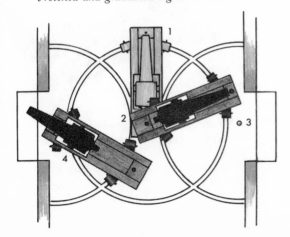

*Heavy pivot guns could be readily moved on system of overlapping rails (racers). Diagram shows gun in fore-and-aft position. 1. To swing to broadside, training trucks were raised off deck by eccentrics, slide pivoted at rear, 2, and pulled over pivot hole in deck, 3. To aim, shifting trucks were raised, training trucks lowered, and slide pivoted at front, 4.*

[143]

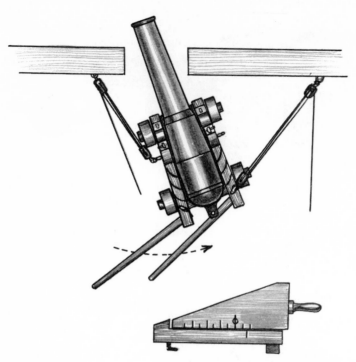

Marked quoin and bed

LEFT: *Gun trained by tackles, and handspikes under horns of carriage.*

*In changing elevation on old-type guns not provided with elevating screws, breech was raised off quoin by handspike placed on step of carriage. The wedge-shaped quoin was shifted forward or backward under breech.*

*Quoins slid in grooved beds. Marks on sides gave distances, and allowed all broadside guns to be ranged simultaneously at a given elevation.*

## NAVAL GUN EXERCISES

"Silence, man the port (or starboard) guns." Crew at attention facing gun.

"Cast off and provide." Gun is cast loose, side and train tackles hooked, breeching cast off, lock cover removed. Gun ports triced up.

"Run in." Gun is hauled back from gun port.

"Serve vent and sponge." Gun captain stops vent and serves with his priming wire. Charge is taken from powderman, and shell from shell box.

"Load." Charge placed in muzzle, pushed down—shell put in. Cap removed from fuse, shown to gun captain and kept for record. Shell pushed home.

"Run out." Captain throws weight on roller hand spike.

"Prime." Captain serves vent again, pricking cartridge, puts in primer.

"Aim." Captain adjusts sight. Takes position directly behind gun out of reach of recoil. Calls "Muzzle right" (or left) to train-tackle men and handspike men.

"Ready—fire." Pulls lanyard. (Second captain stands by with fresh primer in case of misfire.)

"Serve vent and sponge" as before. (Gun has run in on its own recoil.)

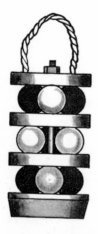

*As flying bits from Army friction primers might cause injuries in confined spaces aboard ship, the Navy used composition-filled tube with explosive wafer on top, fired by gunlock. Lock was made to clear vent after striking, or rush of gas out of vent would have thrown hammer back and damaged it. Pull on lanyard brought 3¼-pound hammer down at same time slot allowed it to pull back from vent.*

*Grapeshot made up of iron balls, usually nine in three tiers, held by bolt. Sometimes shot were canvas-covered and held by rope lashings.*

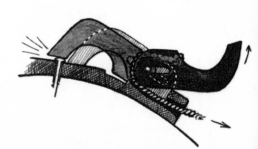

Diagram of naval gunlock
with hammer in three positions

Stand of grape

RIGHT: *Twelve-pdr. howitzer on field carriage. For shore use. Light and easily transportable, these guns saw service in many landing operations.*

LEFT: *Twelve-pdr. boat howitzer on slide carriage. Note compressor slide screws on top of carriage slide. The 12-pdr. was mounted in boats or in the tops. The 24-pdr. was also used in boats, or on deck, the fore end fixed and the inboard end on a truck.*

## NAVAL GUNS

| Type | Bore (in.) | Weight (lbs.) | Length of Bore (in.) | Type of Projectile | Weight of Projectile (lbs.) | Weight of Charge (lbs.) | Range at 5° (yds.) |
|---|---|---|---|---|---|---|---|
| SMOOTHBORES | | | | | | | |
| 15-inch | 15 | 42,000 | 130 | Shell | 330 | 35 | 1700 |
| 11-inch | 11 | 15,700 | 132 | Shell | 136 | 15 | 1712 |
| 10-inch | 10 | 12,000 | 120 | Shell | 100 | 12½ | 1740 |
| 9-inch | 9 | 9200 | 107 | Shell | 70 | 10 | 1710 |
| 8-inch | 8 | 6000 | 95 | Shell | 51 | 7 | 1657 |
| 32-pdr. howitzer | 6.4 | 3000 | 69 | Shot | 32 | 4 | 1469 |
| | | | | Shell | 26 | 4 | 1460 |
| 24-pdr. howitzer | 5.8 | 1300 | 58 | Shell | 20 | 2 | 1270 |
| 12-pdr. howitzer | 4.6 | 760 | 55 | Shell | 10 | 1 | 1085 |
| | | | | | | | |
| RIFLED GUNS | | | | | | | |
| 150-pdr. Parrott | 8 | 16,500 | 136 | Shell | 152 | 16 | 2000 |
| 100-pdr. Parrott | 6.4 | 9700 | 130 | Shot & Shell | 70–100 | 10 | 2000 |
| 60-pdr. Parrott | 5.3 | 5360 | 105 | | 55 | 6 | |
| 30-pdr. Parrott | 4.2 | 3550 | 96.8 | | 25–30 | 3.25 | |

*Diagram of 2-gun turret, showing method of hoisting and loading heavy shot. Far gun is run out for firing.*

A. Magazine hatch
B. Shot hoist in first position
C. Shot hoist in loading position
D. Hoist rail swings to load
E. Hoist rail support
F. Port stopper closed
G. Port stopper open

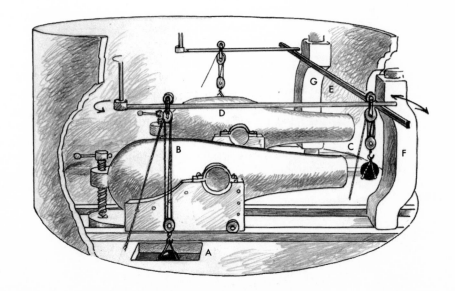

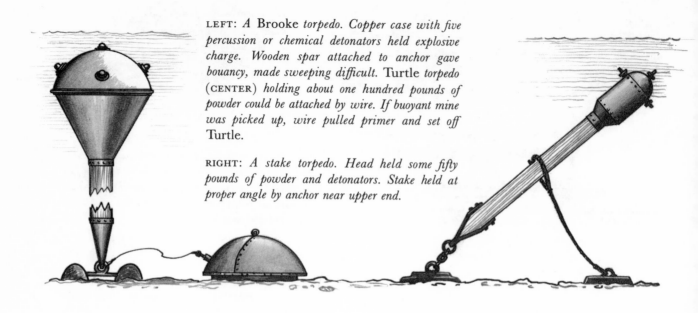

LEFT: *A* Brooke *torpedo. Copper case with five percussion or chemical detonators held explosive charge. Wooden spar attached to anchor gave bouancy, made sweeping difficult.* Turtle *torpedo* (CENTER) *holding about one hundred pounds of powder could be attached by wire. If buoyant mine was picked up, wire pulled primer and set off* Turtle.

RIGHT: *A stake torpedo. Head held some fifty pounds of powder and detonators. Stake held at proper angle by anchor near upper end.*

## MINES, TORPEDOES, AND TORPEDO BOATS

Small mines had been used by the Russians in defense of some of their harbors during the Crimean War, but it was the Civil War which gave the greatest impetus of this type of warfare. Sleeman, in his *Torpedoes and Torpedo Warfare* (1880), wrote: "The prominent position the torpedo now holds as a most important and legitimate function of naval warfare is owing without doubt to the successful and extensive employment of them on the part of the Confederates during this long and bloody struggle."

In its then state of development it was the natural defensive weapon for a weaker naval power, and the variety and ingenuity of some of the infernal machines devised by the Confederates showed great inventiveness. If malfunction due to poor workmanship and faulty materials prevented their accomplishing more than they did, it was not for want of enterprise on the part of their designers.

The fact that the morale effect of a mine field was greater than any physical damage it might do was not lost upon the Confederates, either. More than one stouthearted Northern skipper, who would have thought nothing of laying his ship alongside that of an enemy, hesitated to risk passage of a channel suspected of concealing the deadly containers.

Four monitors and three ironclad gunboats were among some twenty-seven sunk by mines.

(The word, mine, is used here in its modern sense. At that time such weapons were known as torpedoes. Farragut's famous exclamation was in reference to the mine field in which the *Tecumseh* had just gone down.)

Many ships were severely damaged and several had narrow escapes. During one of the attacks on the forts at Charlestown the *New Ironsides* laid for some time over an electrical mine containing three thousand (some say five thousand) pounds of powder, which a frustrated Confederate was vainly trying to detonate.

Although not in any sense a mine, as we understand the word, the Confederates employed a bomb called a "coal torpedoe," which may have caused some losses officially listed as "boiler explosions." This bomb was of iron, cast in the shape of a large lump of coal, and contained ten pounds of powder. Such a bomb would have been planted in a coal heap at a coaling station or on a supply collier. A transport, the *Greyhound,* was sunk by this means in 1864.

An explosion which destroyed several Federal barges at City Point on the James was caused by a clockwork time bomb planted aboard a munitions barge.

The torpedo, as used as an offensive weapon, consisted of a container of explosive mounted on the end of a spar, which was so rigged that it could be carried out of the water, and lowered

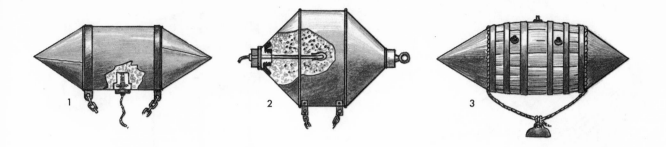

1. *Confederate torpedo consisting of tin cylinder, about 20 inches long and 10½ inches in diameter. Contained charge and bouyancy chamber. Chain was attached to two iron straps. Two cones one foot long were soldered to each end. Firing mechanism was fitted in well in side of cylinder. Filler plug on bottom. Wire to trigger was connected to a float, to another torpedo, or to shore. Pull on wire tripped coiled spring mechanism, releasing trigger which struck ignition primer.*

2. *Electrical ground mine. Fastened by chain to anchor. Watertight plug for electrical wire detonator. Fired by observer on shore.*

3. *Barrel of keg torpedo was pitched inside and out. Usually held about one hundred pounds of powder, and was exploded by percussion or chemical fuses screwed into top and sides. Conical solid pine ends streamlined keg to minimize disturbance by tide.*

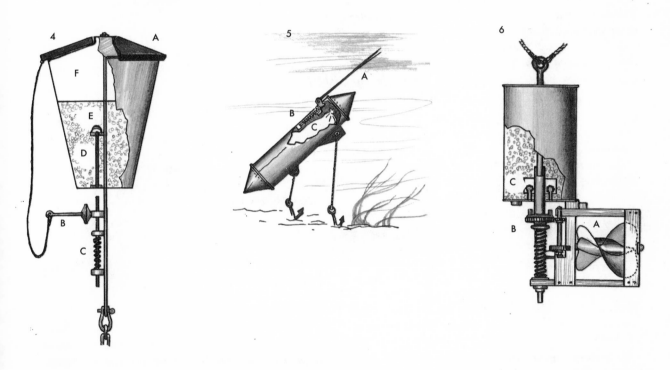

4. *Singer's mine. Vessel struck mine, knocking off heavy iron cap A, which pulled pin B, releasing spring-loaded plunger C, which struck the firing pin D, driving it against detonator E. F is buoyancy chamber.*

5. *Confederate river mine consisted of sheet-iron cylinder, about 5½ feet long and 1 foot in diameter. Anchors held it pointing downstream. Vessel going down-river slid over pronged lever A, but ships coming up caught prongs, moving lever which triggered lock B, firing 70-pound bag of powder, C.*

6. *Confederate drifting mine. Tin cylinder, 16½ inches long, 11½ inches in diameter. Buoyancy chamber in top. Lines from ring to driftwood. Arrested when swept against target, tide and current revolved tin propeller A, turning gears which released spring-loaded plunger B, which struck percussion primers C.*

1. *Frame torpedos were cast-iron shells with percussion detonators mounted on heavy timbers, anchored to the bottom.*

2. *Drifting mine made of tarred keg containing coiled time fuse which led through bottom of keg in watertight gutta-percha tube to iron powder container below. Attached to similar torpedo or piece of driftwood, it floated with current across bows or anchor chain, swung alongside, and when fuse burned down, exploded.*

3. *"Coal" torpedo was hollow chunk of iron, cast in shape of lump of coal, and contained a charge of powder. Whole was coated with tar and covered with coal dust. Hole through which powder was loaded was filled with tar. Planted in Federal coal depots, it blew up when fed into furnaces, exploding boilers.*

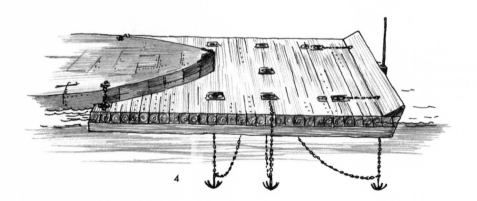

4. *Torpedo searcher built by Federals for use in clearing path through mine fields in Charleston harbor. Heavily built of two layers of 18-inch white pine bolted together. Fifty feet long by 27 feet broad, shaped to fit bow of monitor, to which it was secured by chains and ropes. Originally intended to have torpedos attached to blow up underwater obstructions, but rafts proved so unmanageable that chain grapnels were substituted as being safer. The* Weehawken *pushed one into action but chains and lashings broke getting it across Charleston bar.*

*"When inside it was found that the sea converted the raft into a huge battering ram . . . the raft rose while the vessel fell, and the reverse. . . . After it started the 5-inch iron armor upon the bow I cut it adrift." (One of these broke adrift off Cape Hatteras while being towed to Charleston. Five years later it appeared off St. David's, Bermuda, and was towed ashore for salvage. Its sound condition defied efforts to dismantle it and its remains can be seen to this day.)*

5. *Later in the war, lighter sweeps of frame and cable, which could be raised or lowered from a ship's bows, were used.*

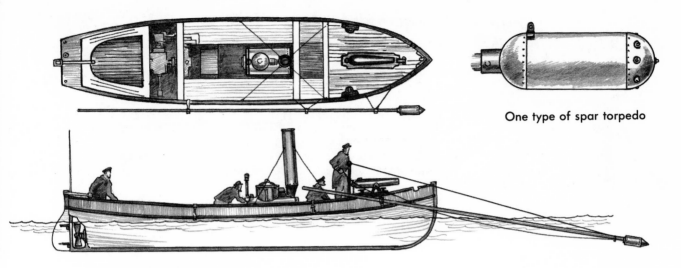

One type of spar torpedo

Thirty-foot steam launch with spar torpedo

*Steam launch such as used by Cushing in his attack on the Confederate* Albemarle. *The spar was not always as long as shown; Cushing's was about fourteen feet long and was lowered into position by a topping lift leading to a stanchion on deck. The torpedo he used was the invention of Engineer Lay, U.S.N., and was fitted to the spar by an iron slide. This was detached from the boom by means of a line leading inboard, allowing the torpedo to float free and rise up under the victim's hull. It was then exploded by a jerk on a separate lanyard which actuated the detonating device.*

*Crews varied. Cushing took seven with him in his daring run. Chances of making a successful spar-torpedo attack on an alert enemy was slight—chances of getting away afterward even slighter.*

when the attack was about to be made. These torpedoes were detonated by contact, the impact against a ship's hull setting off a percussion cap or chemical fuse; by a trigger mechanism fired by pulling a long lanyard at the moment of contact; or by electricity. Of these possibly the lanyard was the surest and safest, and was used by Lieutenant William B. Cushing in his successful attack on the Confederate ram *Albemarle*. The boats used were usually small steam launches.

The Confederates, looking for some means to offset the superior naval forces of the Union, developed a new type of warship. These were small, iron, steam-driven, cigar-shaped vessels. They were submersibles, that is, they could take on enough water ballast to submerge most of their hulls, leaving a small amount of deck, conning tower and smokestack, showing.

These "Davids" (small warriors out to destroy the Union Goliath) carried spar torpedoes. Operating off Charlestown, they severely damaged the *Minnesota* and exploded a charge against the *New*

*Ironsides,* giving her a shaking-up but doing no damage. A true, if crude, submarine vessel, the *Hunley,* which had already earned herself the nickname of the "Peripatetic Coffin" by drowning three crews, including Horace L. Hunley himself, managed to bring her spar torpedo in contact with the *Housatonic,* with results fatal to both vessels.

The daring attacks kept the blockading fleet off Charlestown in a state of constant alert. The ironclads were ordered to have their fenders rigged out, nets hung from them (torpedo nets later became standard equipment in all navies), and picket boats kept in constant movement. Underwater attacks in the dark by an unseen enemy was a menace new to naval warfare, and one not calculated to improve nerves or morale in the blockading fleet.

Fortunately for the Union these little ships were years ahead of their time. Had they been as efficient as they were ingenious, the blockade might have become an impossibility.

[149]

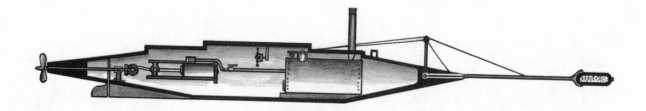

Confederate steam *David* built at Charleston, South Carolina
Length, 54 feet; inside diameter, 5 feet, 6 inches
Crew, captain and three men
Torpedo contained about 100 pounds of powder

Cross section of *David*

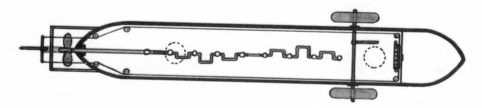

Simplified drawings of Confederate submarine *Hunley*
showing cranks, hydroplanes, and spar torpedo

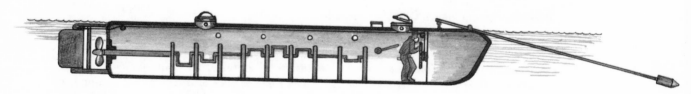

*Hunley*—top view

The *Hunley* (above) was made partly from an old boiler, some twenty-five feet long and four feet in diameter. Water ballast tanks were installed, with pumps to force out the water, which was admitted through sea cocks. Adequate electric motors and batteries did not exist, and steam could not be generated under water, so power was manual—eight men sitting at eight cranks on the end of a propeller shaft—speed about four miles per hour in smooth water. The rudder was moved by a wheel connected to rods running the length of the boat.

Depth was controlled by two lateral fins, five feet eight inches long, on a shaft running through the boat, and worked by a lever. There were two hatches, with eight-inch coamings, in which glass ports were set—the only means of seeing out when rigged for diving. To dive, water was admitted into the ballast tanks until the ports were partly submerged; normal trim was with the deck just under water. The captain then depressed the diving-vane lever and the boat slid under water. A depth gauge was provided. Interior lighting consisted of a candle, which also served as a gauge of the oxygen supply (in a test dive one crew lay on the bottom for two hours and thirty-five minutes before lack of oxygen forced them to the surface). When partly submerged a tube admitted some air to the boat. In an emergency an iron drop keel could be released from inside.

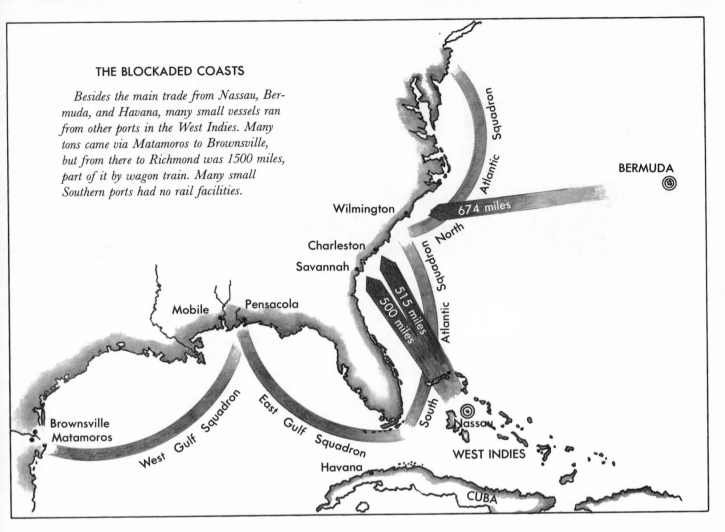

*Besides the main trade from Nassau, Bermuda, and Havana, many small vessels ran from other ports in the West Indies. Many tons came via Matamoros to Brownsville, but from there to Richmond was 1500 miles, part of it by wagon train. Many small Southern ports had no rail facilities.*

# THE BLOCKADE

In a broad sense the whole Federal Navy waged war with the object of strangling the South. Every fort taken, every river forced, every battery destroyed, every ship taken or sunk meant a tightening of the noose. A sailor rolling endlessly in the swells of the Gulf of Mexico might not understand that he was helping beat a Confederate infantry regiment in Virginia, but it was true, nevertheless.

But blockading squadrons do not spring into being overnight, and for the first few months of the war, ships came and went in the Southern ports much as they had always done. To begin with there were many who held Lincoln's proclamation a mistake. U. S. Senator Charles Sumner of Massachusetts said "Had Lincoln proclaimed a closing of the rebel ports [instead of a blockade] there could have been no concession [of belligerency]. The whole case of England is made to stand on the use of the word 'blockade.'"

Also it was obvious that at first the Navy could only maintain a "paper blockade." This was in direct contradiction to the principles for which the War of 1812 had been fought, the right to trade in a belligerent port not actually closed by the presence of a warship. To be legal a blockade must be effective, and must be maintained constantly. In a letter to Lord Lyons, the British minister, Secretary of State William H. Seward tried to deny that the temporary absence of the blockading ship or ships broke the blockade or made necessary new notice of its existence. But the government's position was untenable. The law was that if the port was abandoned or the blockade raised for even one hour, the blockaders had to begin the business of registration and notification all over again.

A neutral entering a port had a right to remain fifteen days, after she was notified of the blockade, while ships approaching a blockaded port could go away unharmed if they had not been notified of the new blockade. And so for several months, until the blockade could be made effective, most of the Southern ports were open.

[151]

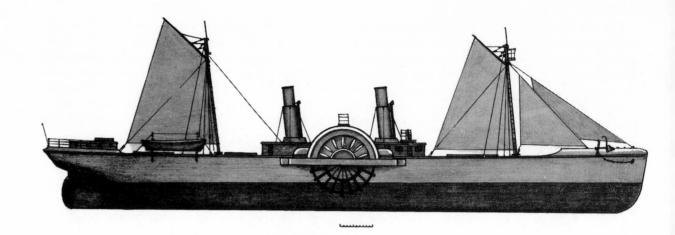

**BLOCKADE-RUNNER**

*The average blockade-runner might be a paddle-wheel steamer of some 400 tons burden (cargo capacity), about 200 feet long, with a 22-foot beam, and 10-foot draft. Engines of 250 H.P. could give her the high speed of 15–16 knots. Low freeboard, short spars, and small superstructures reduced the silhouette. Sails were strictly an auxiliary to the powerful engines and would have been furled when passing through the blockading squadrons.*

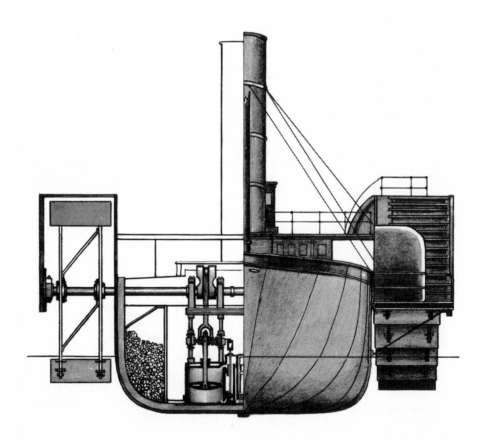

　　　*Cross section of English-built paddle steamer of the Civil War period. Engine of direct-acting type.*

But the South made a grave mistake also. Instead of exporting all the cotton it could while the opportunity lasted, the Confederates chose to hold their cotton in the mistaken belief that the shortage would soon force recognition by England and France. But previous bumper crops had enabled England, the chief importer, to stockpile considerable amounts, sufficient, in fact, to be able to ship some back to New England. Cotton was not really scarce until late in 1862. By then the blockade had tightened, and the Confederates were running short of both money and credit.

WITH the effective and legal establishing of the blockade, there very naturally followed desperate attempts to run it. Nassau in the Bahamas was only five hundred miles from Savannah and five hundred and seventy from Wilmington. It speedily became a focal point for ships attempting to run the blockade, rivaled only by Bermuda. Because large, slow, deep-draft vessels could neither outrun the Federal blockaders nor thread their way through some of the shallow waters off the Carolina coasts, goods were transshipped into swift, light-draft vessels designed especially for the job of blockade-running. Many of these were British-built and British-owned. It may have been an exaggeration, but it was said that at one time half the shipyards in England were building vessels for running the blockade. In some cases they were commanded by officers on extended leave from the Royal Navy.

Theirs was a risky job, but a profitable one if they succeeded in getting in with supplies and out again with a load of cotton. By this time the price of cotton was soaring. Bales which could be bought for six cents a pound in the South were fetching fifty-six to sixty-six per pound in England, and the price of goods smuggled into the Confederacy had also skyrocketed. The profits were enormous. One runner, the *Banshee,* paid her stockholders seven hundred per cent on their investment in eight round trips. Profits on a single bale were at least fifty dollars. A vessel might pay for herself in one successful round trip. It was said an owner could afford to lose his ship after two round trips.

Wages on the blockade runners were high too. When the business was at its peak a successful skipper might expect $5000.00-U.S. for a run to a Southern port and back, and was allowed a little space for his own venture besides. Even the deck hands and firemen earned $250.00 a trip.

The ships themselves were long, low (the twin-screw *Don* had only 8 feet freeboard), rakish-looking craft. As a rule they carried only pole masts, with a crow's nest for the lookouts. Powerful engines, with high-pressure tubular boilers, drove them at speeds up to eighteen knots—a great rate for those days.

They were not armed—use of force by a non-belligerent could have been construed as piracy. Thomas E. Taylor wrote in his *Running the Blockade:*

"The blockading force is entitled to treat such a ship in all respects as an enemy. . . . a crew so captured may be treated as prisoners of war, nor is any resistance to capture permitted, and a single blow or shot in his own defense turns the blockade-runner into a pirate."

They relied on their speed and comparative invisibility in the darkness. (They usually timed their dashes through the blockade to coincide with the dark of the moon.) They were painted a dull gray, and some even lowered the ship's boats to the rail to further decrease their silhouettes. With proper care it was estimated that a runner should be able to slip undetected by a blockader at a cable's length (two hundred yards). Provision was made for blowing off steam under water, and the comparatively smokeless anthracite coal was used.

The blockading vessels were hampered by lack of any efficient form of searchlight or star shells. Flares and rockets were used and late in the war some ships were equipped with locomotive headlights. Many blockaders were painted "Union color," a bluish-gray.

Coming out, the runners were piled high with cotton, "like hay wagons," stacked over the decks and up around the pilothouses. Inward-bound, the cargoes were usually mixed—an unrealistic potpourri of essentials and luxuries: shells and brandy; boots and bonnet frames (Sorrel, Longstreet's chief of staff, wrote that many of the imported boots were worthless "Shoddy things that might be done for in a day's use"); rifles and ladies' dresses; candles; tea; saltpeter; sherry; quinine; soap, and saddles. Not until 1864 did the Confederate Government attempt to put a stop to the wasteful importation of luxuries. The export of all cotton and tobacco was put in the hands of the central government or that of the states. One half of the inbound cargoes had to consist of government freight at fixed rates.

The Confederate Ordnance Department owned and operated a few fast runners. These, of course, confined their cargoes to military material. As the blockade became tighter and risk of loss of ships and expensive cargoes greater, many runners would have preferred to run in light, and make the profit on the cotton on the return trip. The Confederate Government, however, ruled that all ships coming in must carry full cargoes. (Every ship was also required to bring in one barrel of sperm oil for the coastal navigational lights. These had been extinguished at the beginning of the war but were later relighted.)

"Bermuda bacon" was another import. Northerners with more eye for profit than patriotism bought pork for higher than normal prices, then shipped it salted to Bermuda or Nassau, where it found its way to the Confederacy. One gathers that imported bacon was not always of the finest. A disgusted general wrote:

"Some bacon from Nassau was coming through the blockade, and it would not be incredible for the blockading fleet to allow it to come through in hope of poisoning us."

Food in considerable quantities was imported into the Confederacy. There is little doubt that the Southern States could have supported themselves in this respect. Shortages were due to poor food planning and faulty transportation and distribution facilities. Coal, for the blockade-runners, was a great problem. Inefficient arrangements for importing (much came from Halifax, Nova Scotia), and stockpiling at Bermuda and Nassau caused delays. Careful captains were particularly fussy about the quality of their coal, preferring the hard-to-get Welsh anthracite, which gave much heat and little smoke.

Coal was also a problem for the blockaders. Ships of that period could not carry great quantities of fuel, and marine engines were not too efficient, which meant that there were always some ships off-station, coaling. To conserve coal others lay close inshore with fires banked, trusting to a warning rocket or gun from the fast-sailing ships patrolling farther out. Port Royal was the main coaling and repair base for the squadron watching the Eastern coasts.

WHILE the fast, British-built steamers carried a large share of the contraband, they were only a part of the blockade-running operation as a whole. At the outbreak of the war, any sail or steam vessel was used, the older the better, with the idea of cutting losses in case of capture. This proved false economy, however, and it was then that the renowned British yards set to work. By far the largest number of runners were small vessels, schooners mostly. Even the famous yacht *America* was pressed into service.

Nor were profit-minded Yankees averse to an occasional venture, and more than one Northern-owned vessel slipped down the coast to find ultimate refuge in a Southern port. The favorite neutral port was undoubtedly Nassau, and the Nassau-Wilmington run the most popular, but besides Bermuda and Havana a great trade was carried on from the Mexican town of Matamoros, on the Rio Grande.

As the numbers and efficiency of the blockaders increased, the odds against the runners rose. In 1861 it was reckoned that the chance of capture was only one in ten. By 1864 it was one in three. At the war's end, U. S. Navy lists showed 1504 blockade-runners captured or destroyed. The value of the ships and cargoes was estimated at thirty-one million dollars. By this time the blockading fleet was numbered in the hundreds.

As a general rule the fleet Clyde-built runner had the legs on anything in the Federal squadrons, but some of the Northern ships were fast, and occasionally could count on a favorable breeze, which added considerably to their speed. Some of the fastest blockade-runners were among the many ocean-going steamers captured, armed, and taken into the Federal service. These were used to catch other runners in the "set a thief to catch a thief" tradition. Some of the chases were long, hard-run affairs, with the Federal cruiser banging away with her bow chaser, in the hopes of landing a crippling shot, and the runner using every trick in the book to evade capture.

One expedient resorted to by a runner hard pressed by a swift blockader and one which brought anguish to the hearts of her pursuers was to jettison her precious cargo. Every splash alongside the fleeing vessel meant hundreds of dollars in prize money lost, even if she were overtaken in the end.

All captured vessels were condemned in prize court and one half the value went to the captors. It was distributed according to rank. One captain paid his crew one thousand dollars each and even the lowly cabin boy's share amounted to over five hundred dollars.

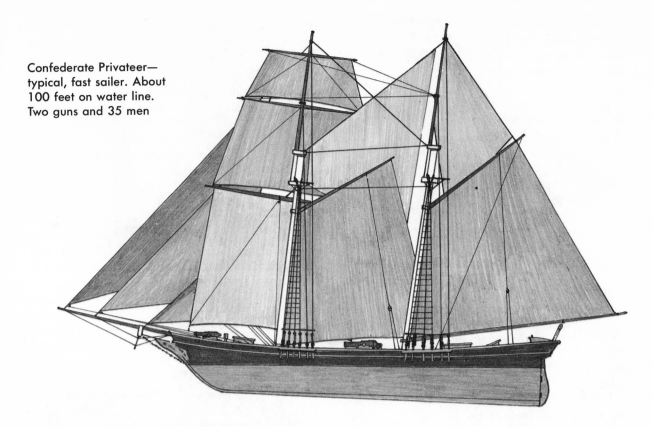

Confederate Privateer—
typical, fast sailer. About
100 feet on water line.
Two guns and 35 men

Privateering is the arming and manning of a vessel by private persons holding a commission from the government (letter of marque) to operate against an enemy, usually his merchantmen. Such warfare had been outlawed by the Declaration of Paris in 1856, but as the United States was not a signatory, the Confederates were legally entitled to equip such ships and send them to sea. These privateers are not to be confused with the cruisers of the Confederate States Navy, such as the *Alabama.*

They comprised a great variety of ships, including steamers, an ironclad (the *Manassas*), submarines, schooners, and armed boats. They were mostly small, carried few guns, and accomplished very little. The big raiders were another story. They were operated by the Confederate Government and were well armed and officered by Southern naval men. Most, like the *Florida,* the *Alabama,* and the *Georgia,* were English-built. The *Nashville* was a Northern ship seized at the outbreak of the war in a Southern port. While having little or no effect on the war, they did great damage to American commerce, damage from which it took years to recover. In all, they took 261 vessels, most of which were destroyed.

Deck view, showing heavy gun on pivot. Ship of this size might carry four small guns on broadside instead

[155]

**C.S.S. ALABAMA**—*Wood; 1040 tons; over-all length, 220 feet; beam, 32 feet; draft, 15 feet; two 300 H.P. engines; speed under power, about 10 knots—under sail and steam, about 15 knots; hoisting-type propeller; coal storage, 350 tons; bark rigged, wire standing rigging.*

*Armament: six 32-pdr. smoothbores; one 100-pdr. Blakely rifle on pivot mount forward; one 68-pdr. smoothbore pivot abaft mainmast. Crew about 120 men, 24 officers.*

Hinged bulwarks allowed pivot guns wide arc of fire

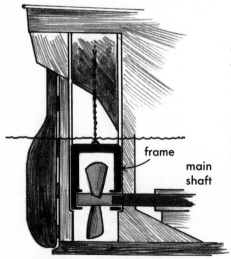

To avoid drag, many war vessels were provided with apparatus for lifting the propeller out of the water. The screw was on a short shaft held by a frame which slid on guides on stern- and rudderposts like a window sash. The main shaft was keyed into the short one and was withdrawn when the frame was raised. The *Alabama* could disengage her shaft and hoist her screw in 15 minutes.

frame

main shaft

Simplified diagram of screw-lifting apparatus

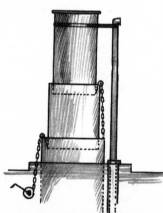

**TELESCOPING FUNNEL** and exhaust pipe. Used on many sailers with auxiliary steampower

# BIBLIOGRAPHY

*Automatic Arms* by Melvin M. Johnson Jr. and Charles T. Haven. William Morrow & Co., New York, 1941

*Letters From Lee's Army* by Susan Leigh Blackford. Charles Scribner's Sons, New York, 1947

*Lincoln's Choice* by J. O. Buckeridge. The Stackpole Co., Harrisburg, Pa., 1956

*Our Rifles* (revised edition) by Charles Winthrop Sawyer. Williams Book Store, Boston, Mass., 1941

*The Story of The Guns* by Sir James Emerson Tennent. Longmans, Green & Co., New York, 1864

*Grape and Canister* by L. Van Loan Naisawald. Oxford University Press, New York, 1960

*The Muzzle-Loading Cap Lock Rifle* by Ned H. Roberts. The Clarke Press, Manchester, New Hampshire, 1944

*The Bullet's Flight* by Franklin W. Mann, B.S., M.D. Standard Printing and Publishing Co., Huntington, W. Va., 1942

*Ammunition* by Captain Melvin M. Johnson Jr. U.S.M.C.R., and Charles T. Haven. William Morrow & Co., New York, 1943

*The Gun Collector's Handbook of Values* by Charles Edward Chapell, First Lieutenant, U.S.M.C.R. Published by author, San Leandro, California, 1940

*The Rifle-Volunteers' Manual* by a Penninsular Officer. Hodson & Son, London, 1861

*Organization and Tactics* by Arthur L. Wagner, Captain, U.S.A. Westermann and Co., New York, 1895

*The NRA Book of Small Arms.* Volume I, *Pistols and Revolvers* by Walter H. B. Smith. The National Rifle Association of America, 1946

*English Pistols and Revolvers* by J. N. George. Smalls-Arms Technical Publishing Co., Plantersville, S.C., 1938

*Single-Shot Rifles* by James J. Grant. William Morrow & Co., New York, 1947

*Twenty-three Years Practice and Observations with Rifle Guns* by Ezekiel Baker. Published by author, London, 1804

*A Practical Course of Artillery* by Charles Gray. Unpublished (as far as known), 1859; original manuscript owned by Jack Coggins

*Hand-book for Hythe* by Hans Busk, M.A., D.L. Routledge, Warne, and Routledge, London, New York, 1860

*The Blue and The Gray* edited by Henry Steele Commager. The Bobbs-Merrill Company, Indianapolis, Ind., 1950

*The History of Naval Tactics from 1530 to 1930* by Rear Admiral S. S. Robison, U.S.N., and M. L. C. Robison. The U. S. Naval Institute, Annapolis, Md., 1942.

*Torpedoes and Torpedo Warfare* by C. W. Sleeman, Esq., Lieutenant, R.N., and Commander, Imperial Ottoman Navy. J. Griffin & Co., Portsmouth, England, 1880

*The Evolution of The Submarine Boat Mine and Torpedo* by Commander Murray F. Sueter, R.N. J. Griffin & Co., Portsmouth, England, 1907

*Instructions for the Exercise and Service of Great Guns.* Harrison & Sons, London, England, 1885 (no author listed)

*Ironclads in Action* by H. W. Wilson, two volumes. Little, Brown & Co., Boston, 1896

*Report of the Secretary of the Navy in Relation to Armored Vessels.* U. S. Government Printing Office, 1864

*Modern Breechloaders* by W. W. Greener. Cassell, Petter, and Galpin, London, 1870

*Naval Gunnery* by Captain H. Garbett, R.N. George Bell and Sons, 1897, London

*Picture History of the U. S. Navy* by Theodore Roscoe and Fred Freeman. Charles Scribner's Sons, New York, 1956

*Decisive Battles* by Major General J. F. C. Fuller. Charles Scribners' Sons, 1940

*Screw Propeller* by John Burne, C. E. Longman, Green & Co., London, 1852

*Iron Ship Building* by William Fairbairn. Longmans, Green & Co., London, 1865

*Development of Navies* by Seardley Wilmot. Seeley & Co., London, 1892

*Evolution of Naval Armament* by F. L. Robertson. Constable & Co., London, 1921

*Warships and Navies of the World* by Chief Engineer J. W. King. A. Williams & Co., Boston, 1881

*Treatise on Marine Engines* by Robert Murray, C. E. John Weale, London, 1852

*Mine and Counter Mine* by Professor A. M. Lowe. Sheridan House, New York, 1940

*Naval Gunnery* by Captain H. Garbett, R.N. George Bell & Co., London, 1897

*British Ships and Shipbuilders* by George Blake. Collins, London, 1946

*Manual of Military Surgery* by John J. Chisolm. C.S.A. War Department, 1864

*Regulations for the Army of The Confederate States, 1862*

*Picture History of the Civil War* by American Heritage. Doubleday & Company, New York, 1960

*The Soldier in Our Civil War* two volumes. Stanley Bradley Publishing Co., New York, 1890

*A Short History of Marine Engineering* by E. C. Smith. The Macmillan Co., New York, 1938

*From Manassas to Appomattox* by Lieutenant General James Longstreet, C.S.A. Philadelphia, 1896

*Decisive Battles* by Sir Edward Creasy. Harpers and Brothers, New York, 1908

*Introduction of the Ironclad Warship* by J. P. Baxter. Harvard University Press, 1933

*History of Our Navy,* five volumes by John R. Spears. Charles Scribner's Sons, New York, 1899

*The Influence of Sea Power upon History* by Captain A. T. Mahan, U.S.N. Little, Brown & Co., Boston, 1897

*The Naval History of the United States* by Willis J. Abbot. Dodd, Mead & Co., New York, 1886

*They Fought for the Union* by Francis A. Lord. The Stackpole Co., Harrisburg, Pa., 1960

*With Sabre and Scalpel* by John A. Wyeth M.D., LL. D. Harpers & Brothers, New York, 1914

*The Civil War, A Soldier's View* by Colonel G. F. R. Henderson, edited by Jay Luvaas. The University of Chicago Press, Chicago, 1958

*Thomas: Rock of Chickamauga* by Richard O'Connor. Prentice-Hall, New York, 1948

*Stonewall Jackson and the American Civil War* by G. F. R. Henderson, C.B. Longmans, Green & Co., 1936

*Sherman, Fighting Prophet* by Lloyd Lewis. Harcourt, Brace & Company, New York, 1932

*General McClellan's Reports and Campaigns* by George B. McClellan. Sheldon & Co., New York, 1864

*Sea Power in the Machine Age* by Bernard Brodie. Princeton University Press, 1941

*The Ship of the Line in Battle* by Admiral Sir Reginald Custance, R.N. William Blackwood & Sons, London, 1912

*Running the Blockade* by Thomas E. Taylor

*Blockade Runners of the Confederacy* by Hamilton Cochran. The Bobbs-Merrill Company, Indianapolis, Ind., 1958

*Recollections of a Confederate Staff Officer* by General G. Moxley Sorrell. Neal Publishing Co., New York, 1905

*War Years with Jeb Stuart* by Lieutenant Colonel W. W. Blackford. Charles Scribner's Sons, 1945

*The Navy: A History* by Fletcher Pratt. Garden City Publishing Co., Garden City, N.Y., 1941

*Surgeon of the Seas* by Charles S. Foltz. The Bobbs-Merrill Company, Indianapolis, Ind., 1931

*Lee's Lieutenants,* two volumes by Douglas Southall Freeman. Charles Scribner's Sons, New York, 1942

*The Twentieth Maine* by John J. Pullen. J. B. Lippincott Company, Philadelphia, 1957

*Mr. Lincoln's Navy* by Richard S. West Jr. Longmans, Green & Co., New York, 1957

*Telegraphy in Battle* by John Emmet O'Brien, M.D. The Raeder Press, Wilkes-Barre, Pa., 1910

*The Life of Billy Yank* by Bell Irvin Wiley. The Bobbs-Merrill Company, Indianapolis, Ind., 1951

*Reminiscences of the Civil War* by General John B. Gordon. Charles Scribner's Sons, New York, 1903

*A Soldier's Recollections* by Randolph H. McKim. Longmans, Green & Co., New York, 1910

*The Story of a Cannoneer Under Stonewall Jackson* by Edward A. Moore. Neale Publishing Co., New York, 1907

*The Long Arm of Lee* by Jennings Cropper Wise, two volumes. J. P. Bell Co., Lynchburg, Va., 1915

*Official Records of the War of the Rebellion*

*The Atlantic Coast* by Rear Admiral Daniel Ammen, U.S.N. Charles Scribner's Sons, New York, 1883

*The History of the American Sailing Navy* by Howard I. Chapelle. W. W. Norton & Company, New York, 1949

*History of 44th. New York Volunteer Infantry.* Eugene Nash, Chicago, 1911

*Cavalry Tactics* by Major General Joseph Wheeler, C.S.A.

*Artillerists Manual 1863* by John Gibbon

*Divided We Fought, A Pictorial History of the War* 1861–1865, edited by D. H. Donald. The Macmillan Co., New York, 1952

*Steam Navy of the United States* by Franklin Bennet. Warren & Co., Philadelphia, 1896

*Lincoln and The Tools of War* by Robert V. Bruce. The Bobbs-Merrill Company, Indianapolis, Ind., 1956

*The Confederate Soldier in the Civil War.* 1895. Reprint, Pageant Books, Inc., Paterson, N.J., 1959

*The Life of Johnny Reb* by Bell Irvin Wiley. The Bobbs-Merrill Company, Indianapolis, Ind., 1943

*The Machine Gun,* two volumes by Lieutenant Colonel George M. Chinn, U.S.M.C. U. S. Government Printing Office, 1951

*Small Arms of the World* by W. H. B. Smith. The Stackpole Co., Harrisburg, Pa.

*The Peacemaker and its Rivals* by John E. Parsons. William Morrow & Co., New York, 1950

*Winchester* by Harold F. Williamson. Combat Forces Press, Washington, D.C., 1952

*The Rifle in America* by Philip B. Sharpe. William Morrow & Co., New York, 1938

*Cavalry Tactic* by Joseph Wheeler. S. H. Goetzel & Co., Mobile, 1863

*Infantry Tactic* by Silas Casey. Evans and Cogswell, Columbia, S.C., 1864

*Reminiscences of General Basil Duke, C.S.A.* Doubleday, Page & Co., Garden City, N.Y., 1911

*History of Morgan's Cavalry* by General Basil Duke, C.S.A. Neal Publishing Co., New York, 1906

*Regulations for the Army of the Confederate States 1862.* C.S.A. War Department. J. L. Power, Jackson, Miss., 1861

*Rifle and Light Infantry Tactics* by William Joseph Hardee. Lippincott, Grambo & Co., 1855

*Handbook of Artillery* by Joseph Roberts. D. Van Nostrand Co., Princeton, N.J., 1860

*Minutiae of Soldiers Life in Army of Northern Virginia* by Carlton McCarthy. C. McCarthy & Co., Richmond, 1882

*Camp and Field Life of the Fifth New York Infantry* by Alfred Davenport. Dick & Fitzgerald, New York, 1879

*Sound of the Guns* by Fairfax Downey. David McKay Company, New York, 1956

*History of the United States Army* (revised edition) by William A. Ganoe. D. Appleton-Century Company, New York, 1942

*Ordnance Manual* by Ordnance Department, C.S.A., 1863

*Field Artillery Journal*

*Rifle and Infantry Tactics* by W. J. Hardee

*Instruction for Field Artillery* by A. W. Stark

*Handbook of Field Fortification and Artillery* by E. G. Vielé

*Instruction for Field Artillery* by U. S. War Department

*Instruction for Siege Artillery* by U. S. Ware Department

*Facts About Ordnance* by Norman Wiard. Washington *Chronicle*, 1862

*Ordnance Manual, 1863* by C.S.A. Ordance Department

*Warfare* by Oliver L. Spaulding, Hoffman Nickerson, and John W. Wright. The Infantry Journal, Inc., Washington, D.C., 1937

*The Tools of War* by James R. Newman. Doubleday, Doran & Company, Garden City, N.Y., 1942

*History of American Sailing Ships* by Howard I. Chapelle. W. W. Norton & Company, New York, 1935

*The Photographic History of The Civil War,* ten volumes. The Review of Reviews, New York, 1912

*Three Main Military Questions of the Day* by Sir Henry Havelock

*This Hallowed Ground* by Bruce Catton. Doubleday and Company, Garden City, N.Y., 1956

*David Glascow Farragut: Our First Admiral* by Charles Lee Lewis. U. S. Naval Institute, Annapolis, Md., 1943

*David Glascow Farragut: Admiral in the Making* by Charles Lee Lewis. U. S. Naval Institute, Annapolis, Md., 1941

*A Stillness at Appomatox* by Bruce Catton Doubleday & Company, Garden City, N.Y., 1957

*Frank Leslie's Illustrated History of the Civil War.* Mrs. Frank Leslie, New York, 1895

*History of the Great Rebellion* by Thomas P. Kettell, L. Stebbins, Hartford, Conn., 1865

*Ordnance and Armor* by Alexander L. Holley, B.P. D. Van Nostrand Co., New York, 1865

*The Rebel Raider* by Howard Swiggett. Garden City Publishing Co., New York, 1937

*First Blood: The Story of Fort Sumter* by W. A. Swanberg. Charles Scribner's Sons, New York, 1958

*Pennsylvania at Gettysburg,* two volumes. Harrisburg, Pa., 1904

*Personal Recollections of a Cavalryman* by Colonel J. A. Kidd. Sentinel Printing Co., Ionia, Mich., 1908

*History of Cavalry* by Lieutenant Colonel George T. Denison. The Macmillan Co., London, 1877

*Manual for Gunnery Instruction, U.S.N., 1864*

*Infantry Tactics* by Silas Casey

*Doctors in Blue* by George Worthington Adams. Henry Schuman, New York, 1952

*Secret and Urgent* by Fletcher Pratt. The Bobbs-Merrill Company, Indianapolis, Ind., 1939

*Ordeal by Fire* by Fletcher Pratt. Harrison Smith & Robert Haas, New York, 1935

*Guns on the Western Waters* by H. Allen Gosnell, Lieutenant Commander, U.S.N.R. Louisiana State University Press, Baton Rouge, 1949

*Our Iron-Clad Warships* by E. J. Reed, C.B. John Murray, London, 1869

*Notes on Ordnance of the American Civil War* by Harold L. Peterson. The American Ordnance Association, Washington, D.C., 1959

*Notes on Ammunition of the American Civil War* by Colonel Berkeley R. Lewis. The American Ordnance Association, Washington, D.C., 1959

*Notes on Naval Ordnance of the American Civil War* by Eugene B. Canfield. The American Ordnance Association, Washington, D.C., 1960

*Rustics in Rebellion* by Geo. Alfred Townsend. University of North Carolina Press, Chapel Hill, 1950

*Battles and Leaders* from *The Century Magazine.* The Century Co., New York, November 1884–April 1888

*History of Morgan's Cavalry* by General Basil W. Duke

# INDEX

## DATE DUE

| | | | |
|---|---|---|---|
| FEB 28/84 | | | |
| JAN 21 '98 | | | |
| | | | |
| | | | |
| | | | |
| | | | |
| | | | |
| | | | |
| | | | |
| | | | |
| | | | |
| | | | |
| | | | |
| | | | |
| | | | |
| | | | |
| GAYLORD | | | PRINTED IN U.S.A |

1st CORPS, 1st DIV.

2nd CORPS, 3rd DIV.

3rd CORPS, 2nd DIV.

4th CORPS, 1st DIV.

## CORPS BADGES ARMY OF THE UNITED STATES

24th CORPS, 2nd DIV.

GENERAL    COLONEL ARTILLERY    CAPTAIN CAVALRY    LIEUTENANT INFANTRY

## SLEEVE BADGES C.S. ARMY

25th CORPS, 3rd DIV.

23rd CORPS, 3rd DIV.

GENERAL

COLONEL—CAVALRY

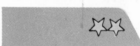

LIEUTENANT COLONEL—STAFF

MAJOR—MEDICAL CORPS

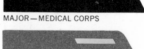

CAPTAIN—ARTILLERY

FIRST LIEUTENANT—INFANTRY

SECOND LIEUTENANT—CAVALRY

## COLLAR BADGES C.S. ARMY

SHERIDAN'S CAVALRY CORPS

WILSON'S CAVALRY CORPS

22nd CORPS, 1st DIV.
(21st CORPS, NO BADGE ADOPTED

20th CORPS, 2nd DIV.

19th CORPS, 1st DIV.

18th CORPS, 3rd DIV.

17th CORPS, 1st DIV.